# The No Holds Barred, Candid Talk About Small Business Success in Florida

How To Maximize The Growth,
Cash Flow And Profitability
Of Your Small Business

12 Simple, Foolproof Steps For Business Success

**Dan Henn, CPA**

"A concise summary of all you need to know in getting started and running your business. I highly recommend this book!"

**Jim McKnight**
**City Manager**
**City of Rockledge, FL**

"This is a very comprehensive, detailed and easy to follow guide for small-business owners in Florida. An excellent resource and ongoing reference book for entrepreneurs."

**Jennifer Sugarman**
**President & CEO**
**Cocoa Beach Regional Chamber of Commerce**

"As a financial advisor, I frequently search for tools to assist my small business clients. Dan's book is the ultimate resource for all that is essential to starting, growing, running, and exiting a business. It is truly a road map to success that I plan to share with all of my business clients – and to frequently refer to myself, for many years to come!"

**Beth Courtney**
**Senior Partner**
**Courtney & Braswell Financial Group**

"If you are serious about being successful in business, this book is your #1 resource. The most complete guide you'll find anywhere for a small business."

**Karen Gregory**
**President & Owner**
**HRSS Consulting Group, LLC**

"It should be mandatory for those that are starting a new business to read this book. So grateful that Dan put together such a comprehensive book, that is a simple read and easy to understand. I would highly recommend it to any new business!"

**Karen Gunn-Bardot Tumbiolo**
**Broker-Owner-CAM**
**Showcase Property Management**

"Congrats to Dan on his new book, *The No Holds Barred, Candid Talk About Small Business Success in Central Florida*. Dan is a passionate, intelligent CPA with a lot to offer to small business owners. I am proud to endorse this insightful book. It is a "must - read" for any small business owner in Central Florida."

**Salim Omar, CPA**
**Author and Educator**

"Any person in, or thinking about owning, a small business, including non-profit initiatives, needs to read this book! Every issue examined and explained represents things that you, the entrepreneur, will face. The content of this book will give you an orientation and a starting point to anticipate and address those issues. Well done, Dan Henn, CPA!"

**Robin Fisher**
**Brevard County Commissioner (2008-2016)**
**State Farm Business Owner**

Published by:

Daniel Henn, CPA, PA
(321) 684-7800
www.cparockledge.com

ISBN-13: 978-0692542248
ISBN-10: 0692542248

# DEDICATION

This book is dedicated to you, my reader – the small business superstar
of tomorrow. In addition, I would like to dedicate this to my
gorgeous wife Christie and my beautiful daughters Alexa and Brooke.
Without their love and support, this book is not possible.

# TABLE OF CONTENTS

# INTRODUCTION:

Have you ever wondered what the difference is between a business that consistently grows and another that struggles just to make ends meet? Or why a business that was started in a basement of a home can outperform some of the best-run "big" companies in sales and profits?

Two businesses, operating in the same marketing arena and selling the same products or services, can have extraordinarily *different* results. How can one business continually grow and prosper, while the other struggles? How can one business owner run a highly successful business and be able to spend time away from the business for trips and vacations with the family, and another owner work day and night only to see his business struggle?

In this book, you will find some of the strategies and processes that will give you a greater chance of being amongst those successful businesses.

But, alongside that, there is one success factor that is probably even more important.

The truth is, for the most part, there is no such thing as a successful or unsuccessful business; there are successful or unsuccessful people, *entrepreneurs* who run businesses. Becoming a successful entrepreneur requires a certain self-image, a certain *mindset*. I like to refer to this mindset as the

**"5 Habits of Highly Successful Small-Business Owners."**

Here they are:

### Habit #1:  *Have a clear vision of their business, and commit their vision to paper*

> *"A man to carry on a successful business must have imagination.*
> *He must see things as in a vision, a dream of the whole thing."*
> Charles M Schwab, American stockbroker

The chances of your small business' success will improve substantially if you have a clear vision of what you want your business to look like, and what you want it to accomplish for you in the future. Your vision is your dream for the future of your business and it should delineate the path you will take to turn that dream into reality. You need a crystal-clear vision, one that you can communicate clearly, with vitality and a strong sense of commitment. Everyone involved in your business must comprehend your vision and, even more important, must believe in its success as much as you do.

Setting direction and guiding the business toward reaching your vision will make it successful. Vision is the owner's business philosophy. It's his "double vision" – his ability to keep the business' long-term dream in mind while micro-managing the business on a day-to-day, hour-by-hour basis.

Successful entrepreneurs commit their vision to paper. In all my years in business, I have found that not doing so is the single most fatal error a business owner can make. There's a direct correlation between having a well-thought-out, written vision statement and the success of your business.

Your vision should be a written statement of what your business will be when it is complete. It is a detailed picture of the future – what your business will look like, act like, smell like, feel like, and how it will perform when it is fully developed. Some of the things your written vision statement should include are: (1) the line of business you are in, (2) your company size, (3) the markets it will serve – demographics and psychographics, (4) the number of employees you will have, (5) the number of locations that you will operate from, and (6) what competitive advantages will differentiate your business from your competitors'.

## Habit #2: Put the proper systems in place

You need systems to be able to deliver a product or service in a predictable and consistent way. All successful businesses have a "how we do it here" manual, also referred to as a "policy and procedures" manual. *Standardize* your procedures so that everyone knows what they are and how to do them. These procedures involve production systems for your products or services, systems to deliver those products or services, systems to track new customers or clients, systems to help you keep up with your finances, systems to hire and train new employees, and the list goes on.

Look at the systems that operate within the McDonald's chain. A McDonald's in the Bronx operates exactly the same way as a McDonald's in Palm Beach. It runs just as predictably and profitably in either place. Why? Because there is absolutely no area in which procedures are not specifically spelled out through documented systems. Every procedure is outlined so clearly that anyone can be put into the system and taught to function at an extremely efficient level in a very short time.

Documented systems can make a difference to your own time, as a business owner. Without such systems in place, everything depends on you. If something happened to you, even for a short period, the entire business would be thrown into chaos. With properly documented systems of management and organization, a key employee (even you!) could leave suddenly, and the business would not suffer. You could replace the employee with minimal disruption. As new problems come up, you can adjust the systems you have in place to accommodate the needed changes.

If you set up the right systems from the start, they help run the business. You can be free to spend your time however you wish: more personal time for yourself, more time for your family, your community, and more time to enjoy a richer, more balanced life.

### Habit #3: Know what they don't know and then quickly get the help to fill the void

Most small-business owners don't realize that having an occupation or skill does not necessarily equate to building a successful business around it. It takes *different skills* to build a business. Let me give you an example. John worked as an engineer for 12 years before he started his own engineering firm. He was considered to be one of the best engineers in his firm before he went on to start his own engineering company. But John had never run a business before, and he did not have the knowledge and skill to operate his new company successfully, despite his engineering expertise. There is a lesson to be learned. The sooner you, the business owner, develop entrepreneurial skills, the sooner you will turn your expertise into business success!

You will need a number of different skills, all of which I will teach you in this book. Financial, marketing, management, and customer fulfillment skills are among those required if you want your business to run like a finely tuned machine.

Can you imagine an athlete training for the Olympic competition without a coach? Of course not! Nor can you develop these skills without qualified help. Your team of advisors can help you think in a new way, show you how to stay on track with your plans, and ultimately achieve your vision.

*We see our customers as invited guests to a party, and we are the hosts. It's our job every day to make every important aspect of the customer experience a little bit better.*
Jeff Bezos

## Habit #4:  Have a mindset of preeminence

**Preeminent (adj.):**  *excelling others, outstanding.*

The business owner has to have the mindset to view his business as a product – not the product or service he is producing, but his *whole* business as the product. It's an entirely new way of thinking, and as soon as such thinking is adopted in any business, the business begins to make massive leaps forward.

As the business owner, your primary objective should be to give your customers or clients the best possible *experience*; to enable others to see your business as a trusted, valued, respected, and expert provider. This mindset can be applied to any type of business. You have the responsibility and the obligation to provide guidance and direction to your customers, and to give them the best short-term and long-term outcome.

Many times, I have seen business owners make one simple, but momentous, mistake. Instead of "falling in love" with their customers, and paying attention to the experience they are having while interacting & being serviced by their business, they fall in love with the size of the company, growth of the company, number of employees, or the market share. The way to greatness today is to transfer your ultimate passion away from products and services, and toward people!  By doing so you will begin to look at your business as a *whole*, and any interaction that the customers have with any *parts* of your business, as part of an overall experience. If you as the business owner are focused on making it the best, most rewarding, most fulfilling, most enjoyable experience for the customer or client, you will dominate everyone else in your business sector.

A strategy of preeminence – of excelling – along with the approach of looking at your business as a whole, is truly transforming. If this is the only idea from these

5 habits that you take to heart and adapt and implement, you will see a significant improvement in your business.

## Habit #5:  Work <u>on</u> their business, not just in it

The successful small-business owner understands the real value and reward that is derived from working *on* the business rather than just working *in* the business. She understands that working on the business means viewing her business as a whole like I described in Habit #4. She sees her business made up of various parts that integrate seamlessly to function as a whole.

Working "on", instead of "in" the business is *strategic* work.  It is the way businesses transform themselves from vision into reality.  It requires asking strategic questions and then doing everything to find answers to those questions.

Smart entrepreneurs do the necessary strategic work, and *regularly* ask the following questions:

- What is my market share?
- Who is my ideal customer?
- Where is my industry headed?
- Who are my competitors?
- What are my competitive advantages?
- What are other successful businesses in my industry doing?
- How do they market their product or service?
- What are other successful businesses outside my industry doing?
- What is the "experience" my customers are having with my business?
- What is the "experience" customers are having at my competitor's place of business?

> *"Learn from yesterday, live for today, hope for tomorrow.*
> *The important thing is not to stop questioning."*
> Albert Einstein

To obtain the greatest value from all the strategies, techniques, success tips and ideas that you will find contained in this book, *begin* with a commitment to develop these habits. In the chapters that follow, you will learn a lot. You will read about many practical ideas – those that worked for me and for hundreds of small businesses, and that will work for you in your business, as well. There are ideas and strategies that you can begin to use immediately to quickly and easily take your business to the next level.

**A word of caution**: You may get tempted or inclined to skip certain chapters or parts of them because you think they don't apply to you. For example, you may own an established business and feel that the chapters on "selecting the right legal structure" or "writing a business plan" are not relevant. Likewise, if you are a newly started business, you may think that the chapter on "planning the exit" is not relevant to you at this time. My humble advice to you is don't assume the irrelevance of a chapter until you have reviewed or at least skimmed over it. The topics and order of the twelve chapters in this book, with the additional chapter on local information have been intentionally, thoughtfully and painstakingly selected because these are *"the essentials"* every small- business owner, doing business here **must** become very familiar with.

Congratulations on your decision to begin your own quest! I promise you, it will be well worth your while. Let's begin our journey.

# 12 Simple, Foolproof Steps For Business Success

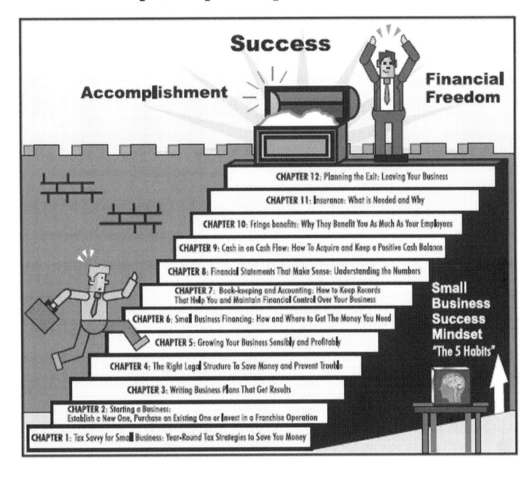

# CHAPTER 1:

## Tax Savvy for Small Business:
## Year-Round Tax Strategies to Save You Money

*I haven't paid taxes in years – one of the reasons*
*I believe everyone should run a business.*
Shirley A., magazine publisher

---

**CASE STUDY**

Jackie, a self-employed individual, operated a small home-based business while her husband, Tony, worked as a professional engineer. Jackie and Tony had prepared their own personal tax returns for the previous five years. A friend of theirs had insisted they have a "professional set of eyes" review their taxes. With great reluctance, this couple set an appointment to do so.

Upon review of their 2013 personal tax returns, $3,121 of overlooked business deductions were uncovered, resulting in *federal and state tax savings* of **$1,953**. A review of the 2011 and 2012 tax returns led to *additional* tax savings of **$2,138**. Total tax savings from this visit **$4,091**. The accountant advised the couple to invest these savings in a tax deferred retirement account to fund their dream – an early retirement.

Their hard-earned money was being handed to the tax authorities, when in fact it legitimately belonged to them. Significant tax deductions had been overlooked, resulting in huge tax savings. Funneling the tax savings to a retirement account would make an early retirement possible. Result? A very happy couple!

---

Every business owner is looking for ways to reduce expenses without reducing quality or losing customers. But few businesses look to the one area almost guaranteed to save money: income taxes. They end up overpaying their taxes because the businesses failed to take all of the tax deductions they were legally entitled to. Many of these businesses are still unaware of their errors.

Don't count on the IRS to help you. They won't tell you about a tax deduction you were entitled to but didn't claim. Discovering legitimate deductions is up to you. Every strategy contained in this chapter will help you reduce your taxes honestly, legitimately, and with the full approval and blessings of the IRS.

As you read this chapter you may recognize tax savings that you failed to claim when filing prior business or personal tax returns. Don't worry. You can go back, amend prior tax returns, and claim a tax refund. Amended tax returns must be filed within three years from the date you filed your original return or within two years from the time you paid your tax, whichever is later.

Our tax system is indeed very complex, and tax laws are ever changing. The Internal Revenue Code, the "Federal Tax Authoritative Guide," is a thick book with over 1.3 million words. Albert Einstein was quoted as saying *"The hardest thing in the world to understand is the income tax."*

The taxes you pay have a tremendous impact on the profits of your business. It is extremely important to consult with an accountant who can help you get the most deductions and assist you in planning for the future.

## Tax Strategies vs. Tax Loopholes or Tax Cheating

In pursuing lower income taxes, it is never necessary to resort to tax cheating or tax loopholes, or even to question the legality of the tax system. There is a big difference between cheating, loopholes, and strategies. This chapter is not about "tax loopholes" or the "gray" (questionable) areas of tax law. This chapter is not about tax tricks, "tax avoidance," or "red flags" to get you audited. Tax strategies are positive, legal use of the tax laws to reduce your income taxes. Tax strategies are legitimate actions you can take to automatically and legally qualify you for additional deductions. These deductions are IRS-approved. Each and every one is money in your pocket. Some tax strategies are straightforward and obvious. Other tax strategies are just as legal, just as easy to use, but less understood. What you read ahead will help you determine your best tax strategy!

> *"The trick is to stop thinking of it as 'your' money."*
> IRS auditor

# Strategy # 1 – Fully deductible business expenses

Business expenses are deductible in full directly from gross income. You can deduct any expenses that are "ordinary and necessary" to run your business, even if they benefit you personally.

This doesn't mean that the IRS will attack all sorts of legitimately claimed business deductions. In practice, the IRS is rather flexible in this regard. It defines "ordinary" as common and accepted in a field of business, and defines "necessary" as helpful and appropriate to that business.

"Ordinary" usually refers to expenses that are frequent and ongoing, such as amounts spent on gasoline or business meals. But it can also apply to something that you pay only once, such as an installation fee for a business telephone line.

In addition to being "ordinary and necessary," it has been held that a business expense must also be "reasonable." Whether an expense is reasonable depends upon the facts and circumstances in a particular situation. For example, it has been held that providing a chauffeured luxury car to an employee was not unreasonable given the nature of the employment and the congested area in which the car was driven. Entertainment and meal expenses are not deductible to the extent that they are lavish or extravagant, given the circumstances.

In applying the "ordinary and necessary" deduction test, you can expect almost any expense that's fairly common for your type of business to pass muster without serious question. Rather, IRS agents use this test to make sure that the expense is actually spent, and: (1) pertains to the business (instead of personal or family needs), (2) is not also being deducted elsewhere on the return (such as in the cost of goods sold computation), and (3) is a current, rather than capital, expense.

**Success Tip**

I want to stress the importance of proper documentation. Many small-business owners forgo worthwhile deductions because they have neglected to keep receipts or records. The IRS requires maintaining adequate records. But don't do it just because the IRS says so. Neglecting to track these deductions can lead to overlooking them. Refer to chapter 7 for assistance on proper record-keeping.

**Success Tip**
The IRS frowns at commingling of business and personal transactions. It is imperative that every small-business owner maintains a separate business bank account for the business. In addition, I highly recommend that a separate credit card be obtained to make business related purchases, especially one that provides with a year-end summary of charges.

# Strategy # 2 – Full home office write-off

The rules allowing a taxpayer to claim the home office deduction were loosened in 1999. No longer does the home office need to be the "principal place of business" for the taxpayer. The home office test can now be satisfied if the taxpayer uses the home office for "administration or management activities" and there is no other fixed location in which the taxpayer performs such activities for his business. The home office still must be used *exclusively* for business purposes to qualify. This will allow more taxpayers who conduct business outside of their office, but use their home to perform administrative tasks, to qualify for the home office deduction.

# Strategy # 3 – Writing off family medical expenses

One of the most under-utilized tax strategies by businesses is the Health Savings Account (HSA). This account offers a variety of benefits, including:

– **Tax Savings**. HSA's are pretax accounts, and contributions to them are deductible from your gross pay amount, potentially putting you into a lower tax bracket.

– **Tax-free Spending.** Money in an HSA account can be spent for tax-free qualifying health care expenses—a rule that applies for your entire life. Just as with a Roth IRA, withdrawals after retirement are not taxed.

– **Insurance Savings.** The HSA qualifying health insurance policy has a lower premium, allowing you to save money on overall healthcare costs. Moreover, the ability to pay cash for health care costs allows you to negotiate for more affordable services and motivates customers to be healthier.

**– Retirement Support.** An HSA can help pay for your retirement. After you turn 65, you have the option to withdraw money for non-health care expenses, and then pay federal income taxes on it. As a HSA holder, you pay ordinary income taxes on nonmedical-related withdrawals, yet with none of the mandatory disbursements required by traditional IRAs.

**– Investment Opportunity.** HSAs allow you to invest money in much the same way you might invest an IRA. It's advisable, though, to stick more with liquid investments if you have a health condition or are at risk of developing one, since you want the money available in case of a medical emergency.

The benefits of HSAs are many, as listed above. These accounts survived the recent federal health-care reform changes—the biggest overhaul of the healthcare system since the 1960s—so it seems a safe bet that HSAs will be around, and available to save you money, for years to come.

These plans are still recognized under ObamaCare as a tax-favored savings account combined with a qualifying high-deductible health insurance plan. It allows taxpayers to get a tax deduction for their healthcare expenses on the front page of their tax returns, enables the unused portions to grow tax-free, offers tax-free distributions for healthcare expenses, and, if not used for healthcare, it can be used like a typical IRA after the age of 59½.

It should be noted that in order to reap the tax savings benefit of an HSA plan, the deadline to have one in place is December 1. For example, to receive a deduction during 2013, you have to have a high-deductible health insurance policy ("HDHP") in place by December 1, 2014. You can always fund the HSA up until April 15, 2015, but you must have the insurance policy in place by the December deadline!

## Strategy # 4 – Writing off your child's college education expenses

For taxpayers challenged with the high cost of providing their children with a college education, this tax strategy is a valuable one to consider. Many business owners don't realize that paying their children under age 18, as well as adult children or grandchildren, is an excellent strategy to minimize their tax liability, in addition to a host of other ancillary benefits.

When children are paid for services they perform for a family business, this generates an expense—i.e. a tax deduction for the parent who is in a much higher tax bracket. The child is in a lower income tax bracket, and so ends up paying little to no tax.

The IRS allows any sole proprietorship or partnership (LLC) that is wholly owned by a child's parents to pay wages to children under age 18 without having to withhold the payroll taxes. For S- and C-Corporations, it is recommended that children be paid out of a family management company that is paid a management fee from the Corporation, or out of a Sole-Proprietorship or LLC with independent income and operations. This is because S- and C-Corporations do not receive the benefit of avoiding FICA when payment is made to children; corporate payment to children requires payroll taxes to be withheld. Children over the age of 18 or grandchildren can be treated as sub-contractors or employees, with the employee status requiring FICA withholding and other typical payroll fees. Additionally, the "Kiddie Tax" only applies to unearned or 'portfolio' income (IRC Section. 1(g)(2)(A) and IRC Reg Section 1.1(i)-1T, Q&A 3), disallowing children from being taxed on their income at the parents' rates.

It must be noted that this strategy does not advocate for children's participation in dishonest business operations. Hiring children to simply perform family chores does not qualify as a valid deduction and will certainly lead to an audit. (See U.S. v. Renfrow, 104 AFTR 2d 2009-5497, 1/26/2009). They have to be legitimately involved in the business, records should be kept of their time worked, and they should be paid a reasonable wage. If done correctly, this under-utilized strategy can yield two significant tax advantages.

First, when you pay your children—under the age of 18—to work, you do not have to withhold any income taxes or payroll taxes. (IRC Code Sec. 3121(b)(3)(A), IRC Reg Section 31.3401(a)(4)-1(b), and IRS Pub No. 15, (2011), p.10) The reasons for this are that the government and insurance carriers assume that 1) your children will not sue you if they are hurt on the job, and 2) your children are also probably on your health insurance plan and you would pay the bill one way or another.

Second, no one pay taxes on an initial amount of income earned each year– the Standard Deduction! (For 2015, this figure was $6,200.) (Rev Proc 2014-61, Sec. 3.14(1), IRB 2014-47). You can still claim your children on your tax return as dependents and take the exemption, even the child tax credit, without your children paying taxes on the first $6,100 of their earned income.

Any income your child earns over and above the standard deduction is taxable at your child's rate. Since the 10 percent tax bracket extends to $9,225 for a single filer, your child could earn an additional $9,225 and owe just $922.50 of federal income tax on the money. Because your marginal tax rate is likely much higher, the extra money your child earns may result in family tax savings.

These accumulated earnings and savings allow you to prioritize your children's futures as you creatively, and legally, prepare for expenses associated with a college education and their other future opportunities. Not only can business owners save thousands of dollars in taxes, but this business setup can draw a family together in ways never fathomed by practicing business owners.

## Strategy # 5 – Make your kids eligible for a Roth IRA

This is an incredible tax saving that I often see being under-utilized. This tax strategy is related to Strategy # 4 but takes it a step further. Hire your children, pay them and put the proceeds in a Roth IRA. All earnings in a Roth IRA are *tax-free*!

The U.S. Tax Court has validated a parent hiring his 7-year-old son to work for his business and allowed the deduction for reasonable wages paid. So if your child takes the yearly $5,000, from age 7 to 18, and invests it under the Roth IRA umbrella at 8% per year, compounded monthly, that child will have accumulated about $67,000 by age 18. If the Roth IRA has been established for at least 5 years, withdrawals can be used tax free for qualified education expenses!

Read on – it gets even better. If you leave all the money untouched, but contribute nothing after your child hits 18, by the time the child is 60, he or she will have accumulated more than $1.9 million that can be withdrawn tax-free. In my opinion, not a bad saving at all!

## Strategy # 6 – Deducting auto mileage to and from your job

Operating a car is expensive. The good news is that if you use your car for business, or your business owns its own vehicle, you can deduct some of the costs of keeping it on the road. Mastering the rules of car expense deductions can be tricky, but well worth your while.

There are two methods of claiming expenses: You can either keep track of and deduct all your actual business-related expenses, or simply deduct a certain amount (56 cents in 2014) for each business mile driven. As a rule, if you use a newer car primarily for business, the actual expense method provides a larger deduction at tax time.

If your auto is used for both business and pleasure, only the business portion produces a tax deduction. That means you must keep track of just how the vehicle is used, and add it all up at the end of the year. Certainly, if you own just one car or truck, no IRS auditor will let you get away with claiming that 100% of its use is business-related.

## Strategy # 7 – Deducting vacation travel expenses

Try to combine business (a meeting with a client or prospective client, checking out some material or resources for your business, etc.) with your vacation travel. As long as your trip is documented in advance, showing intent to build your business in some way, your travel expenses become business expense deductions. Meals, hotel rooms, plane tickets, car rentals, shipping business materials, clothes cleaning, telephone calls, faxes and tips, and even certain expenses for entertainment are deductible as business expenses with proper documentation. But if you take your family along, you can deduct only your own expenses, just as if you had traveled alone.

## Strategy # 8 – Deducting phone, Internet service, and utility bills

If phone calls, Internet service, or utilities are used for legitimate business purposes, then, with proper documentation, they become tax-deductible business expenses. If you have a credit or debit card solely for your business – and you should – the annual fees and interest payments are also tax-deductible business expenses.

## Strategy # 9 – Cutting your taxes when selling appreciated assets

When you are planning to liquidate appreciated assets such as stocks, think twice. Instead, give the actual stock asset to your child or other trusted family member who has a lower tax bracket. When that person sells the assets, he or she will pay taxes at the lower tax rate.

Another excellent method is to donate your appreciated assets to your favorite charitable organization. You are allowed to deduct the full value of the assets as a charitable contribution, and neither you nor the organization will pay any capital gains taxes on the assets.

# Strategy # 10 – Expenses of going into business

Once you're running a business, expenses such as advertising, utilities, office supplies and repairs can be deducted as business expenses. But you cannot take these deductions before you open the business. The costs associated with starting a business are capital expenses, which must be deducted over the first five years that you are in business.

**Success Tip**

If you expect your business to make a profit immediately, you may be able to work around this rule by delaying paying some bills until after you're in business, or by doing a small amount of business just to get officially started. But if, like many businesses, you will suffer losses during the first few years of operation, you might be better off taking the deduction over five years, so you will have some profits to offset.

# Strategy # 11 – Education expenses

You can deduct education expenses if they are related to your current business, trade or occupation, but you must follow strict rules. The expense must be to maintain or improve skills required in your present employment, or be required by your employer or as a legal requirement of your job. The cost of education that qualifies you for a new job is not deductible.

# Strategy # 12 – Legal and professional fees

Fees that you pay to attorneys, tax professionals or consultants generally can be deducted in the year they are incurred. In the event their work clearly relates to future years, these expenses must be deducted over the life of the benefit.

# Strategy # 13 – Renting property to your business

As a business owner, you have the opportunity to be compensated for your financial risk, as well as the services you provide to the business. You do this by retaining any real estate used in your business, in your own name, or in the name of a limited liability company (LLC) you own. Then, you lease the property back to your company. This gives you income that can be increased in later years as the business thrives and you avoid paying self-employment taxes on that income. Simultaneously, it gives your company a deduction. More important, down the road, when the property has appreciated significantly, it will not be double-taxed as it would if your corporation owned it. Real estate is also a good vehicle for family income shifting, when the time comes. (Note: If you have a home office, the IRS expressly forbids this method. If you want to lease part of your own home to yourself, don't try to deduct the rent on your tax return.)

This method is *not* recommended for equipment. Equipment is generally leased as a financing alternative. Since equipment doesn't usually appreciate – in fact quite the opposite: it almost always depreciates – there is little benefit in owning it personally.

The benefit of this strategy is dependent on a number of factors like the tax bracket you are in, the rate of expected appreciation on the property, etc. I recommend that you consult with your accountant.

# Strategy # 14 – Bad Debts

If someone "stiffs" your business, the bad debt you incur may or may not be deductible – it depends on the method of accounting that you use. If you use the accrual method, i.e., you recorded the income you earned, but not yet received, you can deduct it a bad debt expense.

If, however, you use the cash basis of accounting, the bad debt is not considered an expense since you did not record income in the first place.

# Strategy # 15 – Business Entertaining

If you pick up the tab for entertaining present or prospective customers, you may deduct 50% of the cost if it is either:

- "Directly related" to the business, and business is discussed – for example, a catered meeting at your office; or
- "Associated with" the business, and the entertainment takes place immediately before or after a business discussion.

Expenses are "directly related" if you can show:

- There was more than a general expectation of gaining some business benefit other than goodwill.
- You conducted business during the entertainment.
- Active conduct of business was your main purpose.

The IRS presumes that business will generally be conducted in places "conducive" to doing business. This is most significant for what does not qualify, as opposed to what does. Nightclubs, theaters, sporting events, or cocktail parties generally do not meet this standard.

Additionally, country or athletic clubs do not usually pass the test. Any IRS objection can be overcome, however, by clear and proper documentation showing that actual business did take place during the event.

Even if you can't show that the entertainment was "directly related" as discussed above, you can still deduct the expenses as long as you can prove the entertainment was "associated" with your business. To meet this test, the entertainment must directly precede or come after a substantial business discussion. Further, you must have had a clear business purpose when you took on the expense.

**Success Tip**

On the receipt or bill, always make a note of the specific business purpose -- for example, "Lunch with Frank Finnegan of Rahway Manufacturing Co. to discuss widget contract."

**Success Tip**
In circumstances where it's customary to entertain a business associate with his or her spouse, and your spouse also attends, entertainment of both spouses is deductible.

# Strategy # 16 – Fully deduct new equipment

Businesses generally, including unincorporated businesses, may elect to expense (immediately deduct) the cost of most new business equipment up to a fixed annual amount, instead of deducting the cost through depreciation deductions over a period of years.

Beginning in 2008, Congress altered the limits depending on the incentives Congress deemed necessary to stimulate the economy. Since 2010, the deduction maximum has been $500,000, subject to a $2 million limit on purchases. The $2 million dollar limit was enacted to ensure that only small and midsize businesses qualify for the deduction.

In 2015 those maximum deduction and limitation amounts are set to expire and the maximum deduction is planned to revert back to its original limit of $25,000, with a $200,000 limitation on purchases. If the reversion occurs, the advantages of Section 179 would be almost completely eliminated. **Unless Congress passes another extension or revision, the accelerated deduction will be unavailable for the 2015 tax year. At the time of publication, an extension or revision has not been passed.**

# Strategy # 17 - Roth Conversions

This strategy highlights how Roth IRAs can be an effective means to business owners achieving their individual retirement goals. Since 2010, all restrictions on converting to a Roth IRA have been removed, regardless of the level of income. For individuals who have been saving for retirement in a Traditional IRA, they can now convert some or all of the traditional IRA funds into a Roth IRA.

Converting to a Roth IRA means changing the tax treatment in which your retirement savings are placed, from a tax deferral available with a Traditional IRA to a Roth account with post-tax contributions.

With Roth IRAs, you essentially agree to pay any tax now in exchange for tax-free treatment when the funds are withdrawn later. As Roth IRAs have the potential to grow tax-free, this may help you save more over time. Plus, withdrawals are not mandatory during the lifetime of the original owner, allowing Roth IRA assets to pass to your heirs tax-free.

## Strategy # 18 – Interest

If, like many folks, you use credit to finance business purchases, the interest and carrying charges are fully tax-deductible. The same is true if you take out a personal loan and use the proceeds for your business. Many business owners overlook this tax deduction. But be sure to keep good records showing that the money was really put into your business. Otherwise, if you're audited later, the interest expense could be considered personal and the deduction disallowed.

## Strategy # 19 – Examine your business structure

This strategy is probably one of the more common ones I find small-business owners missing out on. How you organize your business structure can have a significant effect on the taxes you pay. By structuring your business as a S-corporation, the business is only required to pay the employer share of FICA taxes on what you take as salary. With S-corporations, a percentage of your earnings can pass through the corporation to you as new dividends, thus reducing your FICA-eligible wages.

Tax and other benefits of various structures can vary from business to business. A qualified accountant can help you determine the most effective way to organize your business.

**Success Tip**
Your business structure should be reviewed annually. To maximize on tax savings, a qualified accountant should review your business structure annually.

## Strategy # 20 – Moving expenses

If you move because of your business or job, you may be able to deduct certain moving costs that would otherwise be non-deductible personal living expenses. To qualify, you must have moved in connection with your business (or job, if you're an employee of your own corporation or someone else's business). The new workplace must be at least 50 miles farther from your old home than your old workplace was. (Technically, moving expenses related to your personal belongings aren't business expenses; there's a special place to list them on your Form 1040 tax return.)

## Strategy # 21 – Contribute to a retirement plan

Not only can you save for a comfortable retirement, but also significantly reduce your taxes by contributing to a tax-deferred retirement plan. Consider establishing a SIMPLE, SEP, or new 401(k) plan.

Keep in mind that if your tax year has already closed and you didn't set up a Keogh or SIMPLE plan, you may want to consider a SEP which allows you to establish and contribute until the due date of your return (including extensions) for the prior year. For example, if you received a six-month filing extension from April 15, you can set up and fund a SEP as late as October 15, 2015, and use the deduction for 2014.

Refer to chapter 10 on fringe benefits where I have discussed the features and benefits of various retirement plans. Meet with your accountant and choose the one that best meets the needs of your business.

## Strategy # 22 – Software

Off-the-shelf computer software placed in service during the tax year is qualifying property for purposes of the section 179 deduction. This is computer software that is readily available for purchase by the general public, is subject to a nonexclusive license, and has not been substantially modified. It includes any program designed to cause a computer to perform a desired function. However, a database or similar item is not considered computer software unless it is in the public domain and is incidental to the operation of otherwise qualifying software.

## Strategy # 23 – Charitable contributions

If your business is a partnership, limited liability company or S-corporation (a corporation that has chosen to be taxed like a partnership), your business can make a charitable contribution and pass the deduction through to you, to claim on your individual tax return. If you own a regular C-corporation, the corporation can deduct the charitable contributions.

**Success Tip**
You may be able to obtain a significant tax write-off by donating old computers or furniture to a school or other nonprofit organization. Keep in mind, however, that you may only receive a deduction if the item(s) has/have not been fully depreciated.

# Strategy # 24 – Taxes

Taxes incurred in operating your business are generally deductible. How and when they are deducted depends on the type of tax.

- Sales tax on items you buy for your business's day-to-day operations is deductible as part of the cost of the items; it's not deducted separately. But tax on a big business asset, such as a car, must be added to the car's cost basis; it isn't all deductible in the year the car was bought.

- Excise and fuel taxes are separately deductible expenses.

If your business pays employment taxes, the employer's share is deductible as a business expense. Self-employment tax is paid by individuals, not their businesses, and so isn't a business expense.

- Federal income tax paid on business income is never deductible. State income tax can be deducted on your personal return as an itemized deduction, not as a business expense.

- Real estate tax on property used for business is deductible, along with any special local assessments for repairs or maintenance. If the assessment is for an improvement – for example, to build a sidewalk – it isn't immediately deductible; instead, it is deducted over a period of years.

# Strategy # 25 – Advertising and promotion

The cost of ordinary advertising of your goods or services – business cards, yellow page ads and so on – is deductible as a current expense. Promotional costs that create business goodwill – for example, sponsoring a peewee football team – are also deductible as long as there is a clear connection between the sponsorship and your business. For example, naming the team the "Toms River Auto Parts Blues" or listing the business name in the program is evidence of the promotion effort.

**Success Tip**

Here are some additional routine deductions that many business owners miss. Keep your eye out for them. Remember that just because you didn't get a receipt doesn't mean you can't deduct the expense, so keep track of those small items and get big tax savings.

## More Easily Overlooked Business Expenses

- audio – and videotapes related to business skills
- bank fees
- business association dues
- business gifts (limited to $25 per person)
- business-related magazines and books
- casual labor and tips
- casualty and theft losses
- coffee and beverage service
- commissions
- consultant fees
- credit bureau fees
- office supplies
- online computer services related to business
- parking and meters
- petty cash funds
- postage
- promotion and publicity
- repairs and maintenance
- seminars and trade shows
- taxi and bus fare
- telephone calls away from the business

# Do You Engage in Tax Planning Year-Round?

Many small-business owners worry about their taxes only during tax season. However, you will save a fortune in taxes, legally, if you make tax planning your year-round concern.

Can you use that extra room in your house as a home office for your business? Can you arrange to use your car more for business purposes, and have you documented your business use mileage? Can you arrange for more of your entertainment expenses to be business related? Have you listed the business purpose on each receipt?

Do you make business and personal purchases, investments, and other expenditures with tax savings in mind? Do you document your expenses well so that they would survive a tax audit? Whenever you are faced with a business or personal financial decision, do you consider the tax consequences?

Make year-round tax planning part of your business management mindset and thus enjoy maximum tax savings. By rearranging your affairs to account for tax implications, you will save a fortune in taxes.

It would be advisable to consult a tax professional or accountant for proper planning and documentation for some of the more complicated tax strategies, but using these strategies could save you thousands of dollars in taxes.

# My final word of tax advice

Changes in tax laws in this country are ongoing. Enjoy the potential tax savings through implementing some of the tax breaks and strategies that I have identified in this chapter while these breaks exist. Don't miss the boat (yacht)!!!

> *"Of course, lower taxes were promised, but that has been promised by every president since Washington crossed the Delaware in a rowboat. But taxes have gotten bigger and their boats have gotten larger until now the president crosses the Delaware in his private yacht."*
> --Will Rogers, 1928

# Frequently Asked Questions on Tax Savvy for Small Business: Year-Round Tax Strategies to Save You Money

## Q. Are My Car and Truck Expenses Deductible?

If you use your car or truck in your business, you may be able to deduct the costs of operating and maintaining your vehicle. You also may be able to deduct other costs of local transportation and traveling away from home overnight on business.

If you use an *electric vehicle, you may qualify* for a deduction from gross income for a part of the cost of a *clean-fuel vehicle* you place in service during the year. The vehicle must meet certain requirements. For more information, see chapter 12 in Publication 535.

**Local transportation expenses.** Local transportation expenses include the ordinary and necessary costs of all the following.

- Getting from one workplace to another in the course of your business when you travel within the city or general area that is considered your tax home. Generally, your *tax home* is your regular place of business, regardless of where you maintain your family home. It includes the entire city or general area in which your business or work is located.

- Getting from your home to a temporary workplace when you have one or more regular places of work. These temporary workplaces can be either within the area of your tax home or outside that area.

Local business transportation does *not* include expenses you have while traveling away from home overnight. Those expenses are deductible as travel expenses.

You *cannot* deduct the costs of driving your car or truck between your home and your main or regular workplace. These costs are personal commuting expenses.

## Q. What are the Methods for Deducting Car and Truck Expenses?

For local transportation or overnight travel by car or truck, you generally can use one of the following methods to figure your expenses.

- Standard mileage rate (SMR).
- Actual expenses.

**Standard mileage rate.** Standard mileage rate refers to deductible costs of operating your car, van, pickup, or panel truck for business purposes. For 2014, the standard mileage rate is 56 cents a mile for all business miles.

If you choose to use the standard mileage rate for a year, you **cannot** deduct your actual expenses for that year except for business-related parking fees and tolls.

*Choosing the standard mileage rate.* Standard mileage rate must be chosen in the first year, but cannot be used if actual expenses have already been chosen as the deductible expense. As long as you use SMR in year 1, you can choose to use it continuously, or switch to actual expenses at a later date. If you use SMR for a leased car, you must use it for the entire lease period.

*Standard mileage rate not allowed.* You cannot use the standard mileage rate if you:

1. Use the car for hire (such as a taxi),
2. Operate two or more cars at the same time,
3. Claimed a depreciation deduction using any method other than straight line, for example, ACRS or MACRS,
4. Claimed a section 179 deduction on the car,
5. Claimed the special depreciation allowance on the car,
6. Claimed actual car expenses for a car you leased, or
7. Is a rural mail carrier who received a qualified reimbursement.

*Parking fees and tolls.* Business-related parking fees and tolls may also be deducted. (Parking fees you pay to park your car at your place of work are nondeductible commuting expenses.)

**Actual expenses.** If you do not choose to use the standard mileage rate, you may be able to deduct your actual car or truck expenses.

If you qualify to use both methods, figure your deduction both ways to see which gives you a larger deduction.

Actual car expenses include the costs of the following items.

| Depreciation | Lease payments | Registration |
|---|---|---|
| Garage rent | Licenses | Repairs |
| Gas | Oil | Tires |
| Insurance | Parking fees | Tolls |

If you use your vehicle for both business and personal purposes, you must divide your expenses between business and personal use. You can divide your expenses based on the miles driven for each purpose.

---

**Example:**

You are the sole proprietor of a specialty foods store. You drove your van 20,000 miles during the year. 16,000 miles were for delivering food to customers and 4,000 miles were for personal use. You can claim only 80% (16,000 ÷ 20,000) of the cost of operating your van as a business expense.

**More information.** For more information about the rules for claiming car and truck expenses, ask your accountant or see Publication 463, *Travel, Entertainment, Gift, and Car Expenses.*

---

## Q. If I Lease a Car, Can I Deduct the Payments?

If you decide to lease, you can deduct lease payments on the car. It's important to keep a detailed log showing how much you use your car for business, as compared to personal use, because that's how much of the lease payment you can deduct as a business expense. From a tax standpoint, life becomes a bit more complicated with leasing, but it's usually worth the effort. For instance, you have to spread any advance payments out over the entire lease period. You can't deduct payments to buy the car, even if they're called lease payments. And, depending on the value of the car, you may have to reduce your lease payment deduction a tiny bit each year of the lease; this reduction is called an "inclusion amount."

## Q. Can I Claim a Deduction for Business-Related Entertainment?

Usually, you can deduct only 50% of entertainment expenses. Qualified business entertainment is defined, so check with your accountant.

Most importantly, you must be able to show some proof that the entertainment expense was either directly related to, or associated with business. So, keep a guest list and note the business (or potential) relationship of each person entertained.

### Q. I am Planning a Trip to a Trade Show. Can I Take My Family Along For a Vacation and Still Be Able to Deduct the Expenses?

Yes and no. You can still deduct your part of the trip, as if you were traveling alone. If your family hops along for the ride, so much the better. But you may not claim a deduction for your family's meals or entertainment.

If you extend your stay and partake in some of the fun after the business part is over, the expenses attributed to the non-business days aren't deductible, unless you extended your stay to get discounted airfare (the "Saturday overnight" requirement). In this case, your hotel room and meals would be fully deductible.

### Q. I Work in my Home Part-Time. Can I Take The Home-Office Tax Deduction?

If you run a business out of your home, you can usually claim a deduction for the portion of the home used for business. Also, you can deduct related costs – utilities, insurance, remodeling, etc.

### Q. What is the Difference Between Current and Capitalized Expenses?

Current expenses are those incurred in the "current" year. Capital expenses are generally those expenses that have a useful life of more than one year, thus are expensed over time.

## Capitalizing Expenses

Capitalized expenses are usually "depreciated." This means that the expense is taken over a number of years, usually in line with a standard "schedule".

There are many rules for how different types of assets must be written off. The tax code dictates both absolute limits on some depreciation deductions, and over how many future years a business must spread its depreciation deductions for all asset purchases. Businesses, large and small, are affected by these provisions (IRC §§167, 168 and 179).

# Repairs and Improvements

The tax code says that repair and improvement expenditures are generally current, unless they do the following:

- Add to the asset's value

- Appreciably lengthens the time you can use it

- Adapts it to a different use

"Improvements" usually refers to real estate – for example, putting in new electrical wiring, plumbing and lighting – but the rule also applies to rebuilding business equipment.

---

**Example**

Gary uses a specialized hydraulic lift in his automotive shop. After 15 years of constant use, the machine is on its last legs. His average yearly maintenance expenses on the machine have been $10,000, which Gary has properly deducted as repair expenses. In 2014, he is faced with either thoroughly rehabilitating the machine at a cost of $80,000, or buying a new one for $175,000. He goes for the rebuilding. The $80,000 expense must be capitalized – that is, it can't all be taken in 2014 when the hydraulic lift is rebuilt. The tax code says that such equipment must be deducted over a period of 7 years.

---

## Q. What Special Deductions can I get if I'm Self-Employed?

You may be able to take an immediate expense deduction for equipment purchased for use in your business, instead of writing it off over many years. Additionally, self-employed individuals may deduct 100% of their health insurance premiums if structured properly. You may also be able to establish a Keogh, SEP or SIMPLE plan and deduct your contributions (investments).

### Q. I Own a Small Business. How can I get my Employees to Participate in the Company's Cafeteria Plan or FSA?

Help your employees understand the benefits of the plan you're offering. Inform them that they can't deduct their medical and dental expenses since they are deductible only to the extent they exceed 10% of their adjusted gross income (AGI). But they can effectively get a deduction for these items if they participate in the company Flexible Spending Account (FSA) or cafeteria plan. These plans permit you to redirect a portion of their salary to pay for these types of expenses with pre-tax dollars.

### Q. Must I Pay Tax on my Employer's Payment or Reimbursement of my Education Expenses?

Maybe not. Up to $5,250 can be tax-free. Exemption can apply to graduate level courses

### Q. Where is a Loss Reported on my Return and How Much Can I Deduct?

If your business deductions are more than your business income for the year, you may have a *Net Operating Loss (NOL)*. A NOL can be deducted from the current or other years' income. In general, partnerships cannot take advantage of this. Partners or shareholders can use their separate shares of the partnership or S corporation's business deductions to impact their individual NOLs. For additional help, see Publication 541, *Partnership,* Publication 542, *Corporation*, Publication 925, *Passive Activities and At-Risk Rules*, and Publication 536, *Net Operating Losses (NOLs) for individuals, Estates, and Trusts.*

A capital loss usually results from the sale of an investment property or a capital asset used in business, or a theft/loss. Publication 544, *Sales and Other Disposition of Assets* provides more information.

# Special Situations

*S-corporations*
An S-corporation shareholder who holds stock at any time during the year may claim his proportionate share of corporate losses on an individual tax return subject

to certain limits. For more information about the limitations, see the instruction for Instructions for Form 1120S, Schedule K-1.

*Partnerships*
Partner losses are allocated per the percentage of ownership during the year, referred to as "partner's distributive share". Reporting of this occurs on Schedule K-1 (Form 1065). Losses are only permitted up to the partnership interest.

## Q. I Invested Personal Funds to Start a New Corporation Last Year. How can I get Credit for this on my Personal Income Tax Return?

The personal funds you invest to start a corporation is known as your "basis" in stock of said corporation. Your personal income tax return will not show this investment unless and until you sell the stock or until the business ceases to operate.

## Q. I Need Help With Form K-1. How do I report this on my Income Return?

If you are a partner in a partnership and have received a 1065 K-1, Please see Instructions for Form 1065, Schedule K-1 for help in preparing your form.
If you are a shareholder in an S-corporation and have received an 1120S K-1, please see Instructions for Form 1120S, Schedule K-1 for help in preparing your form.

## Q. What Deductions Can I take on my Partnership or S-corporation Return?

In general, ordinary and necessary business expenses are deductible on business return. However, there are some items that partnership and S-corporations should deduct at the partner or shareholder level. These are referred to as "separately stated items". For a more complete explanation of business in general, see Publication 535, *Business Expenses* Publication 541, *Partnerships*, and Instructions for Form 1120S.

# CHAPTER 2:

## Starting A Business: Establish a New One, Purchase an Existing One or Invest in a Franchise Operation

*"You see things; and you say, "Why?" But I dream things that never were; and I say "Why not?"*
George Bernard Shaw

# INTRODUCTION

There are a number of different reasons for starting a business. Perhaps you are interested in "trying something new." Perhaps you have found a new way to solve a problem or meet an expressed need, maybe you want independence, or are trying to increase your income. Whatever your reasons for going into business, you must do so with your eyes wide open. If you are like most people, it's likely you haven't thought as much about the downside of going into business as you have about the bright side. A great deal of thought and research should go into making a decision that will affect you and your family for a long time to come.

## Do you have what it takes?

Evaluating your strengths and weaknesses as the owner and manager of a small business is a good place to begin. Carefully consider each of the following questions.

**Are you a "self-starter?"** Will you be motivated to do everything that needs to be done, without someone telling you to do it?

**How well do you get along with different types of personalities?** Customers, vendors, employees, bankers, professionals, and advisors – when you're in business for yourself, you must be able to relate to and get along with all of them. Does that describe you? If not, consider how it would impact your success.

**How are you at making decisions?** Small-business owners are required to make decisions constantly, often quickly, under pressure and independently.

**Do you have the physical and emotional stamina to run a business?** Business ownership can be fun and exciting, but extremely challenging. It's a lot of work, at least in the early years. Can you face 12-hour work days six or seven days a week?

**How well do you plan and organize? Are you a planner?** Research indicates that many business failures could have been avoided through better planning. Good organization of financials, inventory, schedules and production can help avoid many pitfalls.

**Is your drive strong enough to maintain your motivation?** How well do you respond to stress? Business ownership and operation can take its emotional as well as physical toll on you. Are you ready for that?

**How will the business affect your family?** The first few years of business startup can be hard on family life. Have you considered the impact on your spouse? Children? Personal finances? Profitability could take years to achieve. Are you (and your significant others) prepared to decrease your standard of living until the business becomes profitable?

# Common Entry Strategies

There are basically three ways to begin a business. You can start a new business, purchase an existing business, or invest in a franchise operation. There are good reasons for each choice and each carries its own advantages and risks.

# Start a new business

This option permits you the most freedom and the satisfaction of knowing you did it all yourself. Some opportunities which might prompt this choice are: a new invention, a spin-off of an existing product or service, turning a hobby into a business, awareness of a customer ready to buy your product, unfulfilled market need, expansion of a part-time activity or simply chance.

**Advantages of starting a new business:**

- For true entrepreneurs, the real goal and major appeal is in the creation of something new, not necessarily in the management aspect, so starting a new business is appealing.

- The high investment costs associates with buying an existing business or obtaining a franchise can be avoided.

- You are in control. As the owner, you call the shots. You run the business the way you want.

- Great sense of achievement and ability to say "I told you so."

**Disadvantages of starting a new business:**

- You need a good idea, potential customers, and knowledge of marketing, finance and management to succeed.

- There is a high failure rate. (The Small Business Administration reports that 75% of new businesses fail in a year and 25% of first-year survivors fail in the second year.)

- Most new businesses are privately financed with the owner's money and often are undercapitalized.

- There is a lack of formalized structure, which is good for some and bad for others. You'll have to learn to adjust to a need for greater personal drive and motivation to get going and stay active in business.

- It is not unusual for a new business owner to work at least 60 hours, and possibly as many as 80 hours in a week, seven days a week, for the first year or so, which can create stress for yourself and your family not to mention possible burnout.

- Ability for your friends to say "I told you so."

I have identified a four-step process that can reduce the risks of starting a new business.

# Step 1: What business should you choose?

You may already have a very good idea of the business you will choose and feel like you can skip this step. *Don't*. It always helps to test and refine your idea. You can do this very easily. Brainstorm all the businesses you could reasonably consider, write them down, and then eliminate those that you know are not for you. Rule out the ones that require talents and skills you do not possess, and of course those in which you have no interest. Then, gather information and evaluate your idea against other possibilities.

**Success Tip**

You might try one or more of the following sources for information:

- Telephone Yellow Pages can indicate what is and is not available in your area.

- Public libraries have a number of business directories, including the Thomas Register.

- Searching the Internet can help you find and refine your idea.

- Entrepreneurial magazines often have articles about new business ideas that have potential.

- Ask friends, co-workers, neighbors and relatives if they have product or service needs that are not currently being met.

After collecting this additional information and reconsidering your list, narrow the possibilities. Get advice. One of the common errors in choosing a business is *not* asking for help. This is an important way to gather information to complete the selection process. There are four things you can actively do:

**Talk with people who own and operate similar businesses:** Other business owners will usually be willing to share their experience and advice. The local Chamber of Commerce or other business association meetings may provide access to business owners to whom you can talk.

**Work for someone else for a while:** A time-honored way of learning a business is to work in a similar business as an employee. Not only will you get on-the-job training, you'll get a paycheck, and will avoid overhead expenses. When scouting out potential "employer-trainers," it's best to look for one that is successful and well-run.

**Ask for professional advice:** There are four professionals you should get to know early in your business planning: an attorney, accountant, marketing consultant, and banker. Share your plans with them. They may point out factors you hadn't yet considered.

**Share your thoughts with your family, friends and associates:** They may come up with considerations that may discourage you from your idea, or they may offer real encouragement for pursuing another idea. Having the support and involvement of those close to you can be an added benefit.

**Success Tip**
More often than not, you may receive negative reaction from those around you. Don't feel discouraged or forgo your idea. Instead assess the validity of their comments by conducting more research. If you then find truth in their remarks, forgo the current idea and look for other opportunities – don't let your ego get in the way.

**Next**
Once you've narrowed down and refined your idea, you need to decide if this business will be successful.

# Step 2: Is your idea feasible?

At this point, you have examined your personal motivation for business ownership and chosen an interesting possibility. Before you run to the bank, get a loan, and open your business, *Stop*! Take the time to figure out if your business will have a chance to succeed.

A common mistake many new business owners make is to blindly begin a business without evaluating its feasibility. Doing so will allow you to make a more informed "go" or "no go" decision. A sampling of topics that should be honestly appraised includes:

- Is there really a demand for your product or service?

- Have you researched market demand or have you just assumed that people need or want your product or service?

- Does your product or service satisfy an unfulfilled need?

- Will your product or service serve an existing market in which demand exceeds supply?

- Will your product or service be competitive based on its quality, selection, price or location?

- Do you know who your customers will be?

- Will your business be conveniently located for the people you plan to serve?

- Will there be adequate parking facilities for your customers?

- Do you understand how your business compares with your competitors?

- What differentiates you from potential competitors?

Your business must meet the needs and desires of buyers, and do so effectively and efficiently. How do you know? The answer is simple – analyze the market. There are four components to studying a market:

**1. Personal knowledge.** Understanding the specific industry is vital to assessing the market for a product or service. Personal knowledge of the industry develops from having contacts in the business, personal experience and a general feel for the business.

**2. Competition.** Who are your competitors? What are your competitors' strengths and weaknesses? What are your competitors planning to do next? What are your competitors' spending trends? A survey of the competition may be needed to determine if there is a niche or room in the market for another business. Observing competitors' businesses can accomplish this. How busy are they? What problems do other businesses seem to have? What type of customers do they have? Observation helps to determine the size of the market and problems businesses have in serving that market.

**3. Customers.** Do you know who your customers are? Do you understand why they buy your products or services? Another useful method in your planning would be to interview owners of similar businesses outside of your planned market area. If your business will draw customers from a 25-mile radius, similar businesses in towns 60 miles away generally will not be competing for your customers. Business owners may be quite willing to discuss their businesses and to share advice. Often, they have insight and experience that can be invaluable to a new business owner. Also, after developing a profile of a typical customer, talking with a few people fitting that description will help identify needs of customers.

**4. Secondary research.** Finding information that is already published through a library or the Internet is a necessary activity. You must quantify the market and verify your findings from the above three steps. How big is your market? Is it large enough to sustain your business and competition? What is the growth trend for the next five years? Once a market has been identified, what is the size of the actual market that you can compete in?

The following tools are designed to help with research at the library or on the Internet. This research should not be neglected nor should it be the sole source of information used in developing a business or marketing plan.

Local and university libraries contain publications, which can provide much of the information entrepreneurs need. Materials that are not in your local library may be obtained through interlibrary loans. Check with the reference librarians. Most libraries also have Internet connections and the reference librarians can help you with online research.

### Research Tools

Use the following list as your guide to doing secondary research on a specific business or industry.

- Identify the appropriate Standard Industrial Classification (SIC) code for your business. The U.S. Government assigns four-digit numbers to specific business types. Since most government and industrial statistics are gathered and reported by SIC code, identification of the correct code for your business will enable you to locate important data. An SIC code manual is available at most libraries.

- Check for the current periodical literature on the subject.

- Check the Small Business Sourcebook or the Encyclopedia of Business Information Sources to identify major books, trade journals, and organizations for specific business categories.

- Write or call the appropriate industry trade associations that are listed in the Encyclopedia of Associations.

- Write or call for a media kit from trade journals.

- Write or call franchisers for information on their franchised businesses.

- Obtain the financial ratios for the business category. Trade association financial studies, if available, usually provide the most detailed information. Three other popular sources include Robert Morris Associates Annual Statement Studies, Dun & Bradstreet's Business and Financial Ratio, and Financial Research Associates' Financial Studies of the Small Business.

- Examine census material such as income, age and family size of populations in areas as small in size as zip codes in the Census of Population and Housing, Census of Retail Trade, Census of Service Industries, Census of Wholesale Trade, and Census of Manufacturers. The Department of the Census web site is: www.census.gov.

- Search the Internet for information on your topic. Check out popular engines such as: www.google.com, www.yahoo.com, and www.bing.com.

# Step 3: Will you be able to meet the needs of the marketplace?

Once you determine that your idea is indeed feasible, it's time to decide if *you* are going to be able to fulfill the needs of your market. Step 3 will help you do just that.

Conducting what is called a "SWOT" analysis is an ideal method for describing your ability to construct a business that has the potential to meet customer needs and, ultimately, be successful.

In a SWOT Analysis, you essentially nominate the **Strengths** and **Weaknesses** of the business (its internal resources and capabilities), and then you identify the **Opportunities** and **Threats** it faces (factors external to the organization).

This is an easy, understandable way of identifying key issues and communicating them to others. And to make things even simpler to grasp, the typical SWOT analysis is done on a four-cell grid:

| Strengths | Weaknesses |
|---|---|
| **Opportunities** | **Threats** |

The exercise is simple: All you do is list factors in the relevant boxes. Strengths and weaknesses are internal factors; the quality of your product or the skills of your management, for example. (Both might also be weaknesses, of course, if the product quality is low and management incompetent.) Opportunities and threats are external factors, for instance the development of a whole new market (opportunity) or the arrival of a clutch of new competitors (threat).

Sometimes it helps to start without the grid. List any issues at all that might affect the business – internal or external, real or perceived. When you run dry of new ideas, organize the items into the SWOT categories.

**So what are those categories, and what do they mean to you?**

- **Strengths**

In the first box list all the strengths of your company. A few questions that can help you are:

What are your advantages?

What do you do well?

What relevant resources do you have?

What do other people see as your strengths?

---

**Success Tip**

Here's a jump-start tip, especially for a group SWOT session: begin by brainstorming adjectives that characterize your company, write them down as quickly as people say them, and then use those words to construct a more considered profile of your company's strengths. If you're the sole proprietor or the prime mover in the business, try starting with a list of your own positive personal characteristics.

---

- **Weaknesses**

A weakness is something that seriously impedes a firm's effective performance, a limitation or deficiency in resource, skills or capabilities.

What could be improved about the business – markets, staffing, management, and control?

What stumbling blocks do you continue to encounter?

What does your company do that can be improved?

What should be avoided?

What do your competitors do better than you?

Don't try to disguise weaknesses, and don't merely list errors, omissions and mistakes. Look at things from the outsider's perspective, too. For instance, a one-man business might list the proprietor's knowledge as a strength; the outsider might see total reliance on one individual as a weakness. It is best to be realistic now, and face any unpleasant truths as soon as possible.

- **Opportunities**

Where are the good opportunities facing you?

What are the interesting trends you are aware of?

What customer needs are not being met by your competitors?

A useful approach to looking at opportunities is to look at your strengths and ask yourself whether these open up any opportunities. Alternatively, look at your weaknesses and ask yourself whether you could open up opportunities by eliminating them.

- **Threats**

Threats are key impediments to the firm's current or desired position.
What obstacles do you face?
What is your competition doing?
Are the required specifications for your job, products or services changing?
Is changing technology threatening your position?
Do you have bad debt or cash-flow problems?
Could any of your weaknesses seriously threaten your business?

To complete your SWOT haystack, include SWOT analyses produced by other groups or individuals – it always pays to get another point of view. Now sort each category first by relative importance. Then re-sort them in terms of reality – an interesting exercise, which might well require some soul-searching (what evidence do we really have for saying that we are the best?)

Finally, trim the categories to, say, no more than five or six items each, eliminating duplicates and homing in on the really critical issues. You can use this as the basis for strategic planning. If you are preparing a business plan, it's this cut-down summary and the accompanying discussion of strategy that should appear in the document.

The aim of a SWOT analysis is to identify the critical issues in any situation and to organize them in a way that enables you to come up with a sound strategic approach. This should enable you to do the following:

- Build on strengths

- Minimize weaknesses

- Seize opportunities

- Counter threats

Indeed, you might see things in terms of answers to these four questions:

- How can strengths be used to take advantage of opportunities?

- How can strengths be used to avoid or defuse threats?

- How can weaknesses be overcome to take advantage of opportunities?

- How can weaknesses be overcome to counteract or minimize threats?

*But be warned.* SWOTs often reflect an existing viewpoint, and the exercise can easily be (mis)used to justify a previously decided position or some already agreed-upon course of action.

And it's difficult to be objective. You may excel in some aspect of your business. But if there's no demand for those skills and there's no opportunity to sell them, your high opinion of yourself might better appear in the SWOT grid as a weakness.

Besides, one person's threat is another's opportunity. One individual may regard the recruitment of an experienced part-timer as a threat to existing job roles; another might see the opportunity to learn something from the incomer.

**Success Tip**

The secret of a good SWOT analysis is to be as open-minded as possible to suggestions – particularly in a group SWOT. The first SWOT analysis should be done fairly quickly and talked through. Then, it should be followed by another analysis sometime in the future to refine some of the points that came up as a result of your first discussion. SWOT won't help you find a definitive answer to all your questions, but it will help you get your thoughts in order so you can concentrate on fundamental "macro" issues rather than on a sea of "micro" problems.[1]

# Step 4: Financing your small business

Now that you know there are enough customers for your product or service, it's time to determine the financing. Details are listed in Chapter 6.

# Step 5: Find a knowledgeable accountant

Congratulations! If you've completed the first four steps, you now know:

- Whether you have the personal, business and lifestyle requirements to begin a small business endeavor,

- If your idea has been thoroughly examined and refined,

- There are customers for your product or service,

- You have the resources and capacity to meet customer needs,

- You can be financially successful.

With this information, you are on your way to putting together your Business Plan, an important cornerstone of starting a business. But there are still many more questions to answer and choices to make. At this point I recommend you make an appointment with a knowledgeable accountant. He or she can review your information, answer your questions, and point you in the right direction to complete the additional steps needed to start your business.

Some of the additional questions a qualified accountant can help you answer are:

- What legal structure will you have?

- What insurance coverage will be needed?

- What accounting system will you use?

- What equipment and supplies will you need?

- What will you name your business?

- Where will your business be located?

- How will you market your business?

- What permits and licenses do you need?

- Should you rent or lease?

- What do you need to set up an office?

- Should you have a home-based business?

- Have you applied for your state employer identification number and your federal identification number?

- Have you obtained a business license?

- Have you checked zoning and other land use ordinances?

- Have you established a bank account?

- Where will you find qualified employees?

- How much will you pay your employees and yourself?

- How will you price your product or service?

# Buy an Existing Business[2]

By buying an existing business you can avoid lead-time required to launch the business, understand expected income and expenses, acquire an existing customer base, and take hold of an established image. Most successful acquisitions are accomplished by knowledgeable, adequately financed business people. When acquiring a company, it's important to understand the numerous tax and financial maneuverings available for acquiring and financially restructuring an existing company.

# Why Buy an Existing Business?

Evidence clearly shows that your chances of success are best when you buy an existing business or franchise resale. With any new business you have two challenges: developing the product or service, and then seeing what, if anything, people are willing to pay you for it.

In spite of a company's past performance, an existing business or franchise will, at the very least, have a track record from which you will be able to make certain decisions. Even if the company was not profitable in the past, your strengths may lend themselves perfectly to turning it into a viable venture. Additionally, you have the ability to evaluate what the company did in the past that resulted in the current status of the operation.

**Advantages of buying an existing business:**

- The business is "up and running" already.

- It is likely to have an existing customer, employee and supplier base.

- There is a tried and tested business formula to emulate, or some sort of a baseline to improve on.

- The previous owners are likely to lend support and goodwill.

- There is generally more chance of success than starting a similar business from scratch.

- Obtaining outside financing may be easier because of an existing track record.

**Disadvantages of buying an existing business:**

- A large investment is often required.

- The loss of an owner or manager may lead to disruption for the operation.

- Business transfer costs, i.e., attorneys, surveys, accountants etc.

- A large amount of time and travel required to research the opportunities available.

- You may inherit inept employees or employees who are loyal to the previous owner and not to you.

- The present location may be limiting. You may be locked into the existing policies and practices of the business, at least for the foreseeable future.

## Sources of information to purchase an existing business.

I have compiled a list, arranged according to my preference, which can assist you in locating an existing business available for sale.

1. Classified advertisements in newspapers. Popular daily and Sunday newspapers usually have various businesses for sale – look in the classifieds section under the header "Business opportunities."

2. Classified or space advertisements in trade magazines.

3. Business brokers.

4. Professionals: Check with attorneys, accountants and bankers dealing with small business. They may know of a business of the type that you're interested in.

5. Chamber of Commerce: The directors at your local Chamber of Commerce may keep a list of businesses for sale.

# DUE DILIGENCE – Evaluating An Existing Business!

Due diligence refers to the period during which buyers make sure they have all the information they need to proceed with the transaction. At this point buyers are focused on a particular business they are seriously interested in purchasing. Usually, after a buyer signs a letter of intent to purchase a business and the seller accepts the letter, the buyer will have a specified period of time in which to conduct a due diligence investigation of the seller and the company. During this period, a buyer should have access to the business' financial and other records, facilities, employees, etc., to investigate before finalizing the deal.

The seller will try to negotiate the shortest due diligence period possible. Situations where the seller limited the due diligence period to a week or so are not uncommon. Unless you have intimate knowledge of a particular business, it is impossible and even irresponsible to believe you can get a good feel for a business in this short a time. The shorter the period, the greater the number of surprises you will find out later. Moreover, the chances are that you will not be able to learn enough about the business – so you will probably abort the purchase. Or, worse, you will buy the wrong business or negotiate terms and conditions that are highly unfavorable.

You need at least 30 days (20 working days) to investigate even the smallest of companies. Since a proper investigation reaches further than just financials you must allow yourself adequate time to accumulate the information. How do you get the seller to agree to this time frame? Here's my suggestion; let the seller know exactly what it is that you will be investigating. Tell them that you do not want to back out of the deal and if they truly want to move forward with the purchase they must allow you the time to do the proper investigation. Let them know that you want to buy the business, but if they don't let you confirm your commitment through proper due diligence then you will have to walk away before you start. When you position it this way, you'll get what you want!

Your preparation must begin the moment you believe that the business may be worth pursuing. In fact, after you meet the owner the first time and believe that you may be interested, you should begin to organize your plan. No matter how early you are in negotiations, at least start thinking about what it is you need to do. Start lists and note areas and specific details related to the business that warrants further review. Once you get closer to a deal keep detailed "to do" lists, broken down by each sector of the business (i.e. Financials, Employees, Sales, Contracts, etc.). Keep your accountant informed when you anticipate beginning the due diligence. Assemble lists of the materials you will need from the company and begin the due diligence only when you have received all of the supporting documents that you will need from the seller.

The seller must let his people know that they are to provide you with full access to all files and complete cooperation throughout your investigation. Don't let the seller "think" that you are snooping; let them know in the clearest of terms that you are snooping! That's your job. If there is anything that they do not want you to see, then tell them to remove it from the premises.

Note that there is no set amount of time that must pass during due diligence – take as long as you need to answer all of your questions. If you haven't covered them already, you should examine the following areas during the due diligence period:

- **Financial operations**. Inspect the company's books and records, as well as all accounting and bookkeeping methods. Analyze cash flows, both present and projected. Look at accounts receivable. Consider debt and bank or lender relations. Consider services and product pricing and its consistency with industry standards. Get your accountant involved during this analysis.

- **Business operations**. Consider location, vendors, suppliers, management, customer relations, inventories, insurance policies and any other topics specifically related to the business you are considering buying.

- **Marketing**. Review the company's advertising campaigns and public relations programs (if any). Analyze marketing and sales strategies. Look at how your competition markets and advertises their products.

- **Fixed assets**. Examine all appropriate leases and/or deeds. Conduct appraisals for all equipment and assets. Consider depreciation in property and equipment values.

- **Personnel**. Review employees' skills, experience, wages and salaries, payroll procedures and other relevant human resources issues.

**Success Tip**

If you wish more information before doing business with a company, you may want to check them out at Dun & Bradstreet. Dun & Bradstreet is number one globally in providing information about "business-to-business credit, marketing, purchasing, and receivables management and decision support services." You can find Dun & Bradstreet on the Web at http://www.dnb.com/.

# What If You Find Surprises?

If you don't find any surprises, you probably haven't looked hard enough. Address each one on its own and make sure that you scrupulously explore each so that your facts are bulletproof. However, don't get bogged down with minor issues; it's best to take these as "part of the package." Unless you find something that cannot be resolved or is so detrimental that even if the seller lowered the price by 50% you would still walk away, you are best served to take all of these obstacles in stride. Don't publicize them; investigate them. Finding a few surprises doesn't mean that the business is bad. You must weigh the impact against the future viability of the business.

Keep in mind that your objective is to learn what it is you will be getting into and what the future can be with you in charge. The option always exists for you to renegotiate once your investigation is completed. You will be in a much stronger position if you can go to the seller with very specific concerns, which require reevaluation and renegotiation. With this in mind, do not discuss your findings with anyone except your accountant or other advisors. Not the seller, not your broker, not the employees…nobody. It is not their business!

# Business Brokers/Business Transfer Agents

### What Is A Business Broker and Should You Use One?

A business broker attempts to put buyers and sellers together. The requirements to become a business broker vary from state to state, and their individual training, history, specialty and area of expertise are things that you must investigate. Some brokers work independently while others work for a brokerage company. Business brokers work on commission, and if you do not ultimately buy a business, then any work that they have done for you is not compensated.

If you decide to hire a business broker, it is important that you hire the right one. A business broker will provide you with access to businesses available for sale that you would never be able to find on your own. They can narrow the search for you to businesses that fit your criteria and they can help you avoid a lot of wasted time. The one thing that brokers cannot do, no matter how good they may be, is to find a business that is right for you. This is something only you can do. Brokers clearly prefer to work with knowledgeable buyers and if they have to spend their time educating you then they cannot make money. They can be an effective tool for you to use if you can provide them with a clear mandate of what it is that you are looking to buy. Avoid generalities; explain your strengths, weaknesses and objectives and never mislead them.

## Working With Them

Eighty five percent of potential buyers that brokers work with never buy a business. While this is part of the risk involved in their chosen profession, this does not give you the right to waste their time. Accordingly, they may be somewhat hesitant when working with new clients until you demonstrate your sincerity and commitment to buying a business. There is no doubt that if you are a serious and educated buyer then a good broker will go above and beyond the call of duty to service your needs. Be respectful of their time and realize that they have to make a living. If at any time you decide to drop out of the hunt to buy a business then let them know immediately. Conversely, if you do not feel that they are extending their best efforts on your behalf, then find another one.

## How They Can Help You

There are two noteworthy ways that a broker can help you. First, they can provide you with listings and information on businesses that are available for sale that you would not discover on your own. In other words, they have the database from which you can search. Secondly, they can be "used" as the "bad guy." Once you get into negotiations with a seller you should let the broker deliver any bad news or commentary that you may have. The reason for this is because you are going to need the seller's help in completing the deal and thereafter for training and assistance. By letting the broker deal with the bad news you can maintain the integrity of your relationship and keep yourself in somewhat of a third-party-position if renegotiations are needed.

## How They Can Hurt You

If you use the wrong broker they can hurt you significantly. They will be a monumental waste of your time. They can send you looking in the wrong direction altogether. They can try to work both parties and may not make you privy to everything that they are discussing with the seller's broker. If they represent both you and the seller their agenda may be suspect; they may very well be in a conflict-of-interest position. This is specifically why you must control the negotiations and use them properly, or you may find yourself terribly frustrated.

## Where to Find One?

Check your local classifieds to see which brokers seem to have the most prominence and exposure in the "Businesses For Sale/Business Opportunity" section. Start by calling these. Also, if you are aware of any business that has recently changed ownership, call the new owner and ask them for a recommendation. Speak to lawyers, accountants, friends, family and business associates. Ask them if they can suggest anyone.

## Verifying Their References

Get the names of four or five buyers and sellers they have worked for in the past. Contact each one of these and ask them if they could tell you what they believe the broker's strengths and weaknesses are. Be sure to ask each one if they were going to buy or sell a business in the future would they use them again. Tell them the approximate price business you are looking for and ask if they feel that the broker is well-suited for your needs. Ask them what it is specifically that the broker did well or poorly for them.

## Exclusive Agreements

Some brokers may try to get you to sign exclusive representation agreements with them. Under no circumstances whatsoever should you do this! Make it very clear that you will be pleased to work with them and the best measure they can take to ensure that they earn a commission from you is to lead you to the right business. Some brokers may request an application fee. If you believe that the broker is right for you then you can consider it if it's a small amount. They must put in writing that if they do not perform their duties, the money will be refunded, no questions asked. When you buy a business, if they are involved in the transaction then they must also refund the money. They will ask you to sign Confidentiality Agreements for any individual listings they show you. This is for their protection and it is only fair if they show you a business first, then they should make the commission if you buy it. Have a lawyer review it briefly in any case.

### How They Get Paid

The seller is responsible to pay their commission from the proceeds of the sale. Ask the broker to send you a copy of the agreements they have in place with sellers. This way, you can understand the terms and conditions of their agreements, and determine if you have any legal exposure. Generally, the commission is 10% of the total deal regardless of the terms of the agreement; this amount is split between all of the brokers involved. Furthermore, if they work for a brokerage company, part of their share goes to the company. So when all is said and done, they don't make as much as you think. Good brokers earn their money; bad ones should not be allowed to handle your business.

### What If They Don't Hold Up To Your Expectation?

It's very simple; if you do not feel that the broker is working out well, then find another one. Remember, they are entitled to receive a commission for any businesses that they may have shown you, so when you hire a new one, give them all of these details. Have them document how the broker's commission will be split in the event that you buy a business that your previous broker introduced to you.

### Is It Worth The Expense?

Even though your broker may earn a handsome commission from the business you buy, they are always at risk of earning zero if you don't buy. Never begrudge their commission; if they do their job, they are entitled to it. Whenever you meet with your broker over coffee or lunch always pick up the tab. It's a good way for you to express your appreciation of them for doing work on your behalf, not knowing if it will evolve into any compensation. It really is the right thing to do!

## Should You Hire An Accountant To Help You?

I strongly recommend that you use an accountant for this exercise. An accountant can help to run the numbers and verify all of the financial activity. There is so much more that has to be investigated, and your time is best spent on these areas. Hire a professional to help with the financials.

# Buying a Business or Its Assets

A business is simply a collection of assets. Someone who offers a business for sale is trying to sell all these assets together, from the IRS point of view. A buyer may not want all of a business' assets. You want to buy Tony's Pizza Restaurant for its location, but you don't want Tony's business name or the old pizza ovens and furniture. If you make Tony a good enough offer, he may sell just the building to you and not the rest of the assets. However, the tax consequences of this type of sale may be different than if you had purchased all of the assets. How the business is legally structured – sole proprietorship, partnership, limited liability company or corporation – also has important tax consequences for both the buyer and seller.

### Unincorporated Businesses

If you buy a partnership, limited liability company or sole proprietorship, you are getting just its assets — a store lease, inventory, customer list and so on. Normally, you don't take over business-related liabilities, including tax debts. Your contract should require the seller to pay all debts before closing or out of escrow. If not, then the debts remain the seller's personal responsibility after the transfer.

The IRS never releases the seller from unpaid taxes when a business is transferred. But you normally don't have to worry about the seller's tax debts unless the IRS or state-taxing agency has filed a tax lien against the business or the owner.

---

**Example:**

Frank, a sole proprietor, sells his profitable business, Corner Deli, to Mario. Frank has not filed or paid income taxes for the past three years. The IRS hasn't caught on to Frank — yet. Mario takes the business assets free of any tax liability of Frank, who remains personally liable for taxes he should have paid on the business income before the sale.

---

# Corporations

The tax situation is more complex when you buy an incorporated business. Whether you buy corporate shares or its assets instead is a crucial choice, because:

- If you buy only a corporation's assets, you don't assume its liabilities, including taxes.

- If you buy a corporation's shares of stock, however, you end up with both its assets and liabilities – including known and unknown taxes. An example of an unknown tax debt would be one that resulted from an IRS audit that has not yet begun. The seller of the corporate shares is released from all corporate debts unless he personally guarantees them or agrees to be liable for them after the transfer.

Why should you ever consider buying a corporation's stock, given the potential for legal trouble? Because some owners will sell only if a buyer takes corporation stock. There are several reasons why a seller may insist. One, as mentioned, is to rid himself of any potential tax liabilities, since the buyer assumes these along with the stock. But even a perfectly honest seller may have a tax reason for selling stock instead of assets.

## Making Favorable Asset Allocations

A buyer and seller should agree on the allocation of purchase price of assets as part of negotiating the agreement to purchase the business. Because there is almost always flexibility in valuing assets, the buyer should propose the allocation of purchase price in a way that provides the most tax benefit. For the buyer, it is important to have as much as possible allocated to items that he will quickly expense in the business. Otherwise if he has to capitalize the assets, he carries those items on the balance sheet for a long time. He has then paid money for something for which he cannot get a deduction.

Typically, you'll want to allocate as much of the purchase price as possible to inventory and to assets with the fastest tax write-offs – that is, those with the shortest depreciation periods. If it's at all realistic, attribute the lion's share of the price to business equipment. Usually equipment and fixtures can be depreciated over three, five, seven or 10 years. Because of the longer 15-year write-off period, assign smaller values to intangible assets. Commercial real estate, with a depreciation period of 39 years, also provides a longer time period to write off your costs.

# Purchase a Franchise Business

This option allows you to "purchase" a known trademark for delivery of products or services under an established system. You will usually pay a franchise fee, ongoing royalties, and the costs of getting into the franchise. While it can be comforting to have ongoing support services, collective buying and advertising power and market research, not every franchise is guaranteed to be successful. Many small, less-expensive franchises are under-funded, lack a good training program, and fail to provide the necessary support. Many of the large, well-known franchises are too costly for many beginning entrepreneurs. This can be an attractive starting point but be sure to check out the franchise thoroughly.

## Advantages of owning a franchise

- A ready business package that may include setup, training, operations, and marketing programs.
- Public recognition of franchise logo and product achieved through uniform standards in color, design, taste, clothing, etc. This includes quality control measures imposed and enforced by the parent company.
- Lower costs through collective purchasing powers for suppliers because of the economies of scale.
- Ongoing financial relationship that may include assistance and training in budgeting and financial management for your business.
- Finely tuned operating system where the bugs have been worked out at someone else's expense.
- Training and guidance, often in the form of an ongoing program for employees and/or managers.
- Financial assistance, such as startup financing packages. Nearly one-third of parent companies offer startup financing to qualified potential franchisees.

## Disadvantages of owning a franchise

- The high investment cost (franchise fee, royalties, advertising, etc.) may prevent you from looking at several franchise opportunities.
- Royalty fees appear to be never-ending, often as high as 4% to 6%, and tied to gross revenues (not profits). Royalty fees are a variable operating cost and often become a cash drain on small businesses.
- Lack of control: someone else tells you how to run your business.

- Borrowing money can be difficult (not all franchisors offer financing packages). Banks that have had bad experiences with franchises may be less willing to participate in a franchising arrangement.
- The franchisor's ability to terminate the franchise agreement may be somewhat arbitrary.
- The franchisor often reserves the right to place new and more restrictive financial commitments on the franchisee at the franchisor's discretion.

## Ten Questions to Ask Before Buying a Franchise

When you buy a franchise, you're putting big dollars on the line – and your success doesn't entirely depend upon you. The quality of the company that stands behind your franchise also matters a great deal. Thus, it's important to find out as much as you can about the parent company before you lay your money down. Here are 10 questions to ask:

1. **What type of franchise is it?** Most franchises are "package franchises" – businesses such as fast-food restaurants, muffler shops or motels that come complete with a business model laid out by the parent company. That model covers everything from financial controls to hiring guidelines. "Product franchises" include businesses such as car dealerships and gas stations that exist mainly to distribute the parent company's goods. Owners of product franchises have more control over the way they run their businesses.

2. **Does the business lend itself to the franchise model?** Fast-food businesses, for example, greatly benefit from their association with the brand name and products of the franchiser. That might not hold true, however, if the business is a car wash.

3. **What does the offering circular say?** The Federal Trade Commission requires franchisers to provide prospective franchisees with an offering circular that contains basic facts about the company. Read this document; it will contain information about the firm's business experience, legal history, and – perhaps most useful – its other franchises.

4. **How many franchises does the organization have?** Having a large number of franchises indicates a successful, established business. Be careful, though, if a firm's other franchises are located near yours; you could wind up competing with a nearly identical business.

5.  **How much is the franchise fee?** A study by the International Franchise Association showed that 95% of franchise fees were less than $40,000. But you might pay much more for a franchise affiliated with a blue-chip national chain.

6.  **How much will you have to pay in royalties?** Franchisers generally charge royalties equal to 4% to 6% of each franchise's revenues. Some firms charge significantly more, though, and others charge flat fees on an ongoing basis.

7.  **How much money will your business really make?** The parent company's projections probably are optimistic. Run them by other franchisees; the offering circular will tell you how to contact them. When deciding which franchisees to speak to, select the ones that are successful and also the ones that are not doing well. Talking to both groups will give you a better perspective of the potential of your business.

8.  **Can you work with these people?** When you buy a franchise, you're in for the long, expensive haul, so you'd better be able to work with your new bosses. Make sure to visit the company's home office, even if it's in a different state. And ask other franchisees about their experiences with the parent company.

9.  **How will the franchiser help you?** A franchiser may help you select a site for your business, negotiate a lease, advertise for and interview prospective employees, get business licenses, finance the franchise fee or equipment costs or provide other services. Ask what the franchiser will do for you – and get it in writing.

10. **Is the franchise company legitimate?** Some franchisers try to bilk new entrepreneurs. Check with other franchisees, the Federal Trade Commission and the Better Business Bureau to determine the legitimacy of the franchise.

---

**Success Tip**

The following websites contain a wealth of information in this area:

http://www.franchisedirect.com
http://franchisehandbook.com
http://franchisedoc.com
http://www.franchiseopportunities.com
http://www.franchise.com
http://www.franchisesolutions.com

# IN CONCLUSION

Being a successful entrepreneur, a successful business owner, takes more than a great idea. It takes personal desire, fortitude and stamina! Success also requires you to be thorough in your research, and honest in your decisions. Knowing yourself, understanding where your talents are (and where they are not!), testing your ideas, and finally using available resources wisely are all key components of creating a successful business.

# Frequently Asked Questions on Starting a Business

## Q. What are the biggest challenges to starting a business?

**\* You have to do everything!** – The Director of Sales and Marketing one minute, and janitor the next. You are ultimately in charge and responsible for everything.

- **Having to learn everything fast** - this is why it is critical to prepare!
- **Cash flow.** As we will discuss in chapter 9, not having enough cash is a serious problem. Cash is king. And no cash is bad news.
- **Time management.** How do you prioritize when everything has to be done at once? Finding ways to do the most important things first is essential.

**Maintaining balance.** With all of the demands of the business, it's easy for entrepreneurs to lose sight of what motivated them to go into business in the first place. Protect your personal time like you protect your business time. Make sure you take adequate time out for resting and recharging. Remember, you are your business' most valuable asset.

## Q. What are the biggest mistakes new business owners make?

**Not doing market research.**
Just because you have a great idea doesn't mean you have a business. If you take the "if I build it, they will come" approach, you will more often than not be out of business very quickly. Taking a business idea to an informal focus group of friends and colleagues is a good start, but it is critical that you do all kinds of research on your potential market.

**Not doing serious business planning.**
It's a sad fact that many new business owners don't see this obvious relationship between planning and success. They think they can "wing it" and make their plans as they go along. Every business needs a business plan, no matter what size it is. The process of making a plan organizes your thinking and helps you sort out your priorities.

**Thinking you can do it all by yourself.**
Working solo is not working alone. Success depends on developing and using a network of colleagues, friends, mentors and professionals that can provide advice, assistance and direction in tough times.

**Thinking that success will come quickly or easily.**
There are a lot of myths bound up with the concept of starting a business. Success takes long hours, strategic planning, and a commitment to the work involved. The rewards are great, but the effort is, too.

## Q. What's the best way for someone to price their product or service?

It may be obvious that the profitability of any business hinges on the accurate pricing of its products or services, but many small-business owners miscalculate this variable, often with devastating outcomes. If you price your product or service too high, the result will be a low level of sales; if you price too low, though you may reap short-term sales, over-time the business itself will not be profitable and may fail.

There are two contrasting views about how to establish proper pricing. The first is to calculate what the product or service cost to produce, mark this up according to industry guidelines, and establish the price. The second is to experiment selling the product or service at different price points and try to determine what the buyers will pay, my preferred approach.

Whichever approach you choose, here are some crucial pricing do's and don'ts to keep in mind:

- Analyze all the costs that go into producing your product or service, before adding the cost of direct labor, (yours or that of staff), necessary to make the product.
- Don't forget to count yourself as a labor component when calculating the cost of sales.
- Don't overlook direct overhead, the expenses such as rent or utilities for the studio, workroom, or office where you perform your labors.
- Be sure to add a profit margin to the above before determining your wholesale cost.

- Learn the range of prices charged by your competition – this information is invaluable.
- Avoid the temptation to "price down."
- Don't get discouraged if you miscalculate your pricing at first. As your experience and reputation grow, the market perception will change over time and you can adjust your pricing accordingly.

# CHAPTER 3:

## Writing Business Plans That Get Results

**CASE STUDY**

Susan had owned a beauty salon business for a little over 8 years. Revenues had grown steadily but net profits remained stagnant for the past 3 years. Employee turnover and client attrition were high. The day-to-day running of the business was becoming a *big headache*. Susan was wearing too many hats and it was leading to burnout.

Susan knew it was enough. It was time to get her house in order. After reading a book on small business, she realized that her business had added many different services and had hired a number of new employees to perform the services but without the right systems in place. The business was operating very inconsistently. Susan, the owner of the business had become the most senior employee, rather than the visionary, the driving force of the business.

Susan met with her accountant to bring back clarity to the "big picture" to her business. Once the "big picture" was conceptualized, they crystallized it to a one-page document, the vision statement. Through an ongoing coaching meeting, the vision statement was broken down into an action plan.

For Susan, becoming crystal clear about the "big picture" idea brought the *spirit* of the business alive again in her. The breakdown of this vision into an action plan, led to measurable growth of the business. Through the ongoing coaching, systems were designed and implemented that led to consistent performance of services. The business saw a drastic reduction in employee turnover and client attrition. Most important, within seven months, Susan was able to free-up one day a week for personal stuff!

# INTRODUCTION:

## Your Business Plan Is Your Roadmap to Success!

If you were traveling from New York to Alaska, and you had never been to Alaska, you would most likely consult a map for direction and guidance. If you didn't, you could drive in circles for hours, if not days. And if you didn't ask anyone for directions, then you probably would not get there at all. Unfortunately, many small-business owners attempt to do the same thing when they start their business. They start and continue to operate with no such map. The end result is a business that never reaches its full potential. With a business plan as your road map, your journey is not only much simpler, but your confidence is much higher.

A business plan is a written description of your business' future. It's a written document that explains and analyzes your business, and gives detailed projections about its future. In short, it describes what you plan to do and how you plan to do it. A business plan covers all significant areas of the business including business strategy, marketing analysis, financial analysis and operations.

A business plan is the document you create when you take an idea for a commercial endeavor and work through all the factors that will have an impact on the successful startup, operation and management of the business. Smart entrepreneurs go through the process of writing a business plan because they understand how it increases their chances for success. Sure, there are successful businesses whose owners fly by the seat of their pants and never create a written plan. But they succeeded *despite* the lack of a formal plan, not *because* of it. How much better might they have done had their good ideas been coupled with some solid planning?

Those who have decided to embark on a new enterprise have probably already taken some steps, however informal, to confirm the viability of the new business. Creating a *written* plan is the next logical step in that process. For example, a business plan can be the vehicle that carries your new idea from the conceptual and planning phase down the road to the building and operational phases. Or, it may help to establish your business' credentials for purposes of obtaining bank financing or investment by future partners.

A plan for an existing business may just deal with a single aspect of your business, such as a new product introduction, and its impact on financial management and other ongoing operational issues.

# Why Is It That Most Business Plans Never Come To Life and What You Can Do To Bring Life To It?

From my experience, most business plans, once written, sit on a shelf and collect dust. Here are two main reasons why that happens and what you can do about it:

1) Most business plans are written because the business owner thinks of it as an exercise that must be done – *"hey, other business owners have done it"* or *"the banks are going to ask for it when we borrow money."* When the task at hand to prepare a business plan is approached in this way, it lacks the passion, energy and vibrancy that a good business plan should have. Instead, try approaching writing your business plan from the standpoint of the *impact* you want it to have on your customers, your employees, your vendors and your investors. Some key questions that will transform a dry, dull, uninteresting business plan into an energetic and vivacious business plan are: What do you want your business to feel like to those who come in contact with it? What do you want its impact to be? Describe their experiences with your business.

2) Most business plans are static. There is usually no room for change. A well-crafted business plan assumes that you can't predict all the changes that will occur while preparing the plan. Hence, it is more than a one-time product and should be treated as a living, growing document. Because change is a key, built-in assumption in the business plan, essential adjustments can be made to keep it current and relevant. Revisiting your plan gives you the opportunity to step back, examine and organize your thinking about the business, and makes sure you're charting a successful course for the future. Many business owners discard their plans after their initial need to raise money. Keeping your plan up to date not only forces you to step back from the day-to-day activities of running the business but also ensures that the big picture and all its components continue to make sense.

## Why Write A Business Plan?

Writing a business plan is a lot of work. So why take the time to write one? Because good planning leads to good success. Almost without exception, business owners who write a plan are pleased they have one. Those without a plan **wish** they had written one.

Many people believe the only reason to develop a business plan is to convince potential lenders or investors to provide financial backing. This view is a little shortsighted, however. A well-developed plan can also serve as one of your most important management tools. A good plan will provide a blueprint and step-by-step instructions on how to translate your idea into a profitably marketed service or product.

Here are some of the specific and immediate benefits you will derive from writing a business plan.

## 1) Helps You Obtain Money

Venture capitalists and other investors require a business plan before they will consider your proposal seriously. While most banks don't require a business plan, companies that submit them considerably improve their chances of getting the funds they seek. A written plan carries an important message even before it's read: it says that the owner of the company is serious enough to do formal planning. Lenders use it as a screening device to see that you have thought through critical issues facing you as a business owner and really understand your business. Lenders look to profit from taking calculated risks and a business plan allows them to evaluate if your business has a good chance of succeeding.

Keep in mind that in today's times, there are as many potential lenders and investors as there are prospective business owners. A well-thought-out business plan that effectively demonstrates your business concept will have a greater likelihood of success in obtaining funding than a business without one.

## 2) Improves Your Odds of Success

Because writing a business plan forces you to review everything at once, this important exercise teaches you how money flows through your business, the strengths and weaknesses of your business concept, and your likelihood of success. Writing a plan also allows you to see how changing components of the plan increases profits or accomplishes other goals. You can fiddle with individual parts of your business and study the impact it will have. This ability to fine-tune your plan and business can dramatically improve your chances of success.

### 3)   Keeps You On Track

Good businesses – even great businesses – go off track sometimes. The key to recovery is having a sense of destination. This destination is established initially through your business plan. You know what the "track" looks like. And you can keep coming back to it time and time again.

Before a plane takes off, the pilot has a flight plan. He knows exactly where he's going, and flies according to the plan. During the course of the flight, rain, wind, turbulence, human error, air traffic, and other factors may push the flight plan off track. Throughout the entire trip there may be slight deviations from the original plan, but the pilot arrives safely at the intended destination, at least in part because of the original plan.

How does that happen? During the flight, the pilot receives constant feedback. He gets information from instruments that read the environment, from air traffic controllers, and from other airplanes. And based on that feedback, he makes adjustments so that time and again, the airplane keeps returning to the flight plan.

The *hope* lies not in the deviations but in the vision, the business plan, and the ability to get back on track with the vision.

A written business plan gives you a clear course toward the future and easier decision-making capability. It provides the foundation for a tracking system that lets you evaluate your business' progress. This tracking function gives you real-time feedback regarding operations. Some problems and opportunities may represent a change of direction worth following, while others may be distractions that your business plan will enable you to avoid. The black and white of your written business plan will help you face facts if things don't work out as expected.

### *Outline of a Complete Business Plan*

A business plan customarily has a number of major elements or sections. Each of these elements serves a particular purpose in the overall presentation of your plan. The following list identifies and briefly describes each of the documents or document categories that will make up your plan. They are presented in the order in which they *usually* appear in the plan. But don't feel constrained to follow this exact format if another way makes more sense because of the nature of your business. For example, the financial portion of a plan for a business with a 20-year track record is much more important (and comprehensive) than the financial portion of a startup business' plan.

The relative mix of product and services to be offered can also affect the content of a plan. Issues relating to inventory, production, storage, etc., become less significant as the product/service mix moves toward a purely service business. For example, a business that relies on the services of many professional employees would provide substantial details about acquiring and retaining these vital workers.

In any event, it pays to at least mention all the major issues listed below, even the ones that are less significant to your particular business. Someone who's reading your plan will be more confident about your assessment of the situation if you identify such issues and resolve them, however simply. For example, if you plan to work alone and perform all services personally, you might note that you anticipate no need to hire employees or engage independent contractors if the business succeeds at the levels projected in the plan. You don't want to raise any questions in the mind of your audience that aren't resolved somewhere within the plan document.

Remember, there is no requirement that these items be *created* in the order shown. In fact, conventional wisdom has it that the executive summary, which is preceded only by the cover sheet and table of contents, should be prepared after the rest of the plan is complete. Create the plan in any manner that feels comfortable to you. Just remember that, when your plan is completed, all of the following should be thoroughly addressed as they relate to your particular business.

There are three main parts to a business plan:

- The first is the business concept: Here you discuss your business "industry," your business structure, and your products or services.

- The second is the marketplace section: Here you define and analyze the potential buyers of your product or service. You also describe and analyze your competitors.

- The final section is the financial section: This includes your financial reports, e.g., the profit and loss statement, balance sheet, cash flow projections, and ratio analysis.

These three parts further break down into several key components.

## Executive Summary

This is arguably the most important single part of your document. It provides a high-level overview of the entire plan that emphasizes the factors that you believe will lead to success. In essence, it is the business plan in miniature. As such, it should stand alone as a document. It should capture the excitement and essence of the business. Someone who has finished reading your executive summary should be able to say, "*So, that's what these people are about.*"

**Success Tip**
Believe it or not, even those considering investing in your business may not read the entire document. But you can be certain they will read the Executive Summary. Take time to write it, and write it well. Make sure it includes all of what anyone might want to know about your business – in summary form, of course!

A. Describe your business concept
B. Impact you want your business to have on your customers, your employees, your vendors and your investors
C. Key success factors and competitive advantages
D. Describe your current situation
E. Financial situation

## Market Research/Analysis

This presents an analysis of the market conditions that the business faces, sets forth the marketing strategy that the business will follow, and provides a detailed schedule of marketing activities to support sales. Market research looks at the total industry, however it is defined. Analyze the data for both the total market and your specific customers. Your target market represents your potential customers, who may be defined by age, sex, race, affluence, education, physical characteristics, location, etc. Quantify your target market. Is it growing? By how much? What are the spending habits of your targeted customers? Who is your competition and how aggressive is it?

A. Total market
    1. Size
    2. Trends

B. Target market
    1. Customers' demographics
    2. Customers' psychographics
    3. Target market size
    4. Rate of growth of target market

C. Competition
    1. Who are the competitors?
    2. Competitors' strengths?
    3. Competitors' weaknesses?

D. Message
   What words best articulate the "Uniqueness" of your business?

E. Media
   What marketing medium or vehicles will best deliver your marketing message?

F. Pricing philosophy
    1. Sensitivity
    2. Flexibility
    3. Elasticity

G. Growth
    1. Where is the product in its life cycle?
    2. Will the introduction of your product alter the life cycle?
    3. If so, why? And how?

H. Predictions
   1. About the market size
   2. About your target market
   3. About your entry into the field

## Operations, Management and Fulfillment

This is where you detail how operational and management issues will be resolved, including contingency planning. Operations incorporate the physical plant, its capacity and ability to grow, and your needs in terms of contract and equipment purchases (or leases). How adaptable is the plant for updating its process? Is the industry rapidly changing and improving quality? What is the minimum you can manufacture (or sell) to avoid losing money? What salaries are necessary to operate the business?

A. Organizational structure
B. Key personnel
C. Products / services / customer service
   1. Method of delivery
   2. Customer problem resolution
D. Physical facilities
E. Suppliers or vendors
   1. Dependence and reliability
   2. Variety
   3. Control

## Financial Projections

This is another extremely important section. Your projections (and historical financial information, if you have it) demonstrate how the business can be expected to do financially if the business plan's assumptions are sound.

A. Profit and loss projection
B. Cash flow projection
C. Balance sheet projection
D. Ratio analysis

## Outside Advice

    A. Legal
    B. Accounting
    C. Marketing/Advertising
    D. Banking
    E. Other

## Appendix

This is the place to present supporting documents, statistical analysis, product marketing materials, resumes of key employees, etc.

### *Preparing To Write Your Business Plan*

Putting a business plan together requires you to translate your thoughts about how you're going to run your business (and how it will perform), into a form that targets and reaches your intended audience. Your business plan is your first advertisement! As such, it should include details about the one special component that makes it unique. As in marketing, it's important to identify your USP – unique selling proposition, and UVP – unique value proposition. But a business plan is much more than an advertisement – it's a plan for how your business will manifest its USP and UVP. Business plans include information about every aspect of your business. This section details not only the content, but also the format of a business plan. The following are the key things to think about before you can actually start to write your plan:

- Audience: Who is reading your plan? A potential investor? A banker? What do each want to see?

- Choose a time horizon for your plan: How far out into the future will your plan extend?

- Type of business: What are you selling? What is your product? Your service? Who will you sell to?

- Sources of information: Where will you obtain the information on which you will base your plan?

- Reasonable assumptions: Do you really know about the conditions, internal and external, that will dictate how your business will operate? What can you do to learn the facts?

**Success Tip**

**A common question that I am asked is: How long does my business plan have to be?**
A business plan does not have any prescribed length. Typically, plans run about 10 to 20 pages, depending on the concept. Many things determine length: type of product or service, number of products or services, purpose of the plan, etc... The benchmark for a good plan is how well it communicates the full intent of your business and your ideas.

## *Using Your Business Plan and Keeping It Current*

The mark of a good plan is its "usability." Words on a page mean nothing, unless you can put those words into actions. A good plan dictates action. It is a guide for operating your business, especially in its initial stages. The planning process is an important component of your plan. How adaptable is it? Can it be used over and over again? Can you plug new information into the same format, and derive benefit from it? If so, you have the makings of a good business plan. Benefits include:

- An action document for your business. The plan is a blueprint to help you manage your operations. This keeps you focused on your goals.

- A tracking and evaluation tool. Because your plan will set forth a timetable of operational and financial milestones, you can meaningfully interpret your actual operating results against the baseline established by the plan.

**Success Tip**
The following are websites that contain popular business planning software that can help in writing a business plan:
www.paloalto.com
www.liveplan.com
www.businessplanpro.com
www.bizplans.com
www.bplans.com
www.planware.org
www.brs-inc.com

# IN CONCLUSION

Every business needs a plan, just as every destination needs a way to reach it. Business planning, although not flashy or necessarily exciting, is essential to the development and organization of a successful business. Without a plan, there is no way to reach your goal!

Business plans matter to those who start the business, but they are also critical to those who may help bring it to life. Financiers, employees, government officials – these are but a few of the many who rely on business plans to understand what is supposed to happen. Most importantly, business planning forces you – the business owner – to think strategically about all aspects of your business, and keep you on track as you operate.

Elements of a complete business plan include: concept, finance, marketing analysis, and the operations plan. Once complete, the effective business plan serves as a monitoring tool to evaluate success, and can be revised as needed to respond to changing market and operating conditions. Many software packages are available, and offer to the prospective business owner a very complete method of business planning.

# Frequently Asked Questions on "Writing Business Plans That Get Results"

## Q. *What is a business plan and why do I need one?*

A good business plan defines what your business is, and makes clear the intent and purpose of the business. A basic plan includes essential financial information, and specifies how resources will be allocated. The plan is a "blueprint" for how the business is expected to operate, especially in its early stages. Measuring actual vs. projected (i.e., planned) results provides owners with a tool by which to assess progress and success. Perhaps most importantly, a business plan is essential before any bank or investor will loan you money.

## Q. *If business plans are so important, why do so few people actually write one?*

It is in human nature, to put things off and procrastinate. It is a challenge for many business owners to put their assumptions on paper and risk the fact that they may be wrong. In my opinion, if more business did some form of planning, the 80% failure rate of business in the first five years would be greatly reduced.

## Q. *Should I use business-planning software?*

Business-planning software can help you organize your plan and guide you through the process. The big cautionary note here is that many bankers and investors will know a "canned" business plan which often lack originality and much thought. Think of your potential audience and decide from there. There are many excellent software products available on the market. I have named a few of them in the chapter.

# CHAPTER 4:

## The Right Legal Structure to Save Money and Prevent Trouble

---

**CASE STUDY**

Susan and her husband John had been in the residential cleaning business for 12 years. With a lot of hard work, persistence and determination, they had steadily built their residential cleaning business to revenues of over $1M. Their customers were happy with the reliability and consistency they and their team of 14 employees were able to deliver. Things were going well, until an accident occurred that cost them their business and their marriage.

On the advice of a friend who had previously worked as a bookkeeper, Susan and John had set up their new business 12 years ago as a partnership. Legal and accounting matters always intimidated them, and the easiest thing at that time was to heed the advice of their bookkeeper friend. The problem with forming a general partnership is that it provides no protection of your personal assets. By operating as a partnership, Susan and John had unlimited liability for their debts, claims and obligations of the business. This unlimited liability meant that their house, savings and personal assets were exposed to the claims of others.

One summer Monday morning, when Susan was going about her day cleaning at an elderly client's home, a terrible accident happened. Susan had finished mopping the floor and the drying time of the floor was unusually longer due to the high humidity. Susan had not checked to see if her elderly client was at home as she left the wet floor to finish other work in the home. Sadly enough, Susan's elderly customer, not realizing that the floor was wet, walked in and took a bad fall, leaving her paralyzed for life.

---

Within two weeks of the incident, Susan and John were sued. Because they were a partnership, this meant that they, and not the business itself, were sued as well.

The lawyer argued to a jury that Susan had been irresponsible for failing to check if there was anyone else in the home. The jury awarded damages of $14.5 million.

Susan and John were wiped out. As a general partnership, they were completely and personally responsible for every claim the business incurred. They lost their house, their savings, and worst of all, the stress of this all led to their divorce. But this could have been avoided if Susan and John had consulted with an accountant or a lawyer. They could have avoided the disastrous consequences that resulted from relying on a bookkeeper with a one-size-fits-all-mentality.

# INTRODUCTION

No one entity is perfect for every business venture; there are a number of different factors that would favor the selection of one entity over another. Choosing the right business structure can save you money and the pain of many headaches! There are several different legal structures under which you can choose to operate: sole proprietorship, partnership, limited liability company (LLC), S-corporation, C-corporation and non-profit corporation. Each has advantages and disadvantages. In this chapter, I have given you an overlay of the pros and cons.

# SOLE PROPRIETORSHIP

A sole proprietorship is generally the simplest, most-common, least-regulated form of business and does not require any formal action to set up. If you don't incorporate and don't have a partner, the law will *automatically* classify you as a sole proprietorship. To establish a sole proprietorship, all you have to do is obtain whatever licenses and permits needed in your local area and industry to begin operations.

# Advantages of Sole Proprietorship

**Ease and speed of formation:** A sole proprietorship is the easiest and quickest form of business to start. It requires little or no government approval and you usually need to spend only a few minutes with your city or county clerk to obtain a business license or trade name certificate.

**Least expensive to set up:** A sole proprietorship is less expensive to set-up than a partnership, limited liability company (LLC) or corporation. Since no formal set up is required, reduced expenses come from not requiring legal help and additional registration fees with your state regulatory agency.

**Tax savings:** For income tax purposes, the government treats you and your sole proprietorship as one. If you incur a loss in your sole proprietorship, that loss carries over to your personal tax return to help offset earned income from employment. In the early years of a business when losses may be incurred due to start-up costs, this can result in significant tax savings. An added tax savings comes about from not having to pay federal and state unemployment taxes on your profits.

**Success Tip**

A key point to remember is that as a sole proprietorship, you are not considered an employee of your business. This is the point of law often *misunderstood* by new business owners. You *cannot* pay yourself a wage and deduct it as a business expense. You may withdraw (i.e., pay yourself) whatever amount the available cash flow in your business allows, but this "draw" is not a wage, you do not pay payroll taxes on it, and you cannot claim it as a business deduction. The profit of your business, which is computed without regard to your draws, is essentially your "wage" and is included in your personal tax return on Schedule C, "Profit or Loss from Business." You then pay federal income tax, state income tax and self-employment tax.

**Complete control:** Since there are no partners or a board of directors to report to, you are *the* boss. The buck stops with you. You have total control and independence over the business. No unnecessary bureaucracy to deal with means faster implementation of decisions.

**Termination:** The sole proprietorship is not only easy to form but also easy to terminate. No formal dissolution needs to take place.

## Disadvantages of Sole Proprietorship

**Unlimited liability:** One major disadvantage of the sole proprietorship is that you have unlimited personal liability in your business. This means that you are responsible for the full amount of business debts. This liability extends to all your assets, such as home and car. If your business fails while owing money to various creditors, those monies that you still owe can be collected from your personal assets. You can lessen the risk of liability in the case of physical or personal injury by obtaining proper insurance coverage discussed in Chapter 11.

**Limited tax savings for fringe benefits: :** One of the main drawbacks is that the owner must pay self-employment taxes.

**Limited resources:** Because you are a one-owner-operation, your own skills, capabilities and capital resources limit you. This becomes especially important for a business that needs capital or certain skills sets, but can't afford to hire such help. The intellectual and capital resources of one owner can be a limiting factor hampering the growth and development of the sole proprietor.

**Continuity of the business:** When a sole proprietor dies, the sole proprietorship terminates. The sole proprietor's successors can only sell assets, not the business as a going concern.

# PARTNERSHIPS (technically known as the "general partnership")

With the exception that a partnership has two or more owners, it is similar to a sole proprietorship in many ways. Creating a partnership can be very simple, since the law does not require any formal written documents or other formalities for most partnerships. As a practical matter, however, it is a much sounder business practice for partners in a business to have a written partnership agreement that, at a minimum, spells out their agreement on such basic issues as:

- How much will each partner contribute, in cash, property and time, and when will the contributions be made?

- What value will be placed on the contributed property?

- How will the profits and losses be divided among the partners and when and how may such profits be withdrawn?

- What is the purpose of the business, meaning how will it serve each partner? One partner may desire to create a business to sell in a few years with a handsome gain while another partner may want to have a lifelong business. Such issues, and many others, should be clearly spelled out at the onset to avoid conflicts later.

- What function/s or positions in the organization will each partner be responsible for and what will the compensation* be? For example, one partner may decide to take on the financial and operational responsibilities while the other may want to tackle sales and marketing. Having these position responsibilities laid out helps avoid future conflicts.

* Compensation received by a partner who works in the organization is called "guaranteed payments to partners." It is not a regular employee wage for tax purposes. There is no withholding, no employee payroll taxes. It is part of the partner's total partnership income. The partner is responsible to pay estimated taxes based on such income, as well as Social Security and Medicare taxes.

**Success Tip**
If possible, a written partnership agreement should be prepared by an attorney with expertise in this area, and reviewed by an experienced accountant. It is important however, to answer the questions above before your meet with one. Also, refer to the Sample Partnership Agreement.

# Advantages of the Partnership

**Ease of formation:** Although the legal formalities to set up a partnership are greater than a sole proprietor, they are less when compared to the creation of a corporation. Since no government approval is required, all one has to do is to obtain a business license from the city or county clerk, register with the Colorado Secretary of State, and apply for a tax I.D. number from the IRS.

**Added resources (two heads are better than one):** The limitations of the "one-person" situation that a sole proprietor faces can be overcome with a partnership. The additional intellectual and capital resources of two or more partners can be beneficial to the business.

**Tax savings:** For income tax purposes, the profits or losses allocated (Schedule K-1) to you from a partnership are treated as ordinary income or losses. Similar to the sole proprietorship, you can offset losses in the partnership to income generated from other sources of income, resulting in considerable tax savings.

**Termination:** Like the sole proprietorship, no formal dissolution with the government needs to take place. Unless a partnership agreement provides otherwise, a partnership usually terminates when any partner dies or formally withdraws from it.

# Disadvantages of the Partnership

**Unlimited liability of partners:** A major risk inherent in a partnership agreement is that each partner can be held responsible for the debts, taxes, and other claims against the partnership. Note that a limited partner is liable up to his investment in the limited partnership.

If the partnership's assets are not sufficient to pay creditors, the creditors can satisfy their claims out of either partner's personal assets. In addition, when any partner fails to pay personal debts, the partnership's business may be disrupted if his or her creditors proceed to satisfy their claims out of his or her interest in the partnership by seeking what is called a charging order against partnership assets.

**Continuity of the business:** Most state partnership laws provide that when one of the partners dies, quits, or declares bankruptcy, the partnership is then dissolved, jeopardizing the continuity of the business.

**Trust and understanding**: A partnership is an understanding between partners. Much like a marriage, this understanding is nurtured by trust. Unfortunately, many partnerships end in a break-up. Discussing all the vital elements of a partnership agreement and then documenting it can play an important role in alleviating this problem.

## Types of partners

**General partner:** A partner in a partnership whose liability is not limited. All partnerships must have at least one general partner. A general partner is usually also involved in the day-to-day management of the partnership. A limited partnership may also have limited partners who are basically investors and whose liability for partnership debts is limited.

**Limited partner:** Unlike a general partner, a limited partner does not play an active role in the business and has limited liability for losses from the partnership. A limited partner's deductible losses are limited under the passive loss rules.

# C-CORPORATIONS (also known as "the corporation")

An entity formed and operated as a corporation assumes a separate legal and tax life distinct from its shareholders. The label "C-corporation" merely refers to a regular, state-formed corporation. Corporations exist only because state statutory laws allow them to be created.

A corporation issues shares of its stock as evidence of ownership to the person or persons who contribute the money or business assets, which the corporation then uses to conduct its business. Thus, the stockholders (also known as shareholders) are the owners of the corporation, and they are entitled to any dividends the corporation pays. In the event of a dissolution or liquidation, the shareholders receive the corporation assets, after all creditors have been paid.

## Advantages of corporations

**Limited liability\*:** Perhaps the biggest reason why many small-business owners incorporate their business is to limit their liability to the amount invested in the business. As a separate legal entity, a corporation is responsible for its own debts.

Normally, shareholders, directors, and officers are not responsible for corporate liabilities. If the corporation suffers losses, the corporation itself must bear those losses to the extent of its own resources, and not the personal assets of the individual shareholders.

Note, however, that shareholders, directors, and/or officers may be held liable for the debts of the corporation where the court imposes "alter-ego liability" or where the individual has personally guaranteed the corporate debt.

**Ability to raise capital:** Various lenders, including banks, venture capitalists, and others, are generally much more willing to make loans to a corporation that has been operating successfully than to a sole proprietorship or a partnership. The corporation also has the ability to raise capital by selling shares of its stock.

**Two heads are better than one:** The limitations of the "one-man" band that a sole proprietor faces can be overcome with a corporation. Multiple sets of skills can be beneficial to the business.

**Permanence of existence:** A corporation is capable of continuing indefinitely. The death or incapacity of shareholders, directors, or officers of the corporation does not affect its existence.

**Broad range of powers:** As a separate legal entity, a corporation has the power to act in any way permitted by law and by its own corporate charter. For example, a corporation can enter into contracts, buy and sell both real and personal property, sue and be sued, and can even be responsible for breaking the law (i.e., committing a crime).

**Corporate benefits:** As a corporation, you and other members in your business will be able to take advantage of fringe benefits such as pension plans, insurance, company cars, and so forth.

# *Three Exceptions to the Limited Liability Rule

### 1) Personal Guarantees

Where a corporation has not yet established a credit rating, banks and other creditors will often require a personal guarantee from corporate directors before extending credit. Thus, the individuals will be liable for the debt if the corporation defaults on its obligation.

## 2) Tax Obligations

State and federal governments have the power to hold corporate officers and directors personally liable for reporting and payment of taxes.

## 3) Violation of Statutory Duties

Corporate officers and directors have a statutory duty to act responsibly when engaging in corporate activities. Thus, if an individual acts irresponsibly, he or she may be held personally liable for his or her actions.

# Disadvantages of corporations

**Corporate formalities:** A corporation can be created only by compliance with General Corporation Law of the state of incorporation. This requires filing of Articles of Incorporation with the Colorado Secretary of State and payment of the necessary state fees and taxes. Getting this paperwork done takes time, effort and money.

A corporation is required to have a board of directors, corporate officers, annual shareholders meetings, and to maintain separate books and records. If the corporation fails to observe such formalities or becomes too thinly capitalized, the courts may hold the shareholders directly liable for personal debts. This relatively uncommon action is called "piercing the corporate veil."

**Double taxation:** Another potential disadvantage of a corporation is "double taxation." The corporation pays tax once based on its corporate profits and the shareholder pays taxes as ordinary income when profits are distributed to you as the shareholder. Thus, the use of the corporation can obviously be disadvantageous if it results in this double taxation of income.

**Inability to take losses as deductions:** In both the sole proprietorships and partnerships, if you lose money in your business, these losses can be taken as deductions from other earned income, frequently resulting in healthy tax refunds. However, this is not the case with losses incurred by a corporation. When your corporation loses money, such losses remain within the corporation and no immediate benefit is derived from the potential offset against earned income. In such cases, the losses will be carried forward for 15 years and carried back for three or five years as "net operating losses" to offset the taxable income and hence reduce the corporate tax in those years.

# Where to Incorporate

**Under which state's laws should a corporation be formed?** State laws governing corporations vary from state to state. However, if the corporation has significant business or shareholder contacts (a.k.a. "presence") within a state, there is usually not much reason to incorporate outside of that state. For example, forming a corporation in your own state for a business centered in that state is usually the logical choice for the following reasons:

- **Filing Fees:** An out-of-state corporation that will be conducting business in your state must normally "qualify" to do business in that state. This "qualifying" requires the corporation to pay filing fees to that state in addition to whatever filing fees were paid in the state of incorporation. Thus, if you are operating a business in your state and are considering incorporating in Delaware or Nevada solely because of the lower state incorporation fees i.e., avoiding your state's incorporation fees, think twice. Most small businesses conducting business in your state will have to qualify as a foreign corporation in that state and that costs just about as much as it costs to incorporate in your own state in the first place.

- **State Taxes:** An out-of-state corporation doing business in your state will normally have to pay corporation taxes to that state. The corporation may also have to pay corporation taxes in its state of incorporation (even if the corporation is not conducting business in that state). Thus, the corporation is potentially exposed to taxing by more than one state.

- **Securities Laws:** The Corporate Securities Laws of your own state normally apply to any offer or sale of a security "in this state" regardless of the issuer's state of incorporation.

- **Corporate Rules:** Regardless of where the corporation is formed, many provisions of your own state's Corporation Law, for example, apply if the corporation has a sufficient "presence" in that state.

# S-CORPORATION

Many business owners hesitate to the double taxation rules imposed on C-corporation. Setting up your business as an S-corporation alleviates this "double taxation" rule. An S-corporation begins its existence as a general corporation (C-corporation) upon filing the articles of incorporation with the secretary of state. After the C-corporation has been formed, it may elect "S-corporation status" by submitting IRS form 2553 to the Internal Revenue Service (in some cases a state filing is required as well).

Once a corporation makes the Subchapter S-election to be an S-corporation, profits and losses are passed through the corporation and are reported on the individual tax returns of the respective shareholders of the S-corporation. This is the same basic "pass-through" treatment afforded partnerships and LLCs. Thus, the key distinction of the S-corporation is that profits and losses are not taxed at the corporate/business level like they would be if the corporation remained as a C-corporation.

Your decision to be an S-corporation isn't permanent. If you later find there are tax advantages to being a regular corporation, you can easily drop your S-corporation status. On the other hand, the opposite may not be true due to hurdles like the built-in gains tax.

**Success Tip**
A common mistake that I see small-business owners make that costs them thousands of their hard-earned dollars is not evaluating their legal structure every year.

## Qualifying for S-corporation Status

To qualify, your business must meet the specific requirements set forth by the IRS.

These include:

1.  The corporation cannot have more than 100 shareholders who are individuals (though certain types of trusts and estates may qualify).

2.  You must have no nonresident alien shareholders.

3.  You must have only one class of outstanding stock.

4.  All shareholders must consent to the election of an S-corporation.

# THE S-CORPORATION FILING DEADLINE

To qualify as an S-corporation at the federal level, a corporation must timely file IRS Form 2553 with the IRS. This election must be made by March 15 if the corporation is a calendar-year taxpayer in order for the election to take effect for the current tax year.

Rev. Proc. 2013-30 however facilitates the grant of relief to late-filing entities. Generally, the relief under the revenue procedure can be granted when the entity fails to qualify solely because it failed to file the appropriate election under Subchapter S timely with the applicable IRS Campus and all returns reported income consistently as if the election was in effect.

In addition, the revenue procedure also increases the time frame that allows relief, from 24 months from the due date of the election, to 3 years and 75 days of the effective date of the election.

To qualify as an S-corporation at the state level, a corporation must timely file the appropriate forms with the state.

**Success Tip**
Many small-business owners who apply for the S-election don't realize or remember that the S-election needs to be filed for both the federal and at the state level. If not done so, you would get taxed as an S-corporation on the federal level and a C-corporation at the state level. That may not lead to the most advantageous tax set-up for you.

# Advantages of S-corporations

There are several advantages of an S-corporation:

- Receives limited liability protection accorded to corporations. (Refer to "Three exceptions to the limited liability rule" stated earlier.)

- Avoids the double-tax feature of taxation of your corporate profits.

- Permits benefit of offsetting business losses incurred by the corporation against your income.

- Interest you incur to buy S-corporation stock is potentially deductible as an investment interest expense.

- Upon selling your S-corporation, your taxable gain on the sale of the business can be less than if you operated the business as a regular corporation.

- Self-Employment Tax Savings

  In an S-corporation, only earnings actually paid out to an owner as compensation for services are subject to payroll taxes. Any money distributed to the shareholder as a dividend is not subject to payroll taxes...and not subject to self-employment tax.

---

**Example:**

Peter, a retail storeowner, operates as an unincorporated, sole proprietorship. Peter earns a net income of $100,000 during 2013. During the course of the year, Peter withdraws $70,000 as his personal salary leaving the remaining $30,000 in the business as working capital for the year 2014. If Peter operates as a sole proprietorship, he'll owe self-employment tax on the full $100,000 ($100,000 x 15.3% = $15,300).

However, if Peter forms a corporation, elects S-corporation status, and withdraws the same $70,000 as compensation for his services, he would only owe self-employment taxes on the $70,000 in salary ($70,000 x 15.3% = $10,710). Thus, incorporating his business would save Peter $4,590 in payroll/self-employment taxes.

---

# Disadvantages of S-corporations

**Corporate Formalities:** An S-corporation follows the same state formalities as a C-corporation (i.e., filing Articles of Incorporation and paying state fees). In addition, an S-corporation must make a special tax election under sub-chapter S of the Internal Revenue Code by filing IRS Form 2553.

**Passive Investment Income and S-corporations:** If a corporation claims income from a passive investment (e.g., from real estate owned) for three consecutive years, and if that income exceeds 25% of the corporation's gross receipts, S-corporation status may be terminated by the IRS. Most real estate investors, for example, prefer placing real property in an LLC (Limited Liability Company) rather than an S-corporation for this very reason.

**Lack of Flexibility:** S-corporations offer less generous loss deductions compared to LLCs. They also allow lesser classes of ownership (such as voting and non-voting), have less freedom in deciding how profits and losses are to be divided, and are limited to 100 shareholders and to the S-corporation requirement that shareholders be U.S. citizens.

**Minimum State Corporate Tax:** Some states require all S-corporations to pay a minimum corporate tax regardless if the business reports a loss.

# LIMITED LIABILITY COMPANY (LLC)

An LLC is a business entity consisting of one or more "persons" (meaning an individual, general partnership, association, trust, estate or corporations) conducting business for any lawful purpose. This form of business entity is a hybrid between a partnership and a corporation in that it combines the "pass-through" treatment of a partnership with the favorable limited liability accorded to corporate shareholders.

While an LLC has many of the same characteristics as an S-corporation or a limited partnership, it is, in many cases, more flexible. For example, it is possible to use an LLC to allocate profits differently from ownership interests, or to get around the general partner's personal liability in a limited partnership. All 50 states and the District of Columbia allow limited liabilities companies.

# Advantages of LLC

**Limited Liability to Members**: With a few narrow exceptions, LLC members are not subject to the debts and obligations of the LLC and thus enjoy the same "limited liability" of a corporation. Like limited partnerships and corporations, an LLC is recognized as a separate legal entity from its "members."(Refer to "Three exceptions to the limited liability rule" stated earlier.)

**Flexibility**: Should members of an LLC desire additional tax savings, it can elect to change its tax status to that of a regular or S-corporation. LLCs offer more generous loss deductions than S-corporations, allow more classes of ownership (such as voting and non-voting), have more freedom in deciding how profits and losses are to be divided, and are not limited to 100 shareholders nor to the S-corporation requirement that shareholders be U.S. citizens. In Colorado, LLCs do not have to hold shareholders meetings, don't have to keep minutes, and don't issue stock certificates.

# Disadvantages of LLC

**Transferability of Ownership:** No one can become a member of an LLC (either by transfer of an existing membership or the issuance of a new one) without the consent of members having a majority in interest (excluding the person acquiring the membership interest) unless the articles of organization provide otherwise.

**Duration**: An LLC does not have a reliable continuity of existence. The articles of organization must specify the date on which the LLC's existence will terminate. Unless otherwise provided in the articles of organization or a written operating agreement, an LLC is dissolved at the death, withdrawal, resignation, expulsion, or bankruptcy of a member (unless within 90 days a majority in both the profits and capital interests vote to continue the LLC).

**Formalities**: Filing to form an LLC can be complicated, and the paperwork needs to be completed meticulously. The existence of an LLC begins upon the filing of the Articles of Organization with the Secretary of State. The articles must be on the form prescribed by the Secretary of State.

**Operating Agreement Required:** To validly complete the formation of the LLC, members should enter into an Operating Agreement. This Operating Agreement may come into existence either before or after the filing of the Articles of Organization and may be either oral or in writing.

# NONPROFIT CORPORATIONS

A nonprofit organization is a group organized for purposes other than generating profit and in which no part of the organization's income is distributed to its members, directors, or officers. Nonprofit organizations must be designated as nonprofit when created and may only pursue purposes permitted by statutes for nonprofit organizations. Nonprofit organizations include churches, public schools, public charities, public clinics and hospitals, political organizations, legal aid societies, volunteer services organizations, labor unions, professional associations, research institutes, museums, and some governmental agencies.

State laws distinguish between for-profit (stock) corporations and nonprofit (non stock) corporations. In a for-profit corporation, shareholders are authorized to receive stock in exchange for capital investments in the corporation. This capital investment often takes the form of money, equipment, or some other property. Shareholders in a for-profit corporation only receive a return on their investment when dividends are declared and paid.

A nonprofit corporation, however, cannot issue shares and cannot pay dividends. In addition, under the Internal Revenue Code Section 501(c)(3), a tax-exempt corporation cannot pay dividends and, upon dissolution, must distribute its remaining assets to another nonprofit group.

## Advantages of Nonprofit Corporations

### Tax Exemptions

Under Internal Revenue Code Section 501(c)(3) a nonprofit corporation is eligible for certain federal and state tax exemptions. With income tax rates as high as 39% on income over $100,000, tax-exemption status can be invaluable.

### Separate and Perpetual Existence

A nonprofit corporation, like a for-profit corporation, is an entity with a perpetual existence that may outlive all of its founders. In addition, the corporation can act like an individual. It can enter into contracts, incur debt, and own property.

### Employee Benefits

The corporation can employ the principle of a nonprofit corporation. As such, these employees can be eligible for fringe benefits not available to self-employed people.

Examples of these benefits include, sick pay, group life insurance, accident and health insurance, and corporate pension plans.

### Limited Liability for Members and Directors

As with a General, for-profit corporation, directors, trustees, and officers of nonprofit corporations are usually afforded the same limited liability status. Thus, creditors of the nonprofit corporation can only reach as far as the corporation's assets to satisfy corporate debts and not the personal assets of the people involved in the nonprofit corporation.

## Four Exceptions to the Limited Liability Rule

### 1) Personal Guarantees

Where a corporation has not yet established a credit rating, banks and other creditors will often require a personal guarantee from corporate directors before extending credit. Thus, the individuals will be liable for the debt if the corporation defaults on its obligation.

### 2) Tax Obligations

State and federal governments have the power to hold corporate officers and directors personally liable for reporting and payment of taxes. Although, with proper planning and filing, your nonprofit corporation should be exempt from certain taxes, your corporation may still be required to file informational returns and annual reports to the state and federal governments...and don't forget about employee withholding taxes.

### 3) Membership Dues

Members of a nonprofit corporation are personally liable for any membership dues they owe the corporation.

### 4) Violation of Statutory Duties

Corporate officers and directors have a statutory duty to act responsibly when engaging in corporate activities. Thus, if an individual acts irresponsibly, he or she may be held personally liable for his or her actions.

### Other Advantages

- Nonprofit corporations under 501 (c) (3) receive lower postal rates on bulk mail.

- Many organizations offer discounted advertising rates to nonprofit entities.

- Many Internet service providers offer discounted rates to nonprofit corporations.

- Many national chains (Costco, for example) offer lower membership rates.

- Nonprofit corporate employees may qualify for job-training and other work-study programs subsidized by the federal government.

## Disadvantages of Nonprofit Corporations

### Paperwork: Articles of Incorporation, Bylaws and Minutes

Articles of Incorporation must be prepared and filed with the appropriate state entity. In addition, bylaws must be prepared, minutes must be maintained, and certain federal and state tax-exemption filings must be filed to attain a tax-exempt status.

### Federal and State Tax Filings

On the Federal level, IRS form 1023 must be completed to qualify for 501(c)(3) federal tax exempt status. Although certain groups are NOT required to file Form 1023, it is recommended that these exempt organizations nonetheless submit the filing to ensure that the IRS views the organization as a tax-exempt entity.

For example, if your corporation's tax exempt status is for some reason challenged by the IRS, you could be liable for back taxes and severe penalties for the period your company operated as a corporation.

Only after the IRS approves a corporation as a tax-exempt organization can it be rest assured that it is in fact a tax-exempt company.

# IN CONCLUSION

It is reasonably well-accepted and understood that selecting the most appropriate entity is extremely important when you *first* get into business. The fact not clearly understood by most small-business owners is its significance when you are *already* in business. For existing businesses, it is important to know that one type of entity selection may be more advantageous in one year but not in another, due to a shift in circumstances. I recommend that your accountant review the appropriateness of your entity at least once annually. An accountant well-versed in this area will provide excellent insight into which entity is right for you.

Remember that choosing the right business structure can save you money and the pain of many headaches!

# A SAMPLE PARTNERSHIP AGREEMENT

(Attorney review required before use)

Agreement made_____, 20__, between _____, City of _____, Country_____, State of _____, and _____ of _____ (address), City of _____, Country of _____, State of _____, hereinafter referred to as partners.

### *Item One*
### <u>NAME, PURPOSE AND DOMICILE</u>

The name of the partnership shall be _____. The partnership shall be conducted for the purpose of _____ _____.

The principal place of business shall be at _____ _____ unless relocated by majority consent of the partners.

*Item Two*
## DURATION OF AGREEMENT

The term of this agreement shall be for _____ years, commencing on _____, 20__, and terminating on _____, unless sooner terminated by mutual consent of the parties or by operation of the provisions of this agreement.

*Item Three*
## CONTRIBUTION

Each partner shall contribute _____ dollars ($_____) on or before _____, 20__, to be used by the partnership to establish its capital position. Any additional contributions required of partnership shall only be determined and established in accordance with Item Seventeen.

*Item Four*
## BOOKS AND RECORDS

Books of accounts shall be maintained by the partners, and proper entries made therein of all sales, purchases, receipts, payments, transactions, and property of the partnership, and the books of account and all records of the partnership shall be retained at the principal place of business as in Item One herein. Each partner shall have free access at all times to all books and records maintained relative to the partnership business.

*Item Five*
## DIVISION OF PROFITS AND LOSSES

Each partner shall be entitled to _____ percent (_____%) of the net profits of the business and all losses occurring in the course of the business shall be borne in the same proportion, unless the losses are occasioned by the willful neglect or default, and not mere mistake or error, of any of the partners, in which case the losses so incurred shall be made good by the partner through whose neglect or default the losses shall arise. Distribution of profits shall be made on the _____ day of _____ each year.

*Item Six*
## PERFORMANCE

Each partner shall apply all of his or her experience, training and ability in discharging his or her assigned functions in the partnership and in the performance of all work that may be necessary or advantageous to further business interests of the partnership.

*Item Seven*
## BUSINESS EXPENSES

The rent of the buildings where the partnership business shall be carried on, and the cost of the repairs and alterations, all rates, taxes, payments for insurance, and other expenses in respect to the buildings used by the partnership, and the wages for all persons employed by the partnership are all to become payable on the account of the partnership. All losses incurred shall be paid out of capital of the partnership or the profits arising from the partnership business, or, if both shall be deficient, by the partners on a pro-rata basis, in proportion to their original contribution.

*Item Eight*
## ACCOUNTING

The fiscal year of the partnership shall be from _____ to _____ of each year. On the _____ day of _____, commencing in 20___, and on the _____ day of _____ in each succeeding year, a general accounting shall be made and taken by the partners of all sales, purchases, receipts, payments, and transaction of the partnership during the preceding fiscal year, and all the capital property and current liabilities of the partnership. The general accounting shall be written in the partnership account book and signed in each book by each partner immediately after it is completed. After the signature of each partner is entered, each partner shall keep one of the books and shall be bound by every account, except that if any manifest error is found therein by any partner and shown to the other partners within _____ months after the error shall have been noted by all of them, the error shall be rectified.

*Item Nine*
## SEPARATE DEBTS

No partner shall enter into any bond or become surety, security bail, or cosign for any person, partnership or corporation, knowingly condone for any person, partnership, or corporation, or knowingly condone anything whereby the partnership, property may be attached or be taken in execution, without the written consent of the other partners.

Each partner shall punctually pay his or her separate debts and indemnify the other partners and the capital and property of the partnership against his or her separate debts and all expenses relating thereto.

*Item Ten*
## AUTHORITY

No partner shall buy goods or articles into any contract exceeding the value _____ dollars ($_____) without the prior consent in writing of the partners; or the other partners shall have the option to take the goods or accept the contract on account of the partnership or let the goods remain the sole property of the partner who shall have obligated himself or herself.

*Item Eleven*
## EMPLOYEE MANAGEMENT

No partner shall hire or dismiss any person in the employment of the partnership without the consent of the other partners, except in cases of gross misconduct by the employee.

*Item Twelve*
## SALARY

No partner shall receive any salary from the partnership, and the only compensation to be paid shall be as provided in item Five and Fourteen herein.

*Item Thirteen*
## DEATH OF PARTNER

In the event of the death of one partner, the legal representative of the deceased partner shall remain as a partner in the firm, except that the exercising of the right on the part of the representative of the deceased partner shall not continue for a period in excess of _____ Months even though under the terms hereof a greater period of time is provided before the termination of this agreement. The original rights of the partnership herein shall accrue to their heirs, executors, or assigns.

*Item Fourteen*
## ADVANCE DRAWS

Each partner shall be at liberty to draw out of the business in anticipation of the expected profits any sums that may be mutually agreed on, and the sums are to be drawn only after it has been entered in the books of the partnership the terms of agreement, giving the date, the amount to be drawn by the respective partners, the time at which the sums shall be drawn, and any other conditions or matters mutually agreed on. The signatures of each partner shall be affixed thereon. The total sum of the advance drawn for each partner shall be deducted from the sum that partner is entitled to under the distribution of profits as provided for in Item Five of this agreement.

*Item Fifteen*
## RETIREMENT

In the event any partner shall desire to retire from the partnership, he or she shall give _____ Months' notice in writing to the other partners and continuing partners shall pay to the retiring partner at the termination of the months' notice the value of the interest of the retiring partnership. A closing of the books and a rendition of the appropriate profit and loss, trial balance, and balance sheet statements shall determine the value. All disputes arising there from shall be determined as provided in Item Eighteen.

*Item Sixteen*
## RIGHTS OF CONTINUING PARTNERS

On the retirement of any partner, the continuing partners shall be at liberty, if they so desire, to retain all trade names designating the firm name used, and each of the partners shall sign and execute assignments, instruments, or papers that shall be reasonably required for effectuating an amicable retirement.

*Item Seventeen*
## ADDITIONAL CONTRIBUTIONS

The partners shall not have to contribute any additional capital to the partnership to that required under Item Three herein, except as follows: (1) each partner shall be required to contribute a proportionate share in additional contributions if the fiscal year closes with an insufficiency in the capital account of profits of the partnership to meet current expenses, or (2) the capital account falls below _____ dollars ($_____) for a period of months.

*Item Eighteen*
## ARBITRATION

If any differences shall arise between or among partners as to their rights or liabilities under this agreement, or under any instrument made in furtherance of the partnership business, the difference shall be determined and the instrument shall be settled by acting as arbitrator, and his or her decision shall be final as to the contents and interpretations of the instruments and as to the proper mode of carrying the provision into effect.

*Item Nineteen*
## RELEASE OF DEBTS

No partner shall compound, release, or discharge any debts that shall be due or owing to the partnership, without receiving the full amount thereof, unless that partner obtains the prior written consent of the other partners to the discharge of the indebtedness.

*Item Twenty*
## ADDITIONS, ALTERATIONS, OR MODIFICATIONS

Where it shall appear to the partners that this agreement, or any terms and conditions contained herein, are in any way ineffective or deficient, or not expressed as originally intended, and any alteration or addition shall be deemed necessary, the partners will enter into, execute, and perform all further deeds and instruments as their counsel shall advise. Any addition, alteration, or modification shall be in writing, and no oral agreement shall be effective.

In witness whereof, the parties have executed this agreement on
The day and year first above written.

# Frequently Asked Questions on "The Right Legal Structure to Save Money and Prevent Trouble"

## Q. *What is Form 1023 and when must it be filed?*

**A.** Form 1023, *Application for Recognition of Exemption Under Section 501 (c )(3) of the Internal Revenue Service* is used to get exempt status. IRS form 1023 must be filed within 15 months of the date your articles of incorporation were filed. If your filing is timely, the tax-exemption will be retroactive and will apply to the date your articles of incorporation were filed.

## Q. *For What Purposes May a Nonprofit Corporation be Formed?*

Under IRS Code 501(c)(3) a nonprofit corporation may be formed to operate for some religious, charitable, educational, literary, or scientific purpose. These five purposes are usually included as purposes accepted by the individual states as a valid nonprofit corporate purpose.

## Q. *What are some of the limitations imposed upon Nonprofit Corporations?*

Nonprofit corporations must observe the following limitations:

- Pursuit of the following corporate purposes only: Charitable, educational, religious, literary, or scientific purposes.

- No distribution of financial gains to directors, officers or members.

- Corporate assets may only be distributed to another tax-exempt organization upon dissolution of the nonprofit corporation.

- Participation in political campaigns for or against persons running for public office is prohibited.

- Substantial engagement in legislative political activities is forbidden.

## Q. *Is my Corporate Name Available?*

There are a number of options you can use to check if your corporate name is available. A simple telephone call to your local or state trade office will often give you the answer you seek. Go to www.sunbiz.org to search the Florida Secretary of

State, Division of Corporations records to determine if the name you are looking for is available.

## Q. How long is the incorporation process?

Processing times for incorporating a company vary amongst the different states and change constantly depending on the workload at the state office. In many states, the incorporation process can be as short as 48 hours.

## Q. What is a Registered Agent?

Almost *all* jurisdictions require that the corporation designate a registered agent for service of process. However, in most cases, anyone who has a street address (no P.O. Boxes) within the state of incorporation may act as a registered agent for the corporation (i.e. serving of legal documents).

## Q. What are Articles of Incorporation?

An "Article of Incorporation" (AOI) represents the legal beginning of a corporation's existence. An AOI can be simple or complex. An attorney should be consulted in most cases. In general, an AOI contains the corporate name, address, and registered agent.

## Q. What are Bylaws?

Bylaws detail the responsibilities, rights, and duties of directors, shareholders and officers.

## Q. What is a Corporate Officer?

The following are the various corporate officer positions one may have:

- President

- Vice President

- Treasurer

- Secretary (or clerk)

- Assistant Secretary
- Assistant Treasurer

In addition to these required officer positions, a corporation may also have vice presidents and/or assistant secretaries or assistant treasurers.

Typically, the authority and responsibilities of each officer is described in the corporate bylaws and may be further defined by an employment contract or job description.

**The President.** The President has the overall executive responsibility for the management of the corporation and is directly responsible for carrying out the orders of the board of directors. He or she is usually elected by the board of directors.

**The Treasurer.** The Treasurer is the chief financial officer of the corporation and is responsible for controlling and recording its finances and maintaining corporate bank accounts. Actual fiscal policy of the corporation may rest with the Board of Directors and be largely controlled by the president on a day-to-day basis.

**The Secretary.** The Secretary is typically responsible for maintaining the corporate records.

## Q. What is a Corporate Director?

The Board of Directors is essentially the management body for the corporation. The Board consists of individual directors. Their responsibilities include establishing all business policies and approving major contracts and undertakings. In addition, the Board may also elect the President. Ordinary business practices of the corporation are carried out by the Officers and employees under the directives and supervision of these Directors.

The Directors must act collectively for their votes and decisions to be valid. Board members, like officers, have a fiduciary duty to act in the best interests of the corporation and cannot put their own interests ahead of the corporation's. The Board must also act prudently and properly manage the affairs of the corporation. Finally, the Board must make certain that it properly exercises its authority in managing the corporation and does not abrogate its responsibilities to others.

There are many specifics to board management that must be properly understood and executed. It is strongly suggested that new business owners, particularly those unfamiliar with operation and responsibilities of a board of directors, seek the appropriate resources.

## Q. Where can I get a Corporate Seal?

Although not always necessary, many corporations prefer to maintain a corporate seal as a formality. You may contact your local stationer to obtain a corporate seal. A corporate seal includes the corporate name and date of incorporation.

## Q. What is a Federal Employer Identification Number?

A Federal Tax Identification Number (also known as an "EIN Number") is a number assigned to a corporation or LLC by the Federal Government for purposes of taxation. The Federal EIN Number is to a corporation or LLC as a Social Security Number is to an individual. To get an EIN number, you need to prepare your Federal Tax Identification Number Application (IRS Form SS4) at your request. You may contact the IRS with the completed form and obtain the actual "EIN Number" in just minutes! You may also go to www.irs.gov and use the SS-4 wizard to apply online.

## Q. Must I file a D.B.A. ("Doing Business As")?

Individuals and unincorporated entities that regularly conduct business using an assumed name (often referred to as a "d.b.a.") must file an assumed name certificate with the county clerk in each county in which business premises are maintained. If corporations, limited liability companies or limited partnerships (entities created by filing with the secretary of state) do business with a name that is different than the name set forth in the organizational documents, they must file assumed name certificates in the county or counties where the registered office and the principal office are located, and must also file with the secretary of state.

## Q. If I incorporate, will doing so prevent others from using my company name?

Incorporating will not keep another business from using your name. Generally, every business must protect its own business name and the goodwill that it has acquired from the sale of its goods or services in a specific geographic area. Filing articles of incorporation only prevents the secretary of state from filing a document to create another corporation, limited liability company or limited partnership that has the same, a deceptively similar, or similar name as the entity already in existence.

## Q. Can I protect a trade name nationwide?

A. There is no national registration of trade names. Generally, businesses, including corporations, protect their trade names by registering their trade name as a service mark or trademark if the trade name also functions as a service mark or trademark. Because of the legal complexities involved, I recommend that businesses obtain private counsel to get advice on how to protect a trade name in interstate commerce.

## Q. Can the same person be the shareholder, director and all officers of a corporation?

While jurisdictions will vary in their requirements, most states require that there be at least one director and two officers, in a general, for-profit corporation. The required officers are President and Secretary. Most states allow one natural person to hold both offices and be the sole director of the corporation. Usually, that one person may also be the sole shareholder. A corporation may not be a director of another corporation.

## Q. What is the difference between a corporation and an LLC?

Corporations are formed pursuant to state law and have shareholders, are managed by a board of directors, and the daily affairs are administered by officers. Similarly, a limited liability company (LLC) has members and may be managed by one or more managers.

Generally, most people form corporations or limited liability companies in order to shield the shareholders or members and officers or managers from personal liability for the debts and obligations of the entity. There may also be various tax advantages to forming these entities, which may not be available for sole proprietorships and general partnerships.

## Q. Does incorporating a small business start-up offer tax breaks?

Keep in mind that most tax benefits flow to profitable, established corporations, not to start-ups in their first few years. Corporations can offer more tax-flexible pension plans than sole proprietors or partnerships, but few start-ups have the cash flow needed to take advantage of these tax breaks. Similarly, the ability to split income between a corporation and its owners – thereby keeping some income in lower corporate tax brackets – is effective only if the business is solidly profitable

## *Q. Are LLC members who actively participate in a business considered partners?*

Generally, LLC members are treated the same as partners. Unless compensation is in the form of guaranteed payments, an LLC member's share of profits is not considered wages and is not subject to withholding. Each LLC member simply reports his or her share of LLC profits as income on the member's individual income tax return and pays estimated taxes in quarterly installments.

This changes, however, for an LLC member who is active in the business – like a partner in a partnership. In this case, the member pays self-employment taxes on any share of LLC profits. The self-employed tax situation for LLC members has been a subject of controversy and temporary regulations, and the dust has not yet settled around many of the issues. To protect yourself, you might get an opinion from a local tax expert – preferably one who is willing to argue his or her opinion to IRS officials, if it comes to that.

# CHAPTER 5:

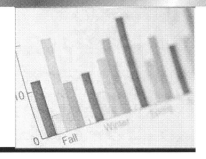

## Growing Your Business Sensibly and Profitably

*"If you do a lot of things to build business, you'll build business. They don't have to be done perfectly to work, although the better you do them, the better they'll work. But the main point is that you have to do them – a lot."*

Joe Girard (02/01/28 –) How To Sell Anything To Anybody

# INTRODUCTION

You may be asking yourself: What is an accountant doing giving advice on how to grow your business? After all, accountants have the reputation of being referred to as "number crunchers," "pencil pushers" and "bean counters." I must confess that when I first got into the profession of accounting, I was just that. I quickly saw the real value I'd bring to my small business clients if I could contribute from a "business advisory" role, rather than a strictly "accounting" one. Since then, I have studied some of the best minds in the field of marketing: I have modified and applied their most effective, most actionable business-building techniques to my own business and to my clients' businesses and noticed positive results. What I will share with you in this chapter are the main highlights. If you start implementing only some of these concepts, you will find your business reaching levels of growth you have never experienced before.

It appears that many small businesses believe in the age-old adage that says, "Build a better mouse trap, and the world will beat a path to your door." In the real world, this little piece of wisdom does *not* hold true. Unless you have invented a totally unique product or service uncommon in the marketplace, it is very likely there are tens or even hundreds of businesses out there that are similar to yours.

Each day, the average American is bombarded by an average of 100 television commercials, 30 radio spots, 194 newspaper ads, and up to 10 direct mail solicitations. This doesn't even include telemarketers!

Competition for your customers' money is fierce. If you want to win the battle for their hearts and money, you must first prove that you understand them, and then you must find the right vehicle to "connect" with them.

Before I share with you specific strategies you can begin to immediately use in your business, let's talk about the fundamentals of marketing.

## Definition of marketing:

It is getting the right message to the right people via the right media. Marketing means: "market first, message second, and media third" – in that order! I often refer to them as the 3 Ms. Let's look at each.

# MARKET

## What is Market?

Not every product appeals to everyone. That's why marketing is so vital; it is the process by which potential customers are identified and "targeted." Your target market is one that has high probability of purchasing your products or services and which you have selected for focused marketing activities. Unfortunately, most small-business owners get to their best prospects randomly – by throwing out their message to everybody and letting the right people find it. This is like getting a message to your uncle in Manhattan by dropping 100,000 copies of your letter out of an airplane as you fly over New York. I refer to this as "blind archery." Imagine launching 100 arrows while blindfolded. You might hit a target or two, but think of what else you'll hit along the way!

And arrows are one thing. A limited supply of dollars is another. If you market wisely, you'll hit the target, and you won't waste money.

# The 3 best ways to target-market

## 1) Geographic targeting

This method targets your prospects by geographical area. It could be the households or small businesses in your town or county. It could be several towns or counties or the entire state, a tri-state area or the entire country. Once you have established your geographical target market, you want to dominate it. You want to strive to become *the* obvious choice for your prospect.

## 2) Targeting by demographics

Demographics are the objective, statistical, behavioral, and even psychological things that particular groups of people have in common. Demographics selection can be as simple as targeting a preferred age group or as complex as targeting women age 30 to 40 who have professional careers, read both "Fast Company" and "Cosmopolitan" magazines, carry the American Express card, and buy clothes over the Internet.

Demographics of people include:

| | | |
|---|---|---|
| Age | Employment status | Income |
| Occupation | Education | Race |
| Marital status | Family status | Gender |
| Physical characteristics | Ethnicity | |

Be aware of the additional demographic influences for business customers:

Industry
Type of business (manufacturer, distributor, retailer, etc.)
Product line
Size of business (sales, number of employees, etc.)

## 3) By Affinity or Association

Do your customers belong to a certain club, religious organization e.g. church, synagogue, mosque or temple? Or are they members of the American Association of Retired People (AARP), the Kiwanis club or any other club.

**Success Tip**

As you formulate your target market, there is an important *distinction* that you want to keep in the forefront of your thinking process. There are essentially two approaches you can take when creating a product or service. One is the "product-oriented" approach which is "I'll create a product and then go out and sell it." This approach is the poorer one. It is focused on the product and its features. The better approach and one that I prefer is the "customer-oriented" approach and it goes as follows: "I'll learn what the market needs, then I'll create the product to satisfy that need." The "customer-oriented" approach focuses on the emotional gratification it provides your customers.

Now that you have defined your market, let's move on to the second M of Marketing, your Message.

# MESSAGE

**Your message is the words that crystallize or articulate the *"uniqueness"* of your business.**

Why is your business unique? What sets it apart? What is that "something special" you can offer that no one else does? How you answer these questions matters very much to how attractive your business will be to potential customers. This can be identified as a "unique selling proposition," or USP. The USP is the heart of your business, and as such it should be the heart of your marketing. All in all, your USP is the most powerful marketing tool you have.

The USP for Federal Express is "When it absolutely, positively has to be there." They based it on a promise of delivery reliability.

Domino's based their slogan on the fact that most pizza eaters don't care how much stuff is on their pizza, but that it is hot, fresh, and delivered quickly. Their slogan goes as "Fresh, hot pizza in 30 minutes or less."

The USP for Avis Rent a Car was "We're number two. We try harder." Avis knew that Hertz, the number one car rental company, was so much bigger that they couldn't compete head on so they positioned themselves as the number-two-car company that worked harder for the customer.

Once you have established your "USP," and made it the foundation of your marketing, the possibilities are limitless!

**Success Tip**
Be specific when creating your USP. Many small-business owners create a USP that has a generalized saying like "Service with a smile" or "The best in town." These don't work because it doesn't communicate uniqueness. Be specific when it comes to your USP. When Domino's stated that your pizza would be, 1) fresh, 2) hot, and 3) delivered within 30 minutes, it was specific and measurable. "Buy it today and install it tonight" – that's specific and measurable.

Once you have defined your target market and your message, you are ready to move to the third M in Marketing, "Media."

## MEDIA – your marketing medium

**Success Tip**
Most small-business owners jump to media quicker than they should. You must understand and define the first M – Market and then the second M, Message before you proceed to the third M – Media.

Your marketing medium is the communication vehicle you use to deliver your marketing message. It's important to choose a marketing medium that gives you the highest return on your marketing dollar. This means you want to choose the medium that delivers your marketing message to your targeted prospects at the least possible cost.

What I have seen most small-business owners do is market their product or service through one "marketing medium" only. So the florist will place a Yellow-Page ad and do nothing else to promote her business. The auto mechanic will place an ad in the newspapers and not explore all the other marketing mediums available. The small- business owner must instead test several marketing mediums and use them in their arsenal of marketing media.

The following types of media are available:

- Coupon type advertising (e.g. Val-Pak, Money-Mailer, etc.)
- Newspaper ads
- Television ads
- Radio ads
- Door-to-door
- Signs and banners

- Classified ads
- Yellow Pages
- Newsletter
- Telemarketing
- Press releases

- Door hangers
- Trade shows
- Word-of-mouth (Referrals)
- Direct mail – sales letter
- Take-one-box

- Online e.g. Google Adwords
- Social Media
- Website
- E-zine ads
- Seminars

- Public speaking
- Publishing a book, articles, etc.
- Charity events
- Networking
- Door-to-door

**Success Tip**
The more skillful you become in matching your *message* to the *market* using the right *media*, the bigger your return on investment on your marketing dollars.

# Three ways to grow your business

Regardless of what your product or service is, there are only three ways to grow your business, i.e., increase revenues and improve profitability. That's it. All paths to growth are a variation on one of these themes. Once you have grasped this idea, your marketing will become more focused, more organized and more powerful. The three ways to grow your business are:

1. Increase the number of customers
2. Increase the average size of the sale per customer
3. Increase the frequency of purchase

Let's look at each one in more detail:

## 1) Increase the number of customers

> *"The purpose of a business is to create and keep customers."*
> Theodore Levitt

There's no denying that customers are very important to any business. It is imperative that you keep a steady stream of customers coming in to your establishment, or taking advantage of your service. They're out there; you just have to find them. Once you identify them as prospects (leads), you must help them believe in the uniqueness of your product or service. When they believe, then you'll have a customer. Here are some ideas on how to turn leads into customers:

    a) **Increase the number of referrals:** Getting new customers through referrals is one of the most cost-effective methods there is for growing a business. It is one that I have implemented in my own accounting and tax business. Referrals from good customers are much easier to sell to because they're already "pre-sold." Credibility and trustworthiness have already been established by the one who referred them. Establish a formalized referral reward program for customers who take the time and make the effort to tell others about the benefit of doing business with you. Simple things like movie passes, restaurant gift certificates, car washes, manicures, or samples of some of the additional products or services you provide make good choices. The reward for a referral should be perceived as high value by your customer, but at a reasonable cost to you.

b) **Establish joint ventures:** Establish joint-venture arrangements with centers of influence. Find companies similar to yours that have already spent considerable time, effort and money establishing and building relationships with their customers. Then work out reciprocal arrangements with those businesses.

c) **Select marketing mediums that can deliver your message to *your* target market in a cost-effective way**. I gave you a slew of marketing medias you could choose from. Find the ones that make sense for your business.

d) **Increase your conversion**: Increase the conversion ratio of prospects into paying customers. You do this by getting better at what you do. You develop your sales skills, your word tracks and your scripts.

e) **Reduce customer loss**: Reduce customer defections – don't let existing customers slip away to do business with the competition. Pay close attention to what the customers are saying. Listen. Respond. And change if necessary.

In his book 'Keeping Customers for Life', Richard F Gershon breaks down the reasons why companies lose customers:

- 68% are upset with the treatment they have received.

- 14% are dissatisfied with the product or service

- 9% begin doing business with the competition

- 5% seek alternatives or develop other business relationships

- 3% move away

- 1% die

The fact that a massive 68% of customers move away following disappointment in the way they have been treated is significant.

Make sure your customers' concerns are also *your* concerns. Let them know you care. Pay attention. If you are losing customers, find out why – and find out quickly.

**Success Tip**

For every 5% increase in customer retention, a business can generate a 30 to 40% increase in profitability over a 12-to-16 month period. Since most businesses lose around 19% of their customers each year, only 81% are left. But if that number were to increase to 86% your business would enjoy a 30 to 40% increase in profitability.

## 2) Increase the average size of the sale per customer

Once you have got the customer in the door or in your database, you want them to spend more money, if it is in their best interest to do so. You can do this by raising prices, up-selling, packaging items/services as attractive solutions or expanding your product line.

Always keep in mind that it can cost a fortune to acquire a new customer. However, once you have the customer, you *must* maximize your sales to them over the life of your business relationship. Here's how you can do it:

a) **Raise your prices:** Customers are often willing to pay much higher prices than you expect for something. Try raising prices in small increments: 5%, 10% or 20% at a time, and then measure the results. Typically, most small-business owners underprice their products or services. They price similarly to competitors. What are people willing to pay for the results you've given them? This should be the first criterion when determining your prices. The market will tell you – in no uncertain terms – what your best price is. All you have to do is test your theories. Make sure you track your results. (For one example of how *not* to test price increases, *please refer to Marketing Mistake #9 later in the chapter for an important discussion on testing*)

b) **Up-sell and cross-sell:** Pay attention to your customers' needs, while at the same time ensuring you have product lines that meet different varieties of needs. Don't be afraid to sell a customer more than what she wants, if you believe she can benefit more from the next level product. A good example of upsell is when you go to a fast food place like McDonalds and you get asked the question, "Would you like to super-size for only 39 cents more?"

Cross-selling means offering your customers the opportunity to add related items to their basic purchase – items that, together, will increase their overall level of satisfaction. If you are not offering other related products or services, look for suitable complements to your current line of products.

c) **Package different products or services together:** Different people want different things, but everyone loves a "package" deal. What do you know about your customers' purchasing habits? Do they often buy items together? If so, use this knowledge to your advantage. Package items together, and price them accordingly. Fast food restaurants do this well. For example, a service business could offer Silver, Gold and Platinum Packages for different customers. By putting them together, you allow clients, who would enjoy the benefit from the additional services, to spend more money by choosing a higher priced service package.

## 3) Increase the frequency of purchase

The third way to grow your business is to increase the frequency of purchase. A prior purchase (and being satisfied with that purchase) is more likely to bring a customer back. Reselling someone is *far* less expensive than selling to someone new. And with trust comes more purchasing. Optimal profits can be earned when you create a structured program that welcomes these folks to purchase more products and services from you.

So keep your customers coming back to you again and again. Here are a few ways you can do that:

a) **Thank you cards / letters:** Everyone likes to receive thank you cards or letters. I can count using my fingers the number of times I have received one when I purchased a product or service. Saying "thank you" shows you care about your customer's wellbeing. And it sets you apart from 99% of businesses who ignore this simple and easy step. Saying "thanks" can be, in and of itself, a UVP (Unique Value Proposition) – few others do it!

Frequent communication with your customers also creates expectations that they will hear from you. This can be used to your advantage as well.

b) **Make new offers:** Keep your customers informed. They may not buy every time you promote something, but they will continually "keep you in mind." Staying in touch with your customers has proven to be an effective way to retain them.

If your sales are year-round, mail postcards or letters to your customers every month or at least every quarter. In every communication, be sure to educate the customer (useful tips and ideas to help the customer) and make an offer on some product or service.

If you are a seasonal business, be sure to send your customers a postcard or letter stating the benefits they would receive from your product or service. In other words, secure the order by re-selling the benefits.

---

**Success Tip**

Establish and maintain a segmented database. Great care should be taken to keep your customer database up to date, clean and meaningfully segmented. Continued communication with past, present and future customers is an effective way to increase sales in your business. There is computer software that is available to help you do that. A few names are ACT, Goldmine and Outlook.

c) **Customer clubs/loyalty programs:** Rewarding customers for frequent purchases is a fast, easy and low cost way to retain customer loyalty. How many free cups of coffee have you earned? If your business lends itself to repeat purchases (and almost every business does) create an opportunity for your customers to reward them for buying from you. Get their names and postal / e-mail addresses for future mailings.

d) **"By invitation only" event:** Any opportunity you can create for your customers to feel more "connected" to your business will pay dividends down the road.

e) **Reactivate old customers:** Inevitably some customers are going to stop doing business with you. They may die or move away or find cheaper services elsewhere. You can't do anything about these people. But some customers stop coming for lesser reasons. They may get busy with work or the kids' sports. They may become ill for a few months. Or they may just forget about you.

Herein lies a gold-mine of opportunity. You should contact these inactive clients – by phone, fax, letter or e-mail and make them a special offer that compels them to buy from you again. Say something like this:

*"We've missed you around the store or office lately, but perhaps you've been busy with other things. That's understandable! Anyway, because we value your patronage (and because we know you appreciate fine widgets/gadgets/ etc,) we'd like to tell you about a terrific new shipment that just arrived. (Describe your product or service here.) As a valued customer, we'd like to offer you the chance to preview this new widgets/gadgets/etc. before anyone else. So, please give us a call before (date) to schedule a free examination. Or, just bring this letter by the store. And, as a valued customer, we'd like to offer you 10% off anything in our store between now and (date). It's our way of saying "welcome back!"*

You might reasonably expect to increase sales by 10%, 20%, even 30% or more simply by reactivating your dormant customer base. Look at it this way. If people trusted you once with their hard-earned dollars, they're more than inclined to do it again. Unless the quality or service of your business has gone down dramatically, the only thing standing between you and newfound profits is a willingness to make the first move. You must reach out to your inactive customers.

# 10 Deadly Marketing Mistakes

One definition of failure is making the same mistakes over and over again, expecting to get different results. Most companies do this in their marketing. They fail to research the markets they are trying to reach. Instead, they market to themselves, advertising the same way and making the same mistakes over and over and over again. And they suffer the same financially disastrous consequences over and over and over again, as well. Below are "10 Deadly Marketing Mistakes" often made by small businesses:

1) **Institutional ads:** Institutional ads represent the most common form of advertising. These ads talk specifically about *you*, and your company. Yellow Page ads are good examples of this form. But institutional ads don't direct the potential buyer to a *buying decision*. Thus, they can be a waste of money. Direct response advertising, on the other hand, makes a complete case for the company, product or service. It overcomes sales objections. It answers all major questions. And it promises results, backing up the promise with a risk-free warranty or money-back guarantee.

2) **Not stressing uniqueness:** Again, your USP is what sets you apart. Advertising that pays little or no attention to this is wasteful, and more important, it shortchanges potential customers on something they might want and need. The USP is the distinguishing advantage you hold out in all your marketing, advertising and sales efforts.

3) **Failing to address customer's needs:** When marketing speaks more about what your business does than how it addresses customers' needs, it is ineffective. Do you know what your customers want? Do you know what they need? More important, are you meeting that need? Unless you consistently do, your customers will eventually abandon you.

4) **Making customers work too hard:** How easy is it to find things in your store? How helpful are your telephone operators when a customer calls with a question? How easy is to order from your business by mail?

Remember, 1) you cannot service too much, 2) you cannot inform too much, 3) you cannot educate enough, 4) you cannot make calling or coming into your business too desirable, 5) you cannot make ordering too easy, and 6) you cannot offer too much follow-up.

By making it inviting, easy, informative, non-threatening, educational and fun to do business with you, you will lift your small business above your competition.

5) **Failing to educate:** Remember how many ads most people see in a day? How does your marketing *focus* your customers' attention? What do you want them to see? Once you identify it, *show it to them.*

6) **Not having back-end sales (cross-selling):** A common problem is business owners who sell only one product or service and don't have anything else to sell as a back-end. The back-end is vital to any business. Your back-end describes the process of customers coming back to you again to buy a similar or upgraded product or service. Look for logical product or service extensions to offer your customers. I have seen numerous successful examples of small businesses capturing higher profits through back-end sales, even though they may have taken a small loss at the initial sales point.

7) **Not knowing the lifetime value of your customer:** The lifetime value of a customer is one of the most valuable things you as a business owner can know. It is simply the total profit of an average client over the lifetime of his or her patronage – including all back-end sales less all advertising, marketing, and incremental product or service fulfillment expenses. Let's say that your average new customer brings you an average profit of $100 on the first sale. He or she repurchases three more times a year, with an average profit of $150 on each reorder. Now, with the average patronage lasting two years, every new client is worth $1,000: ($100 + 3 x $150 + 3 x $150) = $1,000. You could, theoretically, afford to spend up to $1,000 to bring in a client and still break even. The reason this calculation is so important is that by knowing what the value of an average customer is, you can then determine how much you can afford to spend to acquire a new customer, as well as how much you can afford to spend to keep an existing customer from leaving you and purchasing from a competitor.

Lifetime value can be determined as follows:

The average purchase amount.......

*Multiplied by:* The average number of times a customer buys per year......

*Minus:* Product acquisition or production costs, fulfillment and delivery costs, sales commissions, bonuses and salaries, advertising and marketing costs, and other overhead expenses.

*Multiplied by:* The average number of years the customer continues to buy...

*Plus:* The monetary value of their referrals.

8) **Not offering a guarantee:** One of the reasons people don't buy is the perceived risk they believe they are taking in purchasing your product or service. These risks include 1) making the wrong decision, 2) not receiving what they paid for, 3) losing money, and 4) not being satisfied and not being able to recoup their investment. There are a number of risks that people must hurdle over to purchase your product or service. One strategy to overcome these risks is to offer a rock solid guarantee that will make their purchase risk-free, or at least decrease the risk as much as possible.

9) **Not testing your advertising:** I once read somewhere that before Henry Ford would hire anyone for an important position; he would have lunch with them. If the potential employee would salt the food before tasting it, he would not hire the person. The reason? Salting the food before tasting it indicated the person would implement a plan before testing it. It is amazing how few companies ever test any aspect of their marketing and compare it to something else. They bet their destiny on subjective decisions. You don't have the right or the power to predetermine what the marketplace wants, and what the best price, package, or approach will be. If you don't test prices, advertising copy, radio/TV spots and verbal sales messages, you won't know what the market wants, or what it will pay. You're just guessing – which can be disastrous.

10) **Endorsement / Joint Venture:** This method is probably the most under-used, yet one of the least costly and most effective marketing methods out

there. Not utilizing it is a serious marketing mistake made by many small-business owners. Joint ventures can be established with two groups: centers of influence and other businesses that have similar clients to your target market. Work out reciprocal arrangements with them.

# IN CONCLUSION

Effective marketing is more an art than a science. Don't believe for a second that many of these techniques are obvious to everyone – they're not. Only a few know and understand them. As one of those few, you'll not only learn how to make your small business stay alive and thrive, but you'll learn to dominate your marketplace.

Becoming an astute marketer is a process that will take time and money to master. Learning and implementing this one skill will ensure a steady flow of new customers to your door – a very necessary ingredient for a healthy cash flow and continued prosperity of your business. I encourage you, from this point forward, to take on the challenge of becoming a serious student of marketing. Begin the learning process by reading one or more of the books I have recommended in the resource list at the back of this book.

# Frequently Asked Questions on Growing Your Business

### Q. I don't have a database of my customers. How integral is this to the success of business?

Conventional wisdom says that it's five to six times more expensive to attract a new customer than it is to retain a current one. Is a database of existing customers important? You bet it is. For one thing, reselling existing customers is easier, and almost always more profitable.

Once you acquire a customer, there's always the opportunity to sell them additional products (cross selling), or a more expensive version of their original purchase (up-selling). Since you already have a relationship with the customer, these activities are easier and more effective than finding and winning new customers.

# CHAPTER 6:

## Small Business Financing:
## How and Where to Get the Money You Need

# INTRODUCTION:

### The Basics on Financing

Every day thousands of businesses are forced to close their doors. The most common reason given for the high failure rate of small businesses is a lack of adequate capital. Whether you're starting a business or expanding one, sufficient ready capital is essential. But it is not enough to simply have sufficient financing; knowledge and planning are required to manage it well. These qualities ensure that entrepreneurs avoid common mistakes like securing the wrong type of financing, miscalculating the amount required, or underestimating the cost of borrowing money.

Before inquiring about financing, ask yourself the following:

- Can you obtain the capital you need from existing cash flow, or do you need more?

- What do you want to do – expand or protect your business?

- How soon do you need the capital?

- How great are your risks? How does your risk affect what you need?

- In what state of development is the business?

- For what purposes will the capital be used? Any lender will require that capital be requested for very specific needs.

- What is the state of your industry? Are its prospects on the rise or decline? What potential do you have to improve?

- Is your business seasonal or cyclical? Financing needs vary depending on the "term" (short vs. long).

- How strong are your managers? Do they have what it takes to lead your business toward prosperity? If so, it may be time to think about financing. If not, first things first.

- Perhaps most important, how does your need for financing mesh with your business plan?

There are three typical financing arrangements for any business:

1) Self-funding: you put up your own money
2) Debt financing: you borrow money
3) Equity financing: you share ownership with a partner or shareholder in return for money

# Self-Funding

Self-funding is often the more popular option for small-business owners. Without substantial physical assets in the business, banks will often be hesitant to offer a direct business loan. Even if you can get a business loan, a lender often wants you to personally guarantee it. Many business owners also don't want to get involved in the intricacies of equity financing. This leads to most small-business owners choosing the option of self-funding.

There are five ways to raise funds for your small business without obtaining a business loan.

1. **Personal savings**

   Most businesses are financed, at least in part, with personal savings. The benefit of financing the business with your savings is that you don't have to worry about making loan payments. An added benefit of this option is that you enhance your borrowing capacity for the future. The assets that you purchase with your personal savings can later serve as collateral for a business loan, if needed.

## 2. Home equity loans

If you have equity in your home, you can take the proceeds using a home equity loan and use them to operate your business.

## 3. Life insurance

If you own a whole life insurance policy that has a cash surrender value, you may be able to borrow against it. A $500,000 life insurance policy with a cash surrender value of $30,000 enables you to borrow up to $30,000, depending on the percentage stated in your policy.

## 4. Retirement plans

Your Individual Retirement Accounts (IRA) can be source of short-term funding. The rule is that any money withdrawn from an IRA needs to be replaced within 60 days to avoid penalties and taxes. If the withdrawal of funds exceeds the 60-day period, then it becomes a "premature withdrawal" and it becomes subject to ordinary income tax, and if you are under the age of 59½, a 10% penalty on the amount withdrawn.

## 5. Credit cards

With average credit card rates averaging over 15% over the last several years, this is not my preferred method to finance a small business. Some cards have rates as high as or higher than 21%.

However, there are some instances when using credit card debt for the short term is okay. For example, "teaser" rates of new credit card solicitations carry rates as low as 2.9%. With prudent and calculated steps, one can create a longer-lasting low-interest loan than the three-to-six months typical of offerings.

For example, a business owner could play the credit card game by borrowing against a low-rate card and then "rolling over" the debt to another low-rate card as the time for the cheap rate on the original card is expiring. He could repeat this process enough times to go for a year or two paying a very low rate. Obviously this is a tricky game and any oversight in rolling the debt in a timely fashion may wipe out the benefits that would otherwise be derived.

**Success Tip**

Start-up costs are typically funded from personal sources (80%). Only 20% of new businesses use commercial lenders. It's not the first place to look for start-up money.

# Debt Financing

Businesses may use debt financing to operate over a period of time. Funds secured through debt financing must be repaid over a predetermined period of time, usually with interest. Short-term (less than one year) and long-term (more than one year) options are available. Debt financing does not require any change in ownership structure, one advantage of this method. Further, interest paid is deductible as a legitimate business expense. Sources of debt financing include banks, trust companies and credit unions, for example. Other sources include family and friends, suppliers and equipment manufacturers, third-party leasing companies, government agencies and other financing organizations.

Types of debt financing include demand loans, lines of credit, term loans, and leasing and supplier credit. Remember to shop around and compare terms, costs and flexibility. Let's look at each one:

### 1) Short-term loans, demand loans and long-term commercial loans

Usually short-term loans and demand loans are generally used to cover cash-flow shortages, to purchase inventory, or to take advantage of supplier discounts. The loans are usually repaid within 30-to-180 days. A short-term loan is usually secured by a personal guarantee or company assets, or it may be extended solely on the basis of the company's financial statements, track record, and ability to repay the loan. By definition, a demand loan can be called by the lender (i.e., demanded) at any time. This means you must pay back the loan immediately.

Long-term commercial loans provide medium- to long-term financing to cover some or all of the cost of capital equipment, expansion, or renovation of buildings. Term loans are usually secured by the asset being financed, and, depending on the loan's purpose, come with varying repayment schedules.

**Success Tip**
It is highly unlikely that a conventional lending source will finance your business at 100%. In fact, you can expect to come up with 25-30% of the required investment yourself. Your collateral is probably worth far less than you think it is. Be prepared for this when seeking conventional lender financing.

### 2) Line of credit

A line of credit provides a business with money to cover day-to-day operations. As funds are used, the established credit line is reduced. Your line of credit is replenished when you make payments. Like a demand note, it is usually secured by assets, receivables, inventory or other means. The loan has a limit, and interest is paid only on the amount actually borrowed.

### 3) Leasing

Leasing is akin to a long-term rental, and an ideal alternative if you are seeking funding to obtain business equipment. At the end of the lease, you don't automatically own the asset, but you have the option to buy it at its residual value. A lease requires little or no money down and is an alternative to purchasing such items as cars, machinery or office equipment. By leasing instead of buying, your business can usually write off the monthly lease payments.

### 4) Supplier credit

Many manufacturers of cars, machinery or computers provide goods, and extend the privilege of making monthly payments over a specified period of time. Suppliers are more likely to be flexible when working with credit terms, or they may offer discounts for prompt payment, or extend payment terms that work specifically for your business.

# The Five Cs of Credit

Your bank is a commercial institution, not a charitable one. It is in business to make (not lose) money. As a result, when a bank lends money it wants to ensure that it will get paid back. To maximize the likelihood of being paid back, the bank must be confident in the ability of the borrower to pay back a loan – it will take all necessary steps to ensure the creditworthiness of the borrower.

While each lending situation is unique, many banks utilize some variation of evaluating the five C's of credit when making credit decisions. Review each category and see how you stack up.

**Capacity** to repay is the most critical of the five factors. The prospective lender will want to know your company's borrowing history and track record of repayment. How much debt can your company handle? Will you be able to honor the obligation and repay the debt? There are numerous financial benchmarks, such as debt and liquidity ratios, that lenders evaluate before advancing funds.

**Capital** is the money you personally have invested in the business. It is an indication of your financial commitment and how much you have at risk should the business fail. Prospective lenders and investors will expect you to have contributed from your own assets and to have undertaken personal financial risk to establish the business before asking them to commit any funding. If you have a significant personal investment in the business, you are more likely to do everything in your power to make the business successful.

**Collateral** or "guarantees" represents assets that the company pledges as an alternate repayment source for the loan. If for some reason the business cannot repay its bank loan, the bank wants to know there is a second source of repayment.

Most collateral is in the form of hard assets, such as real estate and office or manufacturing equipment. Alternatively, your accounts receivable and inventory can be pledged as collateral. Both business and personal assets can be sources of collateral for a loan. A guarantee, on the other hand, is just that – someone else signs a guarantee document promising to repay the loan if you can't. Some lenders may require such a guarantee in addition to collateral as security for a loan.

**Conditions** focus on the current economic conditions and the intended purpose of the loan. What are the current economic conditions and how does your company fit in? If your business is sensitive to economic downturns, for example, the bank wants a comfort level that you're managing productivity and expenses. What are the trends for your industry, and how does your company fit within them? Are there any economic or political hot potatoes that could negatively impact the growth of your business? Will the borrowed money be used for working capital, additional equipment, or inventory?

**Character** is the overall impression you make on the potential lender or investor. The lender will form a subjective opinion as to whether or not you are sufficiently trustworthy to repay the loan or generate a return on funds invested in your company. Your educational background and experience in business and in your industry will be reviewed. The quality of your references and the background and experience of your employees also will be taken into consideration. Investors want to put their money with those who have impeccable credentials and references. The way you treat your employees and customers, the way you take responsibility, your timeliness in fulfilling your obligations – these are all part of the character question.

## How Your Loan Request Will Be Reviewed

When reviewing a loan request, the lender is primarily concerned about repayment. To help determine this ability, many loan officers will order a copy of your business credit report from a credit-reporting agency. Therefore, you should work with these agencies to help them present an accurate picture of your business. Using the credit report and the information you have provided, the lending officer will consider the following issues:

- Have you invested savings or personal equity in your business totaling at least 25% to 50% of the loan you are requesting? (Remember, a lender or investor will not finance 100% of your business.)

- Do you have a sound record of credit worthiness as indicated by your credit report, work history and letters of recommendation? This is very important.

- Do you have sufficient experience and training to operate a successful business?

- Have you prepared a loan proposal and business plan that demonstrate your understanding of and commitment to the success of the business?

- Does the business have sufficient cash flow to make the monthly payments?

**Success Tip**
Financial projections must demonstrate the business' ability to pay back loans plus interest. Your assumptions must be sound, and based on reality. Conventional loans usually take 60-90 days to fully close. This may be longer, depending upon the information needs of the lender, so be mentally prepared.

# Government Financing Programs

Don't count on the government for financing. Government grants are rare and only available for limited, specific enterprises. Most government loans are in the form of guaranteed loans through local banks. That means the Small Business Administration (SBA) is *not* the lender, but rather a guarantor of a loan made by the lender.

The SBA-guaranteed loan process starts like most other loans – with a local bank. A small-business person can walk into any bank and ask about a loan. The SBA becomes part of the equation once the bank determines that it's not willing to make the loan without the SBA's guarantee.

The SBA will want information similar to that required by a lender – three years of financial statements; accounts receivable and payable; information on leases; cash flow projections; personal financial statements, and so on.

**Success Tip**
The SBA has offices located throughout the country. For the one nearest you, go here:
http://www.sba.gov/tools/local-assistance/districtoffices

# SBA's Major Guaranty Loan Comparison Chart[3]

| | 7(a) Term Loan | SBA Express | Patriot Express | CDC-504 Term Loan |
|---|---|---|---|---|
| **Eligibility** | For-profit business<br><br>Net worth less than $15,000,000<br><br>Net Profit less than $5,000,000 | Same as 7(a) | Same as 7(a)<br><br>Be owned by a Veteran, or active duty military, or national guard member, or reservist, or current spouse, or widowed spouse of a service member who died during service or of a service connected disability | Same as 7(a)<br><br>Create 1 job for each $65,000 in SBA loan funds |
| **Loan Size** | No minimum loan amount<br><br>Maximum loan is $5,000,000 | No minimum loan amount<br><br>Maximum loan is $1,000,000 | No minimum loan amount<br><br>Maximum loan is $500,000 | SBA's debenture minimum is $50,000<br><br>Maximum SBA debenture $5,000,000($5,500,000 for manufacturers) |
| **Use of Proceeds** | • Land- Buildings<br>• Equipment<br>• Fixtures<br>• Inventory<br>• Working Capital<br>• Refinance Debt<br>• Business Acquisition | • Land - Buildings<br>• Equipment<br>• Fixtures<br>• Inventory<br>• Working Capital<br>• Refinance Debt<br>• Business Acquisition | • Land - Buildings<br>• Equipment<br>• Fixtures<br>• Inventory<br>• Working Capital<br>• Refinance Debt<br>• Business Acquisition | • Land - Buildings<br>• Equipment with 10 year useful life |
| **Financing** | Provided by commercial lender<br><br>SBA guaranty is 85% on loans $150,000 or less<br><br>And 75% on loans more than $150,000 | Provided by commercial lender<br><br>SBA Guaranty is 50% | Provided by commercial lender<br><br>SBA guaranty is 85% on loans $150,000 or less<br><br>And 75% on loans more than $150,000 | 50% financing by commercial lender<br><br>40% financed by SBA through a Certified Development Company<br><br>Minimum of 10% by borrower (higher for special purpose property and/or new businesses) |

| | 7(a) Term Loan | SBA Express | Patriot Express | CDC-504 Term Loan |
|---|---|---|---|---|
| **Collateral** | Generally a 1st lien position on assets acquired with loan proceeds<br><br>Loan must be 100% secured if assets available | Generally a 1st lien on assets acquired with loan proceeds | Generally a 1st lien on assets acquired with loan proceeds | Private lender holds first lien on real estate and equipment<br><br>SBA takes second position on project assets |
| **Loan Payment Terms** | 7 to 10 years for working capital and equipment<br><br>25 years for real estate | Revolving loans up to 7 years<br><br>7 to 10 years for working capital and equipment<br><br>25 years for real estate | Revolving loans up to 7 years<br><br>7 to 10 years for working capital and equipment<br><br>25 years for real estate | SBA debenture 10 years for equipment; 20 years for real estate<br><br>Private lender must have minimum of 7 years for equipment 10 for real estate |
| **Interest Rates** | Fixed or Variable<br><br>Maximum of Prime +2.25% for loans with maturity less than 7 years<br><br>Maximum of Prime +2.75% for loans with maturity of 7 years and over<br><br>Additional 2% on loans $25,000 and under; additional 1% on loans $50,000 & under | Fixed or Variable<br><br>Maximum of Prime +6.5% on loans less than $50,000 and Prime +4.5% on loans over $50,000 | Fixed or Variable<br><br>Maximum of Prime +2.25% for loans with maturity less than 7 years<br><br>Maximum of Prime +2.75% for loans with maturity of 7 years and over<br><br>Additional 2% on loans $25,000 and under; additional 1% on loans $50,000 & under | Private Lender loan – negotiated between borrower and lender<br><br>SBA loan – low fixed rate and fixed payment.<br><br>Loan rate set when debenture is sold |
| **SBA Fees** | Fee is charged on guaranteed portion of loan<br><br>For loans $150,000 or less is 2.0%<br>For loans greater than $150,000 up to $700,000 is 3.0%<br>For loans greater than $700,000 is 3.5%<br>For loans greater than $1,000,000 and additional 0.25% is charged on the portion more than $1,000,000<br><br>The SBA guaranty fee can be financed with the loan | | | Contact the local CDC for current fees which are generally less than 3.0% and can be financed with the loan |

## SBA Microloans

Small businesses needing small-scale financing and technical assistance for startup or expansion may be able to obtain up to $50,000 through short-term loans of public money called "microloans." The average loan size is about $10,500 and the maximum maturity for a microloan is six years.

Various responsible nonprofit groups, such as local economic development organizations or state finance authorities, are selected and approved by the SBA. The SBA loans the money to the nonprofit organization, which then pools funds with local money and administers direct loans to small businesses.

These loans are intended for the purchase of machinery and equipment, furniture and fixtures, inventory, supplies and working capital and are administered much like a line of credit. The funds are dispersed with close observation of the recipient, and a self-employment training program usually accompanies the loan. The loan cannot be used to pay existing debts.

## The SBA recommends the following checklist for *established* businesses when applying for an SBA loan

- ❏ Business financial statements for the current and preceding year.

- ❏ Personal financial statements of yourself as the owner or each partner or stockholder owning 20% or more of the corporate stock in the business.

- ❏ A list of collateral to be offered as security for the loan with your estimate of the present market value of each item.

- ❏ State the amount of loan requested and explain exact purposes for which they will be used.

- ❏ Visit your bank. Ask for a direct bank loan, and, if refused, ask the bank to make the loan under the SBA's loan guarantee plan, or to participate with the SBA in a loan. If the bank is interested in an SBA guarantee or participation loan, ask the banker to contact the SBA for discussion of your application. In most cases of guarantee or participation loans, the SBA will deal directly with the bank.

❑ If a guarantee or participation loan is not available, write or visit the nearest SBA office and they will give you the additional information required.

## For *new* businesses, follow this checklist

❑ An updated business plan (see Chapter 3 on writing a business plan.)

❑ Lacking a business plan, a description of the type of business to be established, the experience and management capabilities and competitive strengths.

❑ An estimate of how much you'll need to borrow and the collateral you are willing to put in as security for the loan.

❑ Current personal financial statement.

❑ Projected financial statements of the business for the first 3 years.

❑ Visit your bank with this material. Ask for a direct bank loan, and, if refused, ask the bank to make the loan under the SBA's loan guarantee plan, or to participate with the SBA in a loan. If the bank is interested in an SBA guarantee or participation loan, ask the banker to contact the SBA for discussion of your application. In most cases of guarantee or participation loans, the SBA will deal directly with the bank.

❑ If a guarantee or participation loan is not available, write or visit the nearest SBA office and they will give you the additional information required.

**Success Tip**

Many commercial lenders may not willingly devote significant time to secure an SBA guarantee on a small commercial loan. As the applicant, you should expect to do much of the administrative work yourself. A strong business plan is essential.

# Equity Financing

Equity means ownership. Equity financing describes an exchange of money for a share of business ownership. This form of financing allows you to obtain funds without incurring debt. Equity financing is good if you don't want an obligation to repay a lender. The major disadvantage to equity financing is the dilution of your ownership interests and the possible loss of control that may accompany a sharing of ownership with additional investors. The most basic hurdle to equity financing is finding investors who are willing to buy into your business, especially if you are a new business. No matter how sure you are that your business will succeed, others will not always share your conviction.

## 1) Venture Capital (VC)

A venture capital fund specializes in financing new ventures with capital supplied by investors who are interested in speculative or high-risk investments.

Venture capital is typically targeted at high-growth, high-tech sectors. VC firms speculate on certain high-risk businesses producing a very high rate of return in a very short time. The idea is not to make a percentage return on their money, but to make multiples of their investment.

The availability of venture capital funding to startups is limited to companies with extremely qualified and skilled management, well-engineered processes, and highly marketable products or services.

Compared to traditional lending organizations, VCs more closely scrutinize the features of the product or service being offered, and conduct more extensive analyses of their potential in the market. Due to the amount of money that venture capital firms spend in examining and researching businesses before they invest, they will very frequently have specific preferences for certain type of products, industries and geographic locations.

VC firms can be tough to deal with. In most cases, they insist on owning more than 50% of a business. Although the VCs are not interested in the day-to-day management of business, they are known to exert massive amounts of pressure if business is not growing as projected.

In spite of the elevated costs of financing through venture capital companies, they do offer an incredible opportunity for obtaining large amounts of equity funding for companies that fit their profile.

Venture capital firms are located nationwide. Various resources and information related to this is available through the National Association of Venture Capital http://www.nvca.org, 1655 N. Fort Meyer Dr., Arlington, VA 22209, (703 524-2549).

## 2) Small Business Investment Corps. (SBIC)

An SBIC is a privately owned and operated small-business investment company that partners with the federal government to provide venture capital to small, fast-growing companies. They enjoy unique status under federal securities law, as they encourage more private money to go to smaller companies. Currently, there are 300 SBICs nationwide with private funds and government money to lend.

While there are some general-purpose SBICs, others focus on a particular industry, geographic area, and type of borrower, women, or minorities. Some industries sponsor SBICs to encourage innovation. SBICs differ in the nature of companies they will invest in, the size of investment, stage of company, and so on. Otherwise they bring some of the same concerns as venture capital companies.

## 3) Informal Investors/Business Angels

Another source for external equity financing is through "angels." Angels are private, seasoned investors who are seeking to put their money into promising businesses, hoping to earn a higher return on their investment than through more traditional methods.

Angels can be a very good source of funding if you seek outside investors but you are not interested in, or not a likely target for, a venture capital firm. Angels are not typically interested in controlling the business, although they usually want an advisory role. Although angels tend to be less demanding in their financing terms than venture capital firms, you should still exercise great caution. Angels will still want to play a somewhat active role in your business. Angel financing is appropriate if you are seeking anything from a few thousand dollars to $3 - $5 million.

**Success Tip**

When looking for "angel" investors, do your best to shop for "smart money"; in other words, try to get more from an angel than just financing. Many angels will serve as advisors, or on a board of advisors, to offer the value of their experience and strategic advice on operating the enterprise. In addition, the angels will frequently use their own connections to assist the business in finding additional financing growth opportunities, favorable suppliers, new customers, etc.

## 4) Initial Public Offerings

You may have read about how some small company became an overnight success story by deciding to "go public" through an initial public offering (IPO) of its stock. Going public simply means that a company that was previously owned by a limited number of private investors has elected, for the first time, to sell ownership shares of the business to the general public. Going public involves a rigorous process of regulatory compliance and promotion.

### *Debt or Equity*

Debt and equity financing are simply more opportunities for raising funds. It is good business practice to maintain a commercially acceptable ratio between debt and equity financing. From the lender's viewpoint, the debt-to-equity ratio measures the amount of available assets available for repayment of a debt in the case of default. Too much debt may indicate that your business is overextended and a risky investment. Additionally, you may be unable to weather unforeseen business and economic downturns.

On the other hand, too much equity financing can indicate that you are not making the most productive use of your capital. The capital you have is not being used favorably as leverage for obtaining financing.

# DEBT OR EQUITY FINANCING
## The Pros and Cons of the Choice

|  | Debt | Equity |
|---|---|---|
| CAPACITY | Can you get loans? Do the cash flow and financial structure of your business justify the debt you need to incur? | Can you attract investors or strategic partners? Is the business or investment opportunity attractive enough? Can you "make the case?" |
| COST TO THE BUSINESS | Payment terms, interest, fees, restrictive conditions. | Cost of finding and convincing investors. Dividends or other payouts. |
| FINANCIAL IMPACT ON THE OWNER | Uses "others people's money" to increase size of the business, revenues, profits, and market value, thus leveraging financial benefit to owner (owner has 100%). | Uses "other people's money" to increase size of the business, revenues, profits, and market value – but diminishes owner's share to less than 100%. |
| CONTROL | Owner retains 100% control. Some lenders require restrictive covenants. | Owner may or may not lose control, depending on what percentage of ownership is sold. Always has to acknowledge equity holders to some degree. |
| RISK | Leverages the business (debt-to-equity ratio is the measure). Increases real and perceived risk. Uses up debt capacity. | Stabilizes financial structure and viability. Reduces real and perceived risk. Increases debt capacity, enabling greater expansion later. |

# IN CONCLUSION

When it comes to financing, you essentially have 3 options – put up your own money, borrow it from a bank, or secure it through a business partner. While any or all may work, one thing is certain – your business must be properly financed or it will not succeed. While doing your business planning, spend the time necessary to determine your financing needs and sources.

Remember to keep yourself connected to others who may be able to impart the wisdom of their experience unto you. Other business owners, friends, and associates are resource options; remember, too, the Small Business Administration provides helpful information and resources to all small-business owners. Use them.

Finally, work hard to avoid common mistakes associated with financing your business. Ask yourself the right questions, and spend time evaluating and reevaluating your needs on a regular basis. Understanding the intricacies of financing will go a long way towards securing the financial future of your business.

# Frequently Asked Questions on "Small Business Financing: How and Where To Get the Money You Need"

### Q. What are the alternatives in financing a business?

The money you put up yourself is the best indicator of how committed you are. Risking your money gives confidence for others to invest in your business. Bringing in a partner is one alternative among many. Banks are an obvious source of funds. Refer to other alternatives discussed in this chapter.

### Q. What do I have to do to get a loan?

Consider these questions:

- How will you use the loan?
- How much do you need to borrow?
- How will you repay the loan?

Your lender will want the answers to these 3 questions. Make sure your documentation provides them – clearly. Remember, you have to convince them to take a substantial risk. Think about how you would alleviate that risk for them.

### Q. What is a revolving credit line and how is it used?

A revolving credit line is a flexible method of obtaining immediate cash. Revolving lines have variable rates and loan amounts. Generally, you access cash by writing a check, depositing it into your account, then paying back the "loan" monthly.

### Q. Does it matter what size bank I approach; a big bank or a small bank?

When it come to a banking relationship, it is important to work on building a strong relationship with a *banker*, not just a bank. Having said that, you are usually better off at a smaller bank, especially one with a reputation of lending to small businesses.

Bigger banks have the tendency to assign your account to a junior lending officer, who may eventually move up. Also, the big bank may not be as attentive to your needs as a smaller one. The reason; you are considered a small fish in comparison to their larger, more profitable clients.

# CHAPTER 7:

## Bookkeeping and Accounting:
## How to Keep Records That Help You And
## Maintain Financial Control Over Your Business

---

**Case Study**

Samantha was the owner of Samantha's Retail and Wholesale Outlet Inc., an S-corporation that had been established for 2 years.

She had read an article by an accountant in her local paper titled "Paperwork everywhere – no adequate reporting system." This prompted her to schedule a meeting with him and she arrived in his office with a big black plastic box, one of those that you'd get in an office supply store. The accountant prodded Samantha to share with him what had inspired her to make the appointment and what areas of her business he could address so that she would get the greatest benefit from their meeting.

With concern and frustration on her face, she quickly pointed to the big black box and said *"This is my problem, right here. My records are in here but how do I organize them and what do they mean? If you get me in front of customers, I'm great, but get me in front of paperwork and I don't know where to begin"*

She went on *"You mentioned in your article that there is a wealth of information to be derived from well-kept financial reports. I need to be able to do that. Business was good the first year when I opened my doors, it was terrible last year. To keep afloat, I have had to take a number of loans from family and friends. There is simply too much at stake and I ABSOLUTELY NEED to make this business work."*

Samantha went on to explain the manual check-writing and record-keeping system she had been using. She also shared that she had purchased and installed QuickBooks on her computer at home but wasn't quite sure if she had set it up correctly. She had used it for a few weeks but decided to stick with her manual record-keeping system.

The solution to Samantha's problem was clear to the accountant. She was a very bright and intelligent small-business owner who simply needed some financial guidance. Her manual record-keeping system was far too time-consuming and sapping her energy and focus away from building her business.

The correct installation of her QuickBooks program with some hands-on, customized one-on-one training would make a significant difference in Samantha's business. As they ended the meeting, they both knew the work that lay ahead of them. The accountant sensed the relief in Samantha's voice as they exchanged good-byes.

# INTRODUCTION:

### Managing Your Business Finances

Keeping accurate and clear business financial records can, for many business owners, be the most difficult, and frankly the most stressful, part of running a business. Simply understanding these records is often challenging. And yet maintaining a set of clear and understandable financial records is perhaps the single most important factor that separates successful businesses from those that fail. Good decision-making requires it. And you, the business owner, must take responsibility for obtaining this knowledge. Use the basic principles of sound financial management on a daily basis – you can leave the more complicated accounting work to professionals, but don't underestimate your need to know!

The purpose of this chapter is to provide the small-business owner with a clear, concise, and easy-to-understand system for setting up your business records and keeping the books for the business.

One of the imperatives of success in business is accurate financial records. Without them, how will you know if you are making money, or losing it? How will you know if you are financially strong? How will you anticipate the rough spots? You start with accurate financial records.

**Success Tip**

A simple, well-organized and regularly kept record keeping system can actually be a time-saver by bringing order out of chaos.

## Importance of Good Records

Maintaining good financial records is a must. For all of the things you will want to achieve from the other chapters in this book – saving on taxes, obtaining financing, selling your business, monitoring your business' progress – a solid bookkeeping system is essential.

Develop good habits from the beginning. Although you'd much rather spend your time selling your product or service, take some time to learn about financial records. Accurate and timely financial information is a must. Here are some of the reasons why you need a good financial record-keeping system:

- **To monitor the success of your business.** Am I making money? Are sales increasing? Are expenditures increasing faster than sales? Which expenses are too high? Is spending "in control?"

- **To get the information you need to make decisions.** Which road do you take? How do you know? Each decision you make will probably have financial benefits and consequences. Accurate records help you decipher these, and ultimately help you determine the proper course of action.

- **To obtain bank financing.** Any bank you approach with a plan and a financial application will demand financial statements. More than this, the bank officer may want to know how well you keep financial records. If for no other reason (although there are many good reasons), keep accurate records for this purpose.

- **To obtain other sources of capital.** Potential investors or partners would be foolish to invest or join you in business without good information backing their decision.

- **To budget your money.** Your budget helps you see how well you are doing with income and spending throughout the year, against your stated goals. It is helpful to know how you're doing, so that you can determine where you will end up. Additionally, a budget gives you the opportunity to change course and make corrections as needed, shifting momentum to your favor.

- **To prepare your income tax return.** Whether your business is a sole proprietorship, partnership, limited liability company, S-corporation or C-corporation, you must file an income tax return and pay income taxes. Accurate records will ensure a properly completed tax return. Why pay more than you should? Your record keeping will directly affect the tax return of each partner.

- **To ensure compliance with federal and state payroll tax rules.** Every business must comply with federal and state rules and regulations. Keeping accurate records ensures that these rules are followed. Payroll records, for example, can be complex and prodigious. Poor record-keeping will make timely and simple compliance (not to mention cost-effective compliance) impossible.

- **To properly submit sales taxes.** If you collect sales tax from your customers, good records will make it easy for you to compute the tax due and prepare the required reports.

- **To distribute profits.** How much should each partner receive? Your records, if maintained properly, will show you simply and easily.

**Success Tip**
It is very important to keep your personal and business funds separate. There are 2 reasons for this: 1) The IRS frowns on the commingling of these funds, and 2) it makes it very difficult to properly account for these transactions.

# 6 Tips to Keep Your Business on a Sound Financial Footing

For many small businesses the most common bookkeeping errors are also the easiest to fix. Use these six tips to help keep your business on sound financial footing.

1.  **Use the right accounting system.** Will you use the cash-based or accrual accounting? In the **cash method**, income is "booked" when it is received, and expenses when they are paid. Under **accrual**, income and expenses are counted when they are earned, rather than when funds are received.

    The timing is important especially if you maintain inventory or sell to customers "on credit." As you might expect, the accrual method works best in that case. (Note: if your business has more than $5 million ($10 million if an S corporation or partnership) in sales or maintains inventory, the IRS might require an accrual system.)

2.  **Maintain daily records.** This is a fundamental rule. You will know the financial condition of your business *only* when you maintain accurate records. Use it daily, and you will find how easy it can be. The rewards are substantial.

3.  **Handle and review checks carefully.** Don't take this for granted – checks are as good as cash. Sign checks using a clear, distinctive signature that won't invite forgery. Review canceled checks before anyone else, including your bookkeeper or employees, sees them; that way you can catch unauthorized checks. And if your business is a partnership, it's a good idea to have at least one of the partners co-sign the checks.

4.  **Get a bank statement with a month-end cutoff.** Synchronizing your bank statement with other monthly records will make it much easier to reconcile it and track expenses.

5.  **Leave an audit trail.** Make sure your system allows you (or someone qualified) to retrace your steps. Simple things – keep invoices and checks in numeric order, and maintain separate bank accounts for personal and business needs. Having the ability to reconstruct one year is usually a good standard.

6.  **Use a computer.** Computer bookkeeping software is absolutely essential for all but the smallest businesses. These applications make it easy to track

income and expenses, prepare tax documents, summarize your company's financial activities and back up records for safekeeping. If you're working with an outside bookkeeper, make sure they know how to use a computer.

# Record-Keeping Terminology

**ACCOUNTING** is the *design* of the record-keeping system that a business uses, and the *preparation* and *interpretation* of reports based on the information that is gathered and put into the system.

An accounting system can be represented by the following graphic, which is explained below.

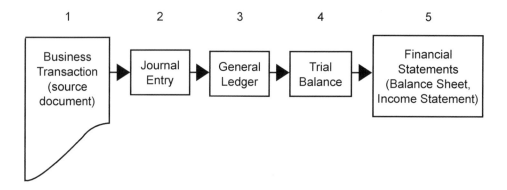

There are five parts to the accounting system. The flow of information during a specified period is commonly referred to as an *accounting cycle*.

The accounting cycle can be described as follows:

1. Business transaction yields a record, called a journal entry.
2. Journal entry totals comprise a book of accounts called the general ledger.
3. The general ledger contains the individual accounts maintained by the business.
4. The individual accounts are listed in the form of debits and credits, known as the trial balance of the general ledger.
5. From the trial balance, business records, i.e., financial statements, are prepared.

A more detailed explanation of each component of the accounting cycle follows:

## Journals

Journal entries are made from original business documents such as sales slips and cash register tapes. Purchase invoices and other business transaction records may also yield journal entries.

## General Ledgers

The summary and totals from all journals are entered into the general ledger. A general ledger is a summary book that records transactions and balances of individual accounts, and is organized into five classes of individual accounts, as follows:

1. Assets – A record of all items that the business owns.

2. Liabilities – A record of all debts the business owes.

3. Capital – A record of all ownership or equity.

4. Sales – A record of all income earned for a specific period.

5. Expenses – A record of all expenditures incurred during a given period.

## Trial Balance

At the end of the accounting period, the individual accounts in the general ledger are totaled and closed. The balances of the individual accounts are summarized in the financial statements.

## Financial Statements

Once your general journal entries are correct and posted into the general ledger, you are ready to prepare financial statements.

The three main types of financial statements are:

- Balance sheet

- Income statement

- Cash flow statement

Usually, an accountant prepares these. But with the help of computer software, you may be able to prepare your own financial statements. If you need to prepare financial statements for third parties, such as a banker, sometimes the third party may request that a professional accountant or certified public accountant prepare the financial statements. Chapter 8 has been devoted to a discussion of financial statements and how to understand and derive value from them. In Chapter 9, I talk about cash flow and how to maximize it.

**BOOKKEEPING** is the actual input of the financial information into the record-keeping system. There are two types of bookkeeping systems: single-entry and double-entry. While single-entry is the easiest, it has fewer built-in checks and balances; this is a significant advantage of the double-entry method.

**Single-entry**. A single-entry system is simple and practical, since it is based on the income statement. A small business may be able to use the single-entry method. The system records the flow of income and expenses through the use of:

1. A daily summary of cash receipts, and

2. Monthly summaries of cash receipts and disbursements.

**Double-entry**. A double-entry bookkeeping system uses journals and ledgers. Transactions are first entered in a journal and then posted to ledger accounts. These accounts show income, expenses, assets, liabilities and net worth or equity. You close income and expense accounts at the end of each tax year. You keep asset, liability, and net worth accounts open on a permanent basis.

For each account, there is a debit and credit. Debits are recorded on the left, while credits are recorded on the right. With a double-entry system, debits and credits must be equal. Non-balanced accounts indicate an error, which should be researched and corrected. Off- the-shelf accounting systems use the double-entry method, are very user-friendly, and are highly recommended, particularly for the accounting novice.

# Important Rules of Bookkeeping

1) Pay bills by check or petty cash. This will make it simple and easy to track your expenses.

2) Track all incoming cash – how much, from where, and when it came in.

3) Draw a salary, rather than taking cash from daily receipts.

4) Establish a business bank account, and deposit all cash receipts on a daily basis. Make sure to separate your personal from your business account, and do the same for personal vs. business related cash.

5) Periodically, have your record-keeping system checked over by a Certified Public Accountant (CPA).

## What should I use: a manual accounting system or a computerized accounting package?

Your decision whether to use a manual or computerized accounting system may depend on the number of transactions that take place in your business. Manual systems (recording transactions by hand in ledgers) may work well for a business with few transactions, however, the plethora of inexpensive software packages – from simple to complex – make manual systems generally moot.

### Manual Record-Keeping

Simply put, manual bookkeeping systems rely on individuals (you, probably) to record all transactions. Should you choose this option, you will find all necessary manual bookkeeping forms at almost any office supply store.

### Computerized Record Keeping

Financial computer software abounds. With minimal research, you should be able to find a software package that suits your business' financial bookkeeping needs, and one that is simple and easy to use.

**Success Tip**

If you are planning to use an accounting software package, consider taking a course that teaches you how to properly set-up and use the accounting software. This step can save you many hours of frustration and headaches in the future. If you prefer, your accountant should also be able to advise you accordingly, and even teach you how to use your new software.

The following are some of the accounting software packages available and website information to get more information on:

o   QuickBooks Desktop is easy to use, highly adaptable.  Excellent for most small businesses.  You may struggle with it if your business needs subsystems – inventory, fixed assets, etc. www.intuit.com

o   Sage Accounting Software (formerly Peachtree) was one of the first comprehensive packages designed for a small business. Several products are available, including those with fixed asset and job costing functions.  Start-ups may find this package a bit advanced, but it should be adaptable for most. www.peachtree.com

o   There are various choices for online (aka cloud) accounting software.  If you have not used accounting software before, these are good options, but if you are an advanced Quickbooks Desktop user, these online choices will be difficult for you to use.

   ▪   Quickbooks Online (QBO) – www.quickbooksonline.com – it is much different that Quickbooks Desktop and a bit cumbersome.

   ▪   Xero – www.xero.com – has many good features, but is also a bit cumbersome versus Quickbooks Desktop.

   ▪   Freshbooks – www.freshbooks.com – user friendly, but also cumbersome

o   Be sure to check the modules these online companies offer in relation to inventory, accounting receivable, invoicing, estimating, quoting, check printing, payroll, point-of-sale system (POS), fixed asset tracking, etc.  Also check if there is a phone and/or tablet app available for you to access remotely. You also need to make sure it has the ability to add your accountant to the access so they can help you with questions or issues.

## The Five Basic Records Required

There are five basic records that are required for any small business record-keeping system:

1.  **Sales records**
    Organize your sales records by "category."  This will make them easier to analyze later.  As an example, suppose you sell both wholesale and retail; you may consider organizing these sales by region or some other market

segmentation. If you are a service provider, you may categorize your revenue records by the type of service you provide.

2. **Cash receipts**

Cash receipts represent cash actually received in the form of sales as well as collection of accounts receivable from monies formerly owed to you.

3. **Cash disbursements**

This refers to monies actually paid on behalf of your business. Cash disbursements may indeed be cash, but can also be paid by check. When recording cash disbursements, include the essentials: date, number, amount and purpose.

Small-business purchases not paid for by check, online bill pay, or credit card are generally paid for with petty cash. Most businesses establish a small cash fund from which these kinds of purchases are made, as required. Funds are kept in a convenient but discrete location, and accessible only by a few. Petty cash expenditures are tracked in much the same way as cash disbursements. Periodically, petty cash is replenished by totaling receipts for cash spent, then issuing another check to "Petty Cash" for the total amount of the receipts.

4. **Accounts receivable**

A good record-keeping system should provide you with a detailed report of accounts receivable, including current information on customers and running a balance of their accounts. To maintain a good accounts receivable system, record credit charges on a regular basis. It is essential that you follow up on all late-paying and delinquent customers.

Accounts receivable should be aged at the end of the month. This means organizing the accounts into those that are current; 30, 60, and 90 days old. This arrangement helps you to take appropriate, timely action.

Some of the key information on the accounts receivable report would be:

    i.   Name of account
    ii.   Account number
    iii.  Invoice date
    iv.  Invoice number
    v.   Invoice amount
    vi.  Terms of invoices

vii. Amount paid
viii. Date paid
ix. Balance

5. **Accounts payable**

   An accounts payable schedule will provide helpful information regarding money that you owe to others. Do you have bills that are past due? If so, perhaps you rely too heavily on trade credit. How do you manage your cash? This is one effective way to determine the answer to this question.

   A payables schedule lists the amounts you owe to others. Accounts payable schedules are generally prepared on a monthly basis.

# Other Important Records

### Payroll records

Payroll is perhaps the most complex function when it comes to accounting. There are myriad state and federal forms that must be completed, and highly specific payroll laws that must be followed.

Each employee must fill in an IRS Form W-4: Employee's Withholding Allowance Certificate. Use this information to compute the federal withholding, Social Security (FICA) and state taxes from each payroll check.

At the close of each payroll period, you must total the accumulated withholdings for all employees. Refer to Publication 15, *(Circular E), Employer's Tax Guide*, for more information on accuracy of deposit rules and penalties.

Prepare Employers Quarterly Federal Tax Return (Form 941) by totaling each employee's withholding for federal taxes, social security and medicare. Also, file the appropriate form with your state.

At the year's end, you are required to prepare not only the information normally required for this quarter, but also summaries of each employee's total earnings and withholdings for the year (Form W-2). Provide this form to each employee by January 31st and the IRS by February 28th of the following year.

Special note – You are an agent for the government for the employee's portion of the social security and medicare as well as their federal withholding. If this portion of the tax does not get paid, even if the business closes, you can be held responsible personally for this portion of the payroll taxes. It is called the Trust Fund Recovery Penalty (TFRP). So, be sure to remit at least this portion to the IRS.

**Success Tip**

It is very easy to fall behind when making tax payments. If you find yourself short of cash, do not be tempted to delay payment of taxes. Delayed payments can easily add up to a much larger sum; the debt may impede the growth of your business and may even force you to close your business, to say nothing of the federal penalties incurred for late payments.

## Insurance

Most businesses have several types of insurance. For each policy, you should have the following information:

- Clear statement of the type of coverage
- Names of individuals covered
- Effective dates and expiration dates
- Annual premium

**Success Tip**

Review your insurance policies on a regular basis. Each year, ask your insurance broker/agent to review the total insurance package to determine if the coverage is appropriate, and to ensure that premiums remain in line with prior quotations.

**Business Equipment**

Keep an accurate list of business equipment. The list should describe the equipment and provide serial numbers, date of purchase and original cost. Keep the list available for insurance or other purposes. You will also need this information to prepare accurate depreciation schedules.

**Auto Mileage Log**

Your transportation expenses are the ordinary and necessary business expenses of getting from one place to another in the course of your business.

There are two methods can be used for calculating this: 1) the actual expense method or, 2) the standard mileage method.

You may be able to take a deduction for car expenses (i.e., gas, oil, repairs, insurance, depreciation, interest, licenses, parking fees and tolls) – the *best* way to track it is get a gas card and charge to it but you still need to keep track of the mileage to determine the business use percentage for the actual method.

OR, you may instead use the standard mileage rate for business of 56 cents per mile for 2014 (57.5 cents for 2015).

# Basic Requirements Of Your Record-keeping System

There are four basic requirements your record keeping system must fulfill:

1. It must be simple to use and easy to understand. The information will be kept current if the system is "user-friendly."
2. Your record-keeping system should be both relevant and accurate. It should be specific to your business in order to minimize time-recording information, and recording only what is needed and necessary. "Accurate" means it should be free of errors, thus conforming to the standards you have for your record-keeping system.
3. Your system should ensure that records are kept current. The information will only be effective if records are done in a timely fashion.
4. Your record-keeping system should be consistent. The same standards and principles should be followed throughout the system, and at all times.

# Small Business Financial Record-Keeping Checklist

The following is a record-keeping checklist that every business should maintain on a daily, weekly, and monthly basis.

## Daily Record-Keeping Tasks

- ❑ Cash on hand balance and bank accounts balance
- ❑ Record all payments made, by check or cash
- ❑ Summarize and record all sales and cash receipts
- ❑ Correct any errors made in recording collections on accounts receivable
- ❑ Record any inventory received or inventory sold

## Weekly Record-Keeping Tasks

- ❑ Review accounts receivable (take action on slow payers)
- ❑ Review accounts payable (take advantage of discounts)
- ❑ Payroll (to save time, I recommend doing this bi-weekly rather than on a weekly basis)
- ❑ If you are a weekly filer, deposit taxes and file reports to federal and state tax authorities (sales tax, payroll taxes, etc.)
- ❑ Record any travel and entertainment expenses (be sure to notate the date, time, people in attendance, and a brief description of the business discussion on the receipt)

## Monthly Record-Keeping Tasks

- ❑ Confirm that all entries have been posted to the right general ledger accounts and correct any misclassifications
- ❑ Prepare / print out a profit and loss statement for the month, within a reasonable time, usually, 10-15 days after the month-end
- ❑ Prepare / print out a cash flow statement for the month
- ❑ Prepare / print out a balance sheet
- ❑ Reconcile your check register against your bank statement
- ❑ Reconcile your petty cash fund
- ❑ If you are a monthly filer, deposit taxes and file reports to federal and state tax authorities (sales tax, payroll taxes, etc.)

❏ Prepare aged accounts receivable report. Report would emphasize accounts that are past due for 30, 60, 90 days, etc. (take action on slow payers)
❏ Reconcile your credit card activity to the statement.

# OWNERS' REVIEW CHECKLIST

Despite all that you have learned here, you may still want to hire someone else to handle your accounting and bookkeeping. That's fine. But there are still some things you, as the business owner, should not surrender responsibility for. What follows are guidelines for you to use on a day-to-day basis:

a) **Compare actual results to budget.** *Each and every month* compare your income and expenses to budget. It's a great way to learn what's working and what's not working with your business. The goal is not to have an accurate budget... but for you to have a thorough knowledge of what is happening and to know if anything unexpected is going on.

b) **Scan the check register.** Periodically (every 3-4 months, or so) take a look at the check register just to make sure all the payees are familiar to you. Multiple checks written around the same time to the same vendor could be an indication that funds are being diverted. (You also might want to reduce the time spent writing and posting multiple checks.)

c) **Review the bank reconciliation.** This should be done on a monthly basis (or if you skip a month take a look at all the reconciliations since your last review.) This step is important, particularly if you have one person doing all the bookkeeping: writing checks, posting entries, preparing financials, etc. Look at any adjustments to the bank accounts, stale items, etc.

d) **Look at canceled checks.** Occasionally (say 1-2 times a year) conduct a thorough review of your bank statements, making sure to flip through the canceled checks. Ensure that all signatures are yours, and that you recognize the vendors. Scan the endorsements on the back.

e) **Review statements from vendors.** Every now and then (maybe 3-4 times per year) take the time to open the mail and look at statements from vendors (many vendors don't send statements, but do send late notices). Here you want to make sure that your business is in good standing with vendors – long overdue invoices might be an indication that a check you thought was going to a vendor actually went in someone else's pocket, or that an invoice has been overlooked.

f) **Review payroll register and hand out the paychecks.** In some industries, "padding" the payroll is a common problem. Regular review of the payroll register will prevent this from occurring.

g) **Review your Accounts Receivable and aging.** Check for "slow paying" customers, and make sure customer payments are being correctly applied.

h) **Take a physical inventory.** Do you know how much inventory you really have? Accountants can be very helpful setting up inventory tracking systems, or you can use one of many available accounting software packages. Physical inventory should be taken at least once a year, but it is generally advisable to do it more frequently.

# BASIC ACCOUNTING TERMS AND DEFINITIONS THAT THE SMALL-BUSINESS OWNER SHOULD KNOW

**Assets:** Items of value held by the business. Assets are considered "balance sheet" accounts. Examples of assets: cash, accounts receivable, and furniture and fixtures.

**Liabilities:** Refers to the amount owed to your creditors. Liabilities are considered "balance sheet" accounts. Examples of liabilities: accounts payable, payroll taxes and loans payable.

**Equity:** The net worth of your company. Also called owner's equity or capital. Equity comes from investment in the business by the owners, plus accumulated net profits of the business that have not been paid out to the owners. It essentially represents amounts owed to the owners. Equity accounts are considered "balance sheet" accounts.

**The accounting equation:** Assets = liabilities + owner's equity. The financial statement called the balance sheet is based on the "accounting equation." Note that assets are on the left-hand side of the equation, and liabilities and equities are on the right-hand side of the equation. Some balance sheets are presented so that assets are on the left, liabilities and owner's equity are on the right.

**Balance sheet:** Also called a statement of financial position, a balance sheet is a financial "snapshot" of your business at a given date in time. It lists your assets, your liabilities, and the difference between the two, which is your equity, or net worth. The balance sheet is a real-life example of the accounting equation because it shows that assets = liabilities + owner's equity.

Once you master the above accounting terms and concepts, you are ready to learn about the following day-to-day accounting terms.

**Debits:** At least one component of every accounting transaction (journal entry) is a debit amount. Debits increase assets and decrease liabilities and equity. For this reason, you will sometimes see debits entered on the left-hand side (the asset side of the accounting equation) of a two-column journal or ledger.

**Credits:** At least one component of every accounting transaction (journal entry) is a credit amount. Credits increase liabilities and equity and decrease assets. For this reason, you will sometimes see credits entered on the right-hand side (the liability and equity side of the accounting equation) of a two-column journal or ledger.

**Double-entry accounting:** In double-entry accounting, every transaction has two journal entries: a debit and a credit. Debits must always equal credits. Because debits equal credits, double-entry accounting prevents some common bookkeeping errors. Errors that do occur are easier to find. Double-entry accounting is the basis of a true accounting system.

In double-entry accounting, every transaction in your business affects at least two accounts, since there is at least one debit and one credit for each transaction. Usually, at least one of the accounts is a balance sheet account. Entries that are not made to a balance sheet account are made to an income or expense account. Income and expenses affect the net profit of the business, which ultimately affects owner's equity. Each transaction (journal entry) is a real-life example of the accounting equation (assets = liabilities + owner's equity).

Some simple accounting systems do not use the double-entry system. You will have to choose between double-entry and single-entry accounting. Because of the benefits described above, I recommend double-entry accounting. Many accounting programs for the computer are based on a double-entry system, but are designed so that you enter each transaction once, and the computer makes the corresponding second entry for you. The double-entry part goes on "behind the scenes," so to speak.

**Cash vs. Accrual Accounting:** There are two basic accounting methods available to most small businesses: cash or accrual. The **cash method** of accounting records the actual flow of cash through a business. It recognizes income when cash is actually collected from a sale. It recognizes expenses when cash is actually paid out, or when a check is written to pay a bill. It is not concerned with matching income and expenses, but rather the actual inflows and outflows of cash. This method of accounting more closely resembles your cash flow. The books are easy to maintain and there is no accounting for accounts receivable or payable. With the cash method, there is also no effective method to accurately reflect inventory costs. Thus the Internal Revenue Service regulations require that the cash method of accounting may only be used by those businesses which are solely service businesses and do not sell any products to their customers.

The **accrual method** reports income and expenses as they are incurred, even if the actual money has yet not changed hands. Most accountants recommend using the accrual method because they feel that this method more accurately reflects what's really going on in the business. It paints a truer picture because it more closely matches income and expenses. It does not, however, track your cash position, so you'll need another mechanism, like the cash plan, to monitor your cash flow. Businesses of all types and sizes can use the accrual method.

Whichever method you use, it's important to realize that either one only gives you a partial picture of the financial status of your business. While the accrual method shows the ebb and the flow of business income and debts more accurately, it may leave you in the dark as to what the cash reserves are available, which could result in a serious cash flow problem.

And though the cash method will give you a truer idea of how much actual cash your business has, it may offer a misleading picture of longer-term profitability. Under the cash method, for instance, your books show one month to be spectacularly profitable, when actually sales have been slow and, by coincidence, a lot of credit customers paid their bills in that month. To have a firm and true understanding of your business' finances, you need more than just a collection of monthly totals; you need to understand what your numbers mean and how to use them to answer specific financial questions.

# IN CONCLUSION

Knowledge of finances and financial record keeping is essential to business success. Good decisions are only made with the benefit of quality information. No matter how skilled you are at creating, manufacturing, selling or marketing your product, any profit you might earn will quickly dissipate if you do not know how to track it, save it, spend or invest it.

# Frequently Asked Questions On "Bookkeeping and Accounting: How to Keep the Books and Maintain Financial Control Over Your Business"

## Q. *What should I know about accounting and bookkeeping?*

First, you should know how important it is to keep adequate records. Without them, you will be unable to obtain critical information about your business, nor able to substantiate many things you are required to. Records are required to substantiate:

1. Your tax returns
2. Any request for credit from vendors or a loan from a bank
3. Your claims about the business, should you wish to sell it.

But most important, you need them to run your business successfully and to increase your profits.

## Q. *I want to start my own small business. What do I have to do to keep out of trouble with the IRS? (especially if it gets selected for audit)*

Keep good records. It's really that simple. Most business owners who find themselves in trouble for non-compliance, could have avoided the situation by making sure their records were sound.

Keep all receipts and canceled checks for business expenses, and keep them organized and in a safe place. Separate the documents by category, such as:

- Auto expenses

- Rent

- Utilities

- Advertising

- Travel

- Entertainment, and

- Professional fees.

Put your documents into individual folders or envelopes. You are responsible for substantiating all of your business deductions; the burden of proof in the event of an audit is on you – *not* the IRS.

### Q. Is it safe and sensible for me to keep my own books and file my own tax returns? (My business can't afford a business accountant or tax preparer.)

Consider the many software options available to small businesses. Maintaining financial records, transactions, and doing your taxes can all be done with the help of appropriate software. And most versions have checks and balances built in, to help you avoid trouble spots.

You may also consider hiring professionals, either in house or outsourced, to manage your day-to-day financial transactions and/or taxes. But make sure you know what they're doing – ultimately, you have to be "in the know."

### Q. How long do I have to keep records for?

Generally, records should be kept to demonstrate compliance with the law and to operate efficiently. And practically speaking, most individuals and businesses retain records based on available space. Record retention is only necessary to the extent that it serves a useful purpose or satisfies legal requirements.

The chart below may be helpful to answer the questions, "What must we keep?" and "How long do we have to keep it?"

Important Note: Once your company has established a record retention policy, it should be strictly enforced. This is necessary in order to negate potential claims that records were destroyed to remove incriminating information from further review. The policy should also provide for appropriate retention periods for records that will likely be needed at a later date. Finally, when a file's number comes up, records should be destroyed (and recycled if possible).

| **Individual Records** | **Retention Period** |
| --- | --- |
| Tax returns | Permanently |
| Forms W-2 | Permanently |

| | |
|---|---|
| Medical bills | Six years from payment |
| Form 1099s | Six years from receipt |
| Keogh and IRA statements | Six years from purchase |
| Year-end brokerage statements | Six years from receipt |
| Schedule K-1s from partnerships or S-corporations | Six years from disposition of interest |
| Insurance policies | Six years from expiration |
| **Business Records** | **Retention Period** |
| General: | |
| Capital stock records | Indefinite |
| Corporate records and minutes | Indefinite |
| Tax returns | Indefinite |
| Accountant's audit reports | Indefinite |
| Monthly trial balances | 7 years |
| Cash: | |
| Cash receipts and disbursements | 7 years |
| Bank statements, cancelled checks and deposit slips | 7 years |
| Bank reconciliations | 7 years |
| Petty cash vouchers | 7 years |
| Inventories: | |
| Perpetual inventory records | 7 years |
| Physical inventory records | 7 years |
| Sales and Receivables: | |
| Sales journals | 7 years |
| Shipping tickets | 7 years |
| Accounts receivable ledgers and trial balances | 7 years |
| Invoices | 3 years |
| Expired contracts | 7 years |
| Purchases and payables: | |
| Purchase journals | 7 years |
| Bills of lading | 3 years |
| Accounts payable ledgers and trial balances | 7 years |
| Purchase orders | 3 years |
| Paid bills and vouchers | 7 years |

| | |
|---|---|
| Expired purchase contracts | 7 years |
| Payroll: | |
| Payroll journals | 7 years |
| Payroll reports | 7 years |
| Form W-4 | 7 years |
| Time cards | 7 years |

## Q. *What other types of tax records should I keep?*

A. Consider keeping some other types of records as well:

- Records of capital assets, such as coin and antique collections, jewelry, stocks, and bonds.
- Records regarding the purchase and improvements to your home.
- Records regarding the purchase, maintenance, and improvements to your rental or investment property.

Keep these records as long as you own the item so you can prove the cost you use to figure your gain or loss when you transfer it.

## Q. *Are there any non-tax records I should keep?*

A. Yes. Here are a few examples:

- Insurance policies, to show casualty or theft loss history; to demonstrate specific medical expenses, or prove certain business losses.
- Records of major purchases, in the event of loss or transfer.
- Family records, such as marriage licenses, birth certificates, adoption papers, divorce agreements, in case you need to prove change in filing status or dependency exemption claims.
- Health records.

## Q. *I need to hire people quickly for a big job coming up. Should I hire independent contractors or employees?*

This is a challenging question for many business people. Generally speaking, the more control you have over workers, the more they are considered your employees.

If you dictate where, when and how your workers do their jobs, consider hiring them as employees.

Independent contractors are generally individuals who have an established business of their own, and offer their services to several businesses.

While classifying your workers as contractors would save you money in the short run (you wouldn't have to pay the employer's share of payroll taxes or have an accountant keep records and file payroll tax forms), but it may get you into big trouble if the IRS later audits you. The IRS may reclassify your "independent contractors" as employees and assess hefty back taxes, penalties and interest against you.

### Q. If you start your own business and send in your quarterly estimated income taxes, must you also file a personal income tax return at the end of the year?

If you have $400 or more of net profit from your business, you will have to file a Form 1040 with a Form 1040, Schedule C, Profit and Loss from Business (Sole Proprietorship) and a Form 1040, Schedule SE, Self-employment Tax. Even if you don't have more than $400 of net profit, I recommend you still file a return to claim any potential losses.

### Q. Is an employer ID number the same as a tax ID number?

Yes. An Employer Identification Number (EIN) and a Taxpayer Identification Number (TIN) are synonymous. EINs are needed when a business has employees (other than the owner), or if you are a corporation, S-corporation, or partnership.

### Q. As a sole proprietor, do I need an employer identification number (EIN)?

Only if (1) you pay wages to one or more employees, or (2) you file pension or excise tax returns. If not, use your social security number.

## Q. We are about to hire employees and need to know how much tax to take out and where to send this money?

Have your employees each complete a Form W-4, Employee's Withholding Allowance Certificate. Publication 15, Circular E, Employer's Tax Guide, and Publication 15-A, Employer's Supplemental Tax Guide, will help you determine how much to withhold, and how to deposit withholdings and taxes.

Generally, employers are required to file Form 941, Employer's Quarterly Federal Tax Return, and annually file Form 940, Employer's Annual Federal Unemployment Tax Return (FUTA), and Form W-2, Wage and Tax Statement, with Form W-3, Transmittal of Income and Tax Statements.

## Q. What is the federal unemployment tax rate?

The federal unemployment tax rate for 2015 is 6.0% and is still considered on the first $7,000 of wages you paid each employee in the calendar year. For specific information, refer to Tax Topic 760, Form 940 or Form 940EZ - Employer's Annual Federal Unemployment Tax Returns, or Publication 15, Circular E, Employer's Tax Guide.

## Q. We have an employee who has reached the limit for social security tax. Does this limit withholding requirements on the employee's portion of social security tax? Is the employer still required to contribute their portion of the social security tax for this employee?

Yes. The employer and employee are subject to the same tax rates and wage limits. Both employee and employer reach the wage limitation at the same time.

## Q. What forms do you use when you have a small business?

This depends upon your type of business entity. See below:

- Sole Proprietorships use Form 1040, Schedule C, Profit and Loss from Business (Sole Proprietorship) or Form 1040, Schedule C-EZ, Net Profit from Business and Form 1040, Schedule SE, Self-employment Tax.

- Partnerships use Form 1065, U.S. Partnership Return of Income and Schedule K-1.

- Corporations use Form 1120, U.S. Corporation Income Tax Return.

- S-corporations use Form 1120S, U.S. Income Tax Return for an S Corporation and Schedule K-1.

Limited liability companies use one of the choices above according to their structure. If you hired employees to work in your business, if you are liable for excise tax, or heavy highway vehicle use tax, other forms and publications would apply.

# CHAPTER 8:

## Financial Statements That Make Sense: Understanding the Numbers

---

**CASE STUDY**

The revenues of Two Rivers Construction Company had grown significantly over the last 5 years. Despite the increase in revenues, the company was now having severe financial problems. The company had no real system to record the financial information and make it understandable for decision-making. The accountant that the owner, Patrick, had retained at the time would visit him to pick up the financial information and return the next month with the required government filings. Early in the following year, Patrick would receive his year-end business tax returns.

This is a very common situation in the small business world. Financial record-keeping should not be maintained **merely** because the government requires it. An accounting service that provides the small-business owner with timely financial information and a monthly financial consult will prove to be dramatically more valuable. The regular monitoring of key financial indicators and receiving an **understandable** report in **layman's terms** gives the small-business owner a better gauge of the financial health of his or her business.

With the advice of a mutual friend, Patrick sought a more comprehensive small business accounting service. Monthly financial accounts with easy to understand explanations gave Patrick an instant advantage over his competitors. With *one glimpse*, he was able to get an accurate picture of his business to make decisions with more confidence. Patrick was better able to catch on to opportunities earlier in his business and financial performance improved drastically.

# INTRODUCTION:

### How Financial Problems *Really* Happen

Most problems are born very, very small, being merely unfavorable indications at first. A problem may be so small as to be barely visible to the "naked eye" – like one stalk of grass going bad in a ten-acre lawn. At the time, nothing seems different. The cause of a problem can be just about anything. Perhaps the time it takes customers to pay you lengthens by one day, on average. No big deal!  Or overhead expenses increase 0.5% during three months. Who cares? A slight change in sales? Maybe just a slight correction – nothing to worry about.  While at the beginning, a change may be extremely small and insignificant,it is important to remember that the cause of a problem is different from the effects it has on your business.

Until you become financially savvy, and pay close attention to the financial status of your business, it may take a long time before any of these consequences become big and important enough to attract your attention. By then, it could be too late. Allowed to go too far, any problem is hard to solve. It may also be very difficult to trace to its root cause. Knowing what might be wrong, and doing something about it right away is always the best way to go.

### The Difference *Early* Problem-Solving Can Make

If you are like most small-business owners, you don't like waiting for the results of yearly accounts. There's a reason for that. Usually, it has to do with receiving too little *meaningful* information *during* the year. Without a clear monthly picture of how the fiscal year is developing, waiting for the final calculation will always hold at least some dread for the business owner.

Finding out about problems *after* the fiscal year has already ended leaves you with few options to correct problems. Worse still, if you miss the problem because it hasn't yet grown large enough to be noticed from the bottom line of *that* year's accounts, it may have a chance to develop into a roaring *monster* – then it may be so huge that it threatens the very existence of the business!

Don't worry. All of this pain and suffering can be avoided**.** It is only if an unfavorable trend goes undetected that it will become your worst nightmare. What you read in this chapter could be the most important part of keeping your business going, responding to the valleys that find their way between the peaks. The degree to which you understand financial statements may be the vital factor in determining if your business will prosper. And the good news is that you can easily avoid all of this unpleasantness, all that loss of time and money – by knowing how to interpret financial data, and by enlisting the help of a trained accounting expert!

## "Financial Intelligence" - Using *Financial Analysis* as Your Early-Warning System

If you saw something wrong in your office, would you fix it or would you just let it be? If you noticed that the coffeemaker was left on in the evening, would you leave it on or turn it off? If you saw a faucet dripping, would you do something or just let it run? Of course – you would fix it!! It's your company and you're the person most responsible for it. You want things to go right, you want the business to progress on, and you want it to reach the goals you've set.

Tracking and monitoring the finances of your small business works exactly the same way as *any* "search and handle" activity in your company. Once you *find* the problem and KNOW what causes it… *you can fix it.*

---

**Success Tip**

What gets *measured* accurately, gets *managed* and what gets managed gets *improved.* The key to building wealth involves a daily exercise of improving your business by inches.

---

# Analyzing Your Financial Position

There are a number of systematic ways to arrange and compare the financial facts about your business, so that they can be used to make sound decisions about future actions. In this chapter, I'll discuss some of the most commonly used tools for financial analysis:

- Financial statements, including the income statement, balance sheet and the statement of cash flows.

- Business ratios that identify key relationships between financial data, and allow you to monitor your liquidity, profitability and efficiency.

- Cost/volume/profit analysis, a way of determining the true cost to you of providing your product or service, and the optimal operation level for your business.

# FINANCIAL STATEMENTS

Financial statements are the tools you use to financially quantify your business. Financial statements present an accurate, objective picture of your business; they reflect the "reality" your business creates.

A sound understanding of financial statements will help you:

- Identify adverse developments in your business's operations before the situation becomes critical.

- Monitor important indicators of financial health (a few examples are liquidity ratios, profitability ratios, efficiency ratios, and solvency ratios).

- Examine your cash flow requirements, and recognize financing needs early.

- Compare and monitor performance against your business plan.

We will discuss three basic kinds of financial statements that can help you determine the present condition of your business. They are:

1) Income Statement
2) Balance Sheet
3) Cash Flow Statement (discussed in chapter 9)

# 1) THE INCOME STATEMENT (also referred to as "Profit & Loss statement" or "P & L")

An income statement is a report that lists and categorizes the various revenues and expenses that result from business operations during a specified period of time, usually a month, a quarter or a year. It describes the financial performance of your business. It tells you or your investors:

- The revenues the business has received or earned during the accounting period

- The costs or expenses that were incurred or disbursed by the business during the period

- The difference between the costs and revenues for the period, or net profit (or loss)

A profit and loss statement operates under the basic premise illustrated by the following profit equation:

$$\textbf{Revenues – Costs = Earnings}$$

This simply means that the profitability of your business is measured by deducting all the costs of doing business from the revenues generated during a specific period. A positive amount indicates a profit while a negative amount means the business incurred a loss.

The profit and loss statement spots the amount of money earned and the amount of money expended. The figures listed in each line item of the income statement serve as important gauges of your business' health. You may choose to prepare a profit and loss statement monthly, quarterly or annually, depending on your needs. You will, at a minimum, need to have an annual profit and loss statement in order to prepare your income tax return. A profit and loss statement, however, provides much more than assistance in easing your tax preparation burdens. It provides you with critical decision- making power!

The P & L statement allows you to clearly view the performance of your business over a period of time. As you begin to collect a series of profit and loss statements, you will be able to conduct various analyses of your business. For example, you will be able to compare monthly performance over a single year to determine which month was the best or worst for the business. You will be able to compare quarterly numbers. The comparison of annual revenues and expenses will allow you to judge the growth or shrinkage of your business over time. Numerous other comparisons are possible, depending on your particular business. How have sales been influenced by advertising expenses? Are production costs higher this quarter than last? Do seasons have an impact on sales? Are certain expenses becoming a burden on the business?

You can use your income statement to determine sales trends. Are sales going up or down, or are they holding steady? If they are going up, are they going up at the rate you want or expect? If you sell goods, for example, you can use the income statement to monitor quality control. Look at your sales returns and allowances. If that number is rising, it may indicate that you have a problem with product quality.

Without a profit and loss statement, it is difficult for the owner of even the smallest business to determine whether or not the business is making a profit. With it, you have a comprehensive grasp of everything your business does and how they relate to one another. Sadly, most business owners evaluate performance of the business by the cash balance in the bank. While keeping track of cash flow is important, relying on it to evaluate your business' performance can be very misleading. This is more fully discussed in Chapter 9.

### The income statement – an indispensable scorecard to track business performance

In finding ways to improve business profitability, the first step is to look at what drives revenue and expenses. The key to maximizing results is to consistently leverage people and processes.

Let's first examine the *revenue* side of the equation stated earlier; **Revenues – Costs = Earnings**. It transforms to one that looks like this:

---

**Revenue (R) = Total Customers (TC) x Frequency (F) x Average Dollar per Visit (ADV)**

Total Customers (TC) = Number of Existing Customers (EC) – Lost Customers (LC) **+ New Customers Gained (NC)**

---

Let me illustrate with a simple example that took place with Samantha's Retail & Wholesale Outlet Inc. For the fourth quarter ended December 31st, 2013, Samantha had 652 of her existing customers purchase from her store. During that same period, she lost 4 customers and attracted 78 new ones to her store due to an appealing referral program. Her total customers totaled 726 for that quarter.

During a meeting with her accountant, Samantha calculated that on the average, a customer shops 1.8 times at her store during any given quarter and the average dollar per visit is $113.

**The following are the KEY FINANCIAL INDICATORS from the above facts.**

| | |
|---|---|
| Revenues (R): | $147,668 (726 * 1.8 * $113) |
| Total customers (TC): | 726 |
| Number of existing customers (EC): | 652 |
| Number of lost customers (LC): | 4 |
| New customers gained (NC): | 78 |
| Frequency of purchases (F): | 1.8 times |
| Average dollar per visit: | $113 |

**The following are the OBSERVATIONS made when her accountant compared the key financial indicators to historical data:**

Total revenues for the fourth quarter had *increased* by 22% (Samantha was very happy about that – she was right on track with her business plan.)

1) New customers gained this quarter were 78, compared to 44 in the fourth quarter of 2012.
   **Reason why:** Her new referral-program initiative she had started was working very well.

2) The frequency of purchase had slightly *increased* to 1.8 times per quarter, from 1.6 from last year.
   **Reason why:** The referral-program promotion letter sent to all her clients was a nice reminder for her clients to visit her.

3) The average dollar per visit had *decreased* from $119 to $113.
   **Reason why:** Samantha's sales staff had slacked on up-selling complementary merchandise to her customers.

**Samantha's ACTION PLAN for the following quarter:**

- To increase the number of visits per quarter, Samantha would have more *frequent* communication with her clients via letters and postcards. She identified an upcoming holiday to send a special discount postcard to all her customers.
- To maintain the increased referrals, Samantha would mention the referral program during any communication with the client, starting with the

upcoming holiday mailing. In addition, she decided to test a new marketing program – all customers that refer a friend become eligible to win a grand prize. Samantha was excited to test this new initiative.

- Samantha would have a staff sales training meeting to review scripts to up-sell her customers and encourage them to invite referrals.

As Samantha regularly measures and monitors these key financial indicators with her accountant's assistance, she is able to uncover hidden opportunities or potential problems. It then gives her the ability to devise an ACTION PLAN that helps her focus her energies and attention for the following quarter on things that make the biggest difference i.e. give her the biggest return on her time. Performing this one simple, yet essential task gives Samantha an immediate competitive edge over most of her competitors.

Continuing, let's now examine the *cost* side of the profit equation:

---

**Revenues – Cost (cost of goods sold + overhead) = Net Profit**

---

Take a look at the two sections *within* cost – "cost of goods sold" and "overhead"

**The following are the KEY FINANCIAL INDICATORS extracted from the "cost of goods sold" section of Samantha's 3-year comparative income statement** (Refer to the table of the income statement that follows):

| | |
|---|---|
| Beginning inventory | $98,148 |
| Ending inventory | $106,495 |
| Purchases | $142,125 |

**The following is the OBSERVATION made when her accountant scrutinized these numbers:**

The ending inventory in Samantha's business has gone up by more than $8,000. Inventory is the merchandise that a business keeps on hand to meet the demands of the customers. Samantha acknowledged she had excess merchandise in one line of her product and getting "rid" of it would free her business up with extra cash she could use for the upcoming holiday promotion.

**Samantha's ACTION PLAN for the following quarter was to:**

- Find out from the supplier if he would be willing to buy back the excess merchandise at cost. Samantha would willingly pay for the shipping costs. That would be the preferred approach.
- If option number one does not materialize, then sell the merchandise off at "50%-off" during the upcoming holiday sale.

**The KEY FINANCIAL INDICATORS in the "overhead" section of Samantha's 3-year comparative income statement are** (Refer to the table of the income statement that follows):

| | |
|---|---|
| Selling expense | $ 28,354 |
| General and administrative expenses | $164,554 |
| Interest expense | $ 7,250 |
| Income taxes | $ 20,072 |

**These are the OBSERVATIONS made:**

Selling expenses should increase only in proportion to increases in sales. Disproportionate increases in selling expense should be followed up and corrected. Samantha realized that her selling expenses had gone up substantially due to a restructured sales commission system that she had devised earlier. Although her selling expenses were higher in 2013 than in previous years, Samantha knew that the new commission system gave stronger incentives to her sales assistants to sell more, as was indicated by the total sales for the year. For now, Samantha was happy to leave things as they were. No action required here.

General and administrative expenses should also be closely watched. Increases beyond what you determine reasonable may indicate a need for cost-cutting measures. A further scrutiny of Samantha's indicated increases in telephone and insurance. The rest of the expense categories were within budget, and income tax expense had pleasingly decreased due to two tax saving strategies that she had implemented following a prior meeting with her accountant.

**Samantha's ACTION PLAN for the following quarter:**

- Speak to her insurance agent about better rates and to review the deductibles in her business insurance policy.

- Call two other telephone service providers for rates.

Samantha decided she would delegate both these responsibilities to her part-time bookkeeper and she would overlook its effective execution.

It is critical that you measure both sides of the profit equation, especially revenue and expense driving activities. As you can see from the example that I have illustrated, these activities are crucial to the overall performance of a company, and they can be measured and leveraged. It is also important that you select those indicators that best measure those activities within your business.

**Success Tip**

Too often, I see small-business owners overlooking to track their revenues and expenses by "profit centers." Your financial reporting system should be set up such that it has the ability to generate reports that give you a breakdown of your revenues and expenses by the *type* of service provided or by the *type* of product sold, i.e. by each profit center. This information can be extremely useful in identifying profit centers that are the "winners" in your business and subsequently, channeling your resources and energies accordingly.

## Two Types of Income Statements

There are generally two approaches to the income statement – the "functional" and the "contribution" methods. They both start with revenues and they both arrive at the same bottom line, but they organize operating costs differently and are useful in different ways for different audiences.

### 1) The "Functional Method"

For the purposes of external reporting, the functional method is best. Costs are separated into your business' "major function" categories – production, marketing and sales, and general and administrative. Outsiders, who don't know the operation of your business as well as you do, get a clearer picture from the functional categorization of costs.

**Success Tip**

If you are using the functional method and don't want to change to the contribution method, I strongly suggest that you begin learning and using break-even analysis explained later.

The "functional income statement" for Samantha's Retail & Wholesale Outlet Inc. showing three years' information is presented next

| Samantha's Retail & Wholesale Outlet Inc. *Functional Format* Income Statement Years Ended December 31, 2013, 2012, and 2011 | | | |
|---|---|---|---|
| | **2013** | **2012** | **2011** |
| Sales | $452,512 | $374,114 | $321,124 |
| (Sales returns and allowances) | (1,215) | (1,133) | (1,198) |
| *Sales (net)* | *$451,297* | *$372,981* | *$319,926* |
| | **2013** | **2012** | **2011** |
| **Cost of goods sold** | | | |
| Beginning inventory | 98,148 | 85,354 | 74,512 |
| Cost of goods purchased | 142,125 | 134,001 | 112,127 |
| (Ending inventory) | (106,495) | (98,148) | (85,354) |
| *Cost of goods sold* | *$133,778* | *$121,207* | *$101,285* |
| Gross profit | $317,519 | $251,774 | $218,641 |
| **Expenses** | | | |
| Selling expense | $28,354 | $16,451 | $12,354 |
| General and administrative expense | 164,554 | 138,954 | 124,554 |
| *Total operating expenses* | *$192,908* | *$155,405* | *$136,908* |
| Income from operations | $124,611 | $96,369 | $81,733 |

| | | | |
|---|---|---|---|
| Interest expense | $7,250 | $7,540 | $4,505 |
| *Pretax income* | *117,361* | *88,829* | *77,228* |
| Income taxes | (20,072) | (17,766) | (15,445) |
| **Net income** | **$97,289** | **$71,063** | **$61,783** |

## 2) The "Contribution Method"

The contribution method is recommended for "internal" reporting, partly because it is simpler to construct and use. It helps to more clearly understand the financial dynamics of your business. It is the more preferable method when you want to understand the profitability of your products and services, and when deciding how to make intelligent pricing decisions.

Here's the contribution format income statement for Samantha's business:

| Samantha's Retail & Wholesale Outlet Inc. *Contribution Format* Income Statement For Year Ended December 31, 2013 | | |
|---|---|---|
| Sales (net) | $451,297 | |
| Less Variable Costs: | | |
| Cost of Goods Sold | 133,778 | |
| Sales Commissions | 28,354 | |
| *Total Variable Costs* | 162,132 | |
| **Contribution Margin** | **289,165** | **64%** |
| Less: Fixed Costs: | | |
| Advertising | 5,548 | |
| Depreciation | 13,115 | |
| Insurance | 7,017 | |
| Payroll Taxes | 7,500 | |
| Rent | 30,200 | |

| | | |
|---|---:|---|
| Utilities | 15,224 | |
| Wages | 85,950 | |
| Interest | 7,250 | |
| Income taxes | 20,072 | |
| *Total Fixed Costs* | 191,876 | |
| **Net Operating Income** | **$97,289** | |

You can tell at a glance that Samantha's Retail and Wholesale Outlet Inc. has a contribution margin for the year of 64%. This means, for every dollar of sales, after subtracting costs directly related to the sales, 64 cents remained to contribute toward paying for the fixed costs and for profit.

## 2) The Balance Sheet

The balance sheet lists everything your company owns (assets), everything your company owes to others (liabilities) and the owners net worth (equity) at a specific point in time. Your business' financial position (health and value) can be ascertained by looking at your balance sheet.

A balance sheet is often referred to as a "snapshot" because it provides a clear picture of the business at a given moment, although it does not necessarily reveal how the business arrived there or where it's headed. In order to learn a business' "whole story," it is important to review all financial information, from all financial statements and records; together, they will tell you everything you need to know. The balance sheet consists of three categories of items: assets, liabilities, and stockholders' or owners' equity.

**Assets.** Assets are generally divided into two groups — current assets and fixed (long-term) assets. They are usually presented in order of liquidity, with current assets (cash and those that will be converted to cash within one year) appearing first. Let's take a look at the current assets section of the balance sheet of Samantha's Retail and Wholesale Outlet Inc. as of December 31st, 2013:

| Current Assets | |
|---|---|
| Cash and cash equivalents | $ 19,451 |
| Short-term investments and marketable securities | $ 1,500 |
| Accounts receivable | $ 74,651 |
| Inventories | $106,495 |
| Prepaid expenses | $ 2,750 |
| Other current assets | $ 5,000 |
| **Total Current Assets** | **$209,847** |

Fixed assets (those that will not be converted to cash within one year) usually are presented after current assets, and look like this for Samantha's business:

| Fixed Assets | |
|---|---|
| Machinery and equipment | $136,332 |
| Capitalized leases | $ 14,991 |
| (Less accumulated depreciation and amortization) | ($ 35,450) |
| Other fixed assets | $ 4,500 |
| **Total Fixed Assets** | **$120,373** |
| **Total Assets** | **$330,220** |

**Liabilities.** Liabilities are normally presented in order of their claim on the company's assets (i.e., liabilities due within one year are presented before liabilities due several years from now).

This is the liability section of Samantha's balance sheet:

| Current Liabilities | |
|---|---|
| Accounts payable | $ 52,412 |
| Line of credit with bank | $ 15,000 |
| Income taxes currently payable | $ 7,453 |
| Current portion of long-term debt | $ 5,250 |
| Other current liabilities | $ 2,445 |
| **Total Current Liabilities** | **$ 82,560** |

| Long-Term Liabilities | |
|---|---|
| Long-term debt | $ 85,000 |
| Capital lease obligations | $  5,550 |
| Other long-term liabilities | $  7,214 |
| **Total Long-Term Liabilities** | **$ 97,764** |
| **Total Liabilities** | **$180,324** |

**Equity.** Stockholders' equity (also known as owner's equity or net worth) is presented properly when each class of ownership is presented with all its relevant information (for example, number of shares authorized, shares issued, shares outstanding, and par value). If retained earnings are restricted or appropriated, this also should be shown.

Stockholders' equity for an incorporated business normally would look like this:

| Stockholders' Equity | |
|---|---|
| Preferred stock, $10 par value (authorized 1,000 shares; issued and outstanding 100 shares) | $  1,000 |
| Common stock, $20 par value (authorized 5,000 shares; issued and outstanding 500 shares) | $ 10,000 |
| Additional paid-in capital | $ 25,000 |
| Retained earnings | $113,896 |
| **Total Shareholders' Equity** | **$149,896** |

**These are the OBSERVATIONS made after her accountant examined the above sections of the balance sheet together with historical data:**

Samantha's accounts receivable had increased from $45,321 as of December 31st, 2012 to $74,651 as of December 31st, 2013. An examination at the aging accounts receivable report indicated an *early warning* sign; two of Samantha's regular wholesale customers were 60 days overdue on their accounts.

Samantha's long-term note payable had decreased from $100,000 as of December 31st, 2012 to $85,000 as of December 31st, 2013. Samantha was happy that her regular payment schedule was helping her reduce this debt that she had incurred during the early years of her business operation. No action required but to stay on with her payment plan.

Accounts payable on December 31<sup>st</sup>, 2013 was $52,412. $22,400 of this amount consisted of a payable to a vendor who offered a generous 4% discount for payment within 30 days of delivery. If Samantha were to take advantage of these payment terms, it would bring about a saving of $896.

**ACTION PLAN:**

- Samantha will call her two customers immediately to assess the reason for the delay in their payments.

- Samantha to review her credit policy document with her accountant at the next meeting to be sure that she had clearly stated her credit terms.

- Samantha to instruct her bookkeeper to transfer funds from the business line of credit account to the regular checking account. The bookkeeper would then make a timely payment to the vendor to receive the discount. It clearly made sense to utilize the low interest bearing credit facility for this purpose.

**Success Tip**

Small-business owners sometimes confuse the difference between a balance sheet and an income statement. Here's my simple explanation: Balance sheets provide a cumulative overview of a business's assets and liabilities at a given point in time. The income statement provides a summary of the "flow" of transactions over a specific time period, usually by the month, quarter, or year. Another way to look at each report is this: income statements show detailed activity between balance sheets!

# Business Ratios

The true value of financial statement figures emerges when they are compared to one another. The process by which these comparisons are made is called "ratio analysis."

Ratio analysis has been developed to help establish the state of health of various financial aspects of your business. When you routinely calculate and compare changes in your business ratios from one period to another, you identify strengths as well as problem areas requiring attention and improvement. Also, by comparing your ratios to those in other businesses, you can see possibilities for improvement in key areas. The various sources of industry ratios include trade or business associations, commercial services and your accountant.

Conducting ratio analyses may sound intimidating, but it really is very simple. When used effectively, ratios are a powerful tool because they allow you to clearly understand the relationship expressed and its effect on the business. Various ratios can be easily established from key figures on the financial statements. These ratios can be expressed in the format "2:1," (a ratio), 150% (a percentage), or 4/1 (a fraction). There are a few key income statement and balance sheet items that, when compared with each other, provide insights into the efficiency, profitability, and solvency of your business. Here are a few important ones that I've found to be helpful in understanding the financial dynamics of a small business:

Financial ratios fall into four categories:

- Profitability ratios

- Liquidity ratios

- Efficiency ratios

- Solvency ratios

## Profitability Ratios

Measures of profitability are essential because they allow you to assess changes in your business' profit performance. There are four types of profitability ratios. The first two ratios are derived from the "functional" income statement:

- Net profit margin

- Gross profit margin

- Return on assets

- Return on investment

**1) Net Profit Margin** (also known as Return on Revenues or Return on Sales)

This ratio demonstrates the amount of net income derived from every dollar of net revenues. Essentially, it is the net profit, commonly known as the "bottom line" as a percentage. I consider this ratio to be the key financial indicator of the profitability of the business, and one that needs close monitoring.

> **Net Profit Margin = Net Profit / Sales**

In Samantha's case, net income for 2013 was $97,289 and sales were $452,297, her profit margin was 21.51% ($97,289 / $452,297 = .2151; expressed as a percentage it translates to 21.51%). Explained in other words, it means that for every dollar of sales, the company is earning 21.51 cents. For 2012, it was 19%. Clearly, Samantha's profitability had improved over the year.

The higher the net profit margin, the more profitable the business is. Note that this number will vary significantly depending upon the industry you are in. This ratio should be reviewed against other similar businesses to get a clear understanding of positive or negative trends over time. Samantha knew her net profit margin was above the industry average, but somehow implicitly felt that she could improve it with a closer watch on her expenses.

If you decide that your net profit margin ratio is lower than desired, you may be able to raise it by the doing the following:

1) Increase your sales revenue (a function of the number of customers, frequency of purchase and the pricing structure).
2) Reduce operating costs.
3) Increase the price of your products or services

**2) Gross Profit Margin**

The gross profit margin is an indication of the mark-up on goods that are sold to customers. This ratio is useful for businesses that maintain inventory and generate sales from it.

Your gross profit margin can be calculated using figures taken from the income statement.

**Gross Profit Margin = Gross Profits\* / Sales**

**\* Gross Profit = Sales – Cost of Goods Sold\*\***
**\*\* Cost of Goods Sold = Beginning inventory + Purchases – Ending Inventory**

**The higher the gross profit margin, the better**. If your gross profit margin is declining over time, it could mean a number of things. Perhaps you have a larger inventory at the end of each period. Maybe your selling prices are not rising as fast as the costs of the goods you sell. In either case, knowing your gross profit margin and making comparisons to industry standards can help you make important day-to-day financial decisions.

Samantha's gross profit margin was 70.36% ($317,519 / $452,512). This ratio was unusually high in the industry because Samantha had prudently positioned her business so that it would command higher prices for its merchandise in exchange for premium services.

**3) Return on Assets** (also known as Investment Turnover)

Return on assets is the ratio of net income to total assets. It indicates the ability of a business to generate net profit from its assets.

**Return on Assets = Net Profit / Total Assets**

Generally, the higher the ratio, the stronger the business. A high return on assets can result from two things: 1) a high profit margin; 2) a rapid turnover of assets, or a combination of both.

For Samantha, it calculated to 29% ($97,289 / $330,220), a very good return.

**4) Return on Investment, commonly referred to as ROI** (also known as Return on Equity)

This ratio is another valuable tool to measure profitability. The ratio of Net Income to Owners Equity shows you what you've earned on your investment in the business.

The return on equity ratio can be calculated using the following formula:

**Return on Investment = Net Profit / Owner's Equity**

One of the primary reasons to go into business is the potential return on your investment. In this regard, comparing your business' ROI to your stock portfolio ROI allows you to objectively assess the worthiness of your capital, time and energy on it rather than passive investments like the stock market. You should strive to have the highest net profit for the smallest amount of money invested in the business.

Plugging Samantha's figures into the equation, her ROI came to 64.90% ($97,289 / $149,896).

# Measures of Liquidity

Liquidity refers to the ability of your business to quickly generate the cash needed to pay your debts. Generally speaking, the more liquid the business, the better its state of financial health. On the other end, not having enough liquidity in the business might mean it did not have sufficient cash to meet its short-term debts. Liquidity ratios are sometimes also called working capital ratios.

There are two types of liquidity ratios:

- The current ratio

- The quick ratio

**The Current Ratio**

This is my favorite measure of liquidity. It indicates the short-term resources (current assets) the company has available to meet its short-term obligations (current liabilities). The current ratio is hence calculated using information on your balance sheet. You simply divide current assets by current liabilities.

**Current ratio = Current assets / current liabilities**

In Samantha's case, her current assets were $209,847 and the current liabilities were $82,560. Her current ratio would be 2.54

Current Ratio = $ 209,847 / $82,560 = 2.54

I am often asked this question: What is a healthy current ratio? The general rule of thumb says that current assets should be about twice as much as current debts, although this rule will vary slightly between industries.

If you decide that your current ratio is too low, you may be able to raise it by the doing the following:

1) Pay off some current liabilities.
2) Convert non-current assets into current assets.
3) Increase your current assets through long-term borrowing or equity contributions.
4) Put more of your profits back into the business.
5) Delay purchases to reduce accounts payable and quicken the invoicing of pending orders to increase receivables.

**The Quick Ratio** (also known as the Acid Test Ratio)

The quick ratio, also known as the acid test ratio, is another measure of liquidity. It is similar to a current ratio, although inventory is not considered. Why remove inventory from the equation? By removing inventory, this ratio (also referred to as the "quick" ratio) gives you a better picture of your ability to meet your short-term obligations, regardless of your sales levels. The quick ratio thus takes into consideration only the real liquid assets. Usually a quick ratio of about 1.0 is considered satisfactory, although again, it varies between industries. It shows that your quick current assets can cover your current liabilities. Over time, a stable current ratio with a declining quick ratio may indicate that you've built up too much inventory.

> **Quick Ratio = (Current Assets – Inventory) / Current Liabilities**

Samantha's current assets were $209,847, inventory was $106,495 and her current liabilities were $82,560, therefore, her acid test ratio would be.

Quick Ratio = ($209,847 - $106,495) / $82,560 = 1.25

If you decide that your quick ratio is too low, you may be able to raise it by doing the same as noted above, or converting inventory to cash or to accounts receivable.

## Efficiency Ratios

One of the key objectives as a business owner is to maximize the use of your assets. Understanding and monitoring the following ratios will help you determine the efficiency in the use of the business assets. They are:

- Inventory turnover ratio
- Accounts receivable turnover
- Fixed asset turnover
- Total asset turnover

**Inventory Turnover ratio**: This ratio tells how often a business' inventory turns over (or sells) during the course of the year. This ratio is obtained by dividing the "Total Sales" of a company by its "Total Inventory." The ratio is regarded as a test of efficiency, and indicates how rapidly the company is able to move its merchandise. The efficiency of your inventory management may have a considerable influence on your cash flow.

---

**Inventory Turnover Ratio = Net Sales / Inventory**

---

Plugging Samantha's numbers in the above equation, her inventory turnover ratio calculated to 4.24 ($451,297 / $106,495)

It could also be calculated as:

---

**Inventory Turnover Ratio = Cost of Goods Sold / Inventory**

---

**Success Tip**

Since inventories are the least liquid form of asset, a high inventory turnover ratio is generally considered positive. However, an unusually high ratio compared to your peers may indicate that your business is losing sales due to inadequate stock on hand. A low turnover may indicate overstocking, or obsolete inventory.

**Accounts Receivable Turnover:** Accounts receivable represent sales for which payment has not yet been collected. The Accounts Receivable turnover ratio is a good way to gauge the effectiveness of your company's payment terms. It indicates how quickly you are getting paid!

---

**Receivable Turnover = Net Sales / Average Accounts Receivables**

---

For Samantha, that came to 7.02 ($451,297 / $64,295). This ratio seemed too high and her accountant suspected an error. Sure enough, as they began to review it, they realized that they would get a more realistic picture if they used net sales derived from the wholesale side of the business only. The retail side of her business did not generate any accounts receivable and any sales generated from it should be left out of this equation. The re-calculated ratio was 1.34 ($86,124 / $64,295). Her accountant explained to Samantha that this ratio was low and her efforts to collect from her two customers and a review of her credit terms will help alleviate this potential problem.

**Success Tip**
A high number indicates the number of times that your accounts receivable turns over during the course of the year. The more your accounts receivable turns over the better it is because that means a shorter time between sales and cash collection.

**Fixed Asset Turnover:** Fixed asset turnover is the ratio of sales to the value of your fixed assets. It indicates how well your business is using its fixed assets to generate sales.

---

**Fixed Asset Turnover = Sales / Fixed Assets**

---

**Success Tip**
Generally speaking, the higher the ratio the better. A high ratio indicates your business has less money tied up in fixed assets for each dollar of sales revenue. A declining ratio may indicate that you've over-invested in plant, equipment, or other fixed assets.

**Total Asset Turnover:** The ratio of total sales to total assets is yet another efficiency ratio that points out how well you are using all of your business' assets (rather than just fixed assets or inventories to generate revenue).

---

**Total Asset Turnover = Total Sales / Total Assets**

---

A high asset turnover ratio indicates a higher return on assets.

# Solvency Ratios

The final group of ratios can help you determine how much financial risk your business must assume. "Financial risk" refers to the degree to which your obligations impose on your cash flow. Solvency ratios help you assess if your current level of debt is appropriate for your company. Commonly used solvency ratios are:

- Debt to equity

- Debt to assets

- Coverage of fixed costs

- Interest coverage

**Debt to Equity** (also known as Leverage Ratio): This ratio shows how your company's equity (net worth) relates to its debt.

---

**Debt to Equity Ratio = Total Debt / Equity (Net Worth)**

---

For Samantha, it calculated to 1.20 ($180,324 / $149,896). She was in line here.

High debt to equity ratios may be evidence that your business' debt is too high. In this case, additional borrowing should be avoided. Low ratios may indicate that you are being too conservative in your borrowing practices, and may benefit from increasing debt.

**Coverage of Fixed Charges (also known as** "times fixed charges earned"): **This ratio** shows your ability to meet fixed obligations of all types.

> **Coverage of Fixed Charges = Net Income, *Before* Taxes and Fixed Charges (Debt Repayment, Long-Term Leases, Preferred Stock Dividends etc.) / Fixed Charges**

The higher the number the better, because it shows the ability of the business to meet its fixed obligation needs without hampering its operations.

**Interest Coverage** (also known as the "times interest earned ratio"): This ratio is very similar to the "times fixed charges earned" ratio but more narrowly focuses on the interest portion of your debt payments. It measures how many times your interest obligations are covered by earnings from operations.

> **Interest Coverage = Operating Income / Interest Expense**

The higher the ratio, the more able the business is to meet interest payments. If this ratio is declining over time, it's a clear indication that your financial risk is increasing.

**Break-Even Analysis**

The break-even analysis is a simple but very underutilized technique in the small business world. The use of this technique gives you a better understanding of the financial impact or success of the business decisions you make. It does that by showing you the correlation between your sales volume, the fixed and variable costs in your business, and your net profits.

It helps answer questions such as the following:

1) How much in sales do you need to break even?

2) How much profit will you make for any given level of sales?

3) How will changing your prices impact your profitability?

4) What are your most profitable products or services?

Break-even analysis is an indispensable tool that helps answer these, and many more, questions about your business.

The *first step* in performing a break-even analysis is breaking down your costs between fixed costs and variable costs.

## Step 1:

**Fixed costs**: These costs do not vary in direct proportion with revenues. They may increase slightly with increases in revenues. For example, if revenues increase by 20%, your fixed costs may increase by, say, 4%. A few typical examples would be insurance, rent, supplies, interest on debt, depreciation, and the cost of administrative staff.

**Variable costs** (also called "direct costs"): These costs are in direct proportion to revenues. If revenues increase by 50%, then variable costs increase by 50%. A few examples of variable costs would be sales commissions, cost of materials used to manufacture products, shipping charges and wages of labor involved in the manufacture of the goods.

Most costs will easily fall in one of the two categories explained above. You will, however, run into some costs where this may not be the case, such as a telephone bill. This kind of expense has a fixed portion (the base fee) and a variable portion (calls made related to sales). It would, however, be too tedious to break it into these two components. In such cases, judgment should be used to classify the entire telephone bill as either a variable or fixed expense.

After breaking all your costs between variable and fixed costs in Step 1, you are ready for Step 2, calculating your break-even point.

## Step 2:

**Calculating your break-even point involves the following formulas:**

> **Contribution Margin per Unit = Sales Price per Unit – Variable Costs per Unit**

> **Contribution Margin Ratio = Contribution Margin per Unit *divided* by Sales Price per Unit**

> **Break-Even Revenues = Fixed Costs *divided* by Contribution Margin Ratio**

| Calculating the Break-Even Point | | | |
|---|---|---|---|
| | | | |
| Sales (10,000 units @ $10 per unit) | $100,000 | $10 per unit | 100% |
| | | | |
| Variable Costs | $(60,000) | $6 per unit | 60% |
| | | | |
| Contribution Margin | $ 40,000 | $4 per unit | 40% |
| | | | |
| Fixed Expenses | $(15,000) | | 15% |
| | | | |
| Operating Profits | $ 25,000 | $2.50 per unit | 25% |
| | | | |
| **Contribution Margin Per Unit** | **$4 per unit** | | |
| | | | |
| **Contribution Margin Ratio** | **$4 per unit / $10 per unit = 40%** | | |
| | | | |
| **Break-even Revenues** | **$15,000 / 40% = $37,500** | | |
| | | | |

Break-even revenues or sales are $37,500. Sales of more than that will produce a profit while sales below that produce a loss. It is imperative that every small-business owner knows what the break-even revenues are for his or her business.

**Success Tip**
Your goal as a small-business owner is to keep the breakeven point as low as possible. Product cost, volume and price together with your fixed costs all play an important role in determining the break-even point as well as the ultimate success of your small business.

# IN CONCLUSION

Small-business owners who know their numbers have a tremendous advantage over those who do not. Your financials tell a story and understanding the story behind your numbers can be one of the most important element for long-term success. Such reports, complimented with a meaningful explanation of the numbers in "plain English" should be a basic component of your relationship with your accountant. If you don't already have this process in place, talk with your accountant and assess his or her capacity or willingness to provide this information. If that fails or if you are still not satisfied, consider finding an accountant who values the importance of such service and, more important, can provide it.

# Frequently Asked Questions on Financial Statements That Make Sense

## Q. *What financial statements will I need?*

You should prepare and understand three basic financial statements:

(1) The balance sheet, which is a record of assets, liabilities and capital; and

(2) The income (profit and loss) statement, a summary of your earnings and expenses over a given period of time.

(3) Cash flow statement, a record of cash in-flows and cash outflows.

## Q. *Is there a formal report I can expect from my accountant at the year-end verifying that he or she has reviewed the numbers in my business?*

The Accountants' Report is a formal document issued by an accountant that is commonly one of three:

1) Compilation report: non-expression of opinion or any form of assurance on a presentation in the form of financial statements information that is the representation of management.

2) Review report: expression of limited assurance on financial statements as a result of performing inquiry and analytic procedures.

3) Audit report: a statement that the audit was conducted in accordance with generally accepted auditing standards (GAAS), which require that the auditor plan and perform the audit to obtain reasonable assurance about whether the financial statements are free of material misstatement, as well as a statement that the auditor believes the audit provides a reasonable basis for his or her opinion.

# CHAPTER 9:

## Cash In On Cash Flow:
## How to Acquire and Keep a Positive Cash Balance

---

**Case Study**

Anthony Wilkins opened his company in the spring of 2007, providing architectural services to large multi-million real estate developers. He had the experience, the contacts, and the entrepreneurial drive to build a successful business.

As he had anticipated, the contracts came in and business began to boom. Anthony got on-board, the brightest and most qualified architects and administrative staff to tackle the large, multifaceted commercial projects his company was awarded. Bigger clients required Anthony to be on the road for longer periods of time. No problem, he had good help.

Within 6 years, the business went bankrupt. What was the problem? *Poor cash flow.* Anthony did not have his finger on the cash inflows and cash outflows in his company. He had underestimated the weekly cash outflow required to run the company. He had underestimated that a company requires cash reserves to make it through the slack times. Had Anthony taken the time to learn better cash management or hired a savvy accountant to help him in this area, he would not have ended up in a horrifying bankruptcy. Anthony forgot the golden rule, no cash, equals no business.

---

# INTRODUCTION:

## Cash Flow: Lifeline of Your Business

As the saying goes, "cash is king!" Cash flow is the lifeblood of any business organization. Small-business owners are often so concerned with other matters that they fail to pay proper attention to managing their cash resources properly.

More businesses go ***out*** of business for this above all other reasons. The hard reality is this – *When you're out of* cash, *you're out of business.* The fortunate thing is that proper cash management, like many other skills, *can* be learned. Once understood and implemented, you will wonder how you got along without using "cash management" as an integral tool in managing your small business. This chapter will show you how.

## What is Cash Flow?

Cash flow is the movement of money in and out of your business over a period of time; these movements are called inflow and outflow. Inflows for your business primarily come about from the sales of goods, collections of your receivables, borrowed money, investment income from interest, and finally, sale of assets.

Outflows for your business are measured by the checks you write and the cash you disburse to pay expenses. Some examples of cash outflow are payroll, operating costs such as utilities, rent and telephone, purchasing inventory, and any loan repayments.

A **positive cash flow** results if the cash inflows are greater than the cash outflows. A **negative cash flow** results when the opposite takes place; cash outflows exceed cash inflows.

## Cash Flow Verses Profit

Although cash is critical, people think in profits instead of cash. We all do. When you imagine a new business, you think of what it would cost to make the product, what you could sell it for, and what the profits per unit might be. We are trained to think of business as sales minus costs and expenses, which are profits. Unfortunately, we don't spend the profits in a business. We spend cash. Profitable companies go broke because they had all their money tied up in assets and couldn't pay their expenses. Working capital is critical to business health. Unfortunately, we don't see the cash implications as clearly as we should, which is one of the best reasons for proper cash planning. We have to manage cash, as well as profits.

Cash flow and profit are two concepts that are very *different* from each other and very often misunderstood by many small-business owners. The two major differences between cash flow and profit come about due to:

1) **Difference in timing when transactions are recorded**. Profits are the excess of revenues over expenses. Revenues are recorded in the books when your customers buy from you, with cash or on credit. Even though you haven't received the cash, the sale shows up on your income statement and is part of your profits (assuming you are on the accrual basis). As part of your management review, if you were to look only at your income statement for that period of time, you'd think all was well because your books are showing a healthy profit. Your cash flow statement, however, shows a very different picture. This difference between when a sale is made and the cash is received can have serious financial consequences on your business if not understood and reviewed regularly. The example below illustrates this more clearly.

### Income statement prepared using the Accrual basis – January 1 to June 30, 20XX

| | | |
|---|---|---|
| Sales | $50,000 | *Assume sale of one piece of merchandise* |
| Cost of goods sold | -$20,000 | |
| Gross Profit | $30,000 | |
| Operating expenses: | | |
| Various expenses | -$12,000 | |
| **Net Profit** | **$18,000** | A *nice, healthy profit* |

### Cash flow statement - January 1 to June 30, 20XX

| | | |
|---|---|---|
| Cash Inflow | $0 | *You sold the merchandise on credit & haven't received payment* |
| Cash Outflow | -$32,000 | |
| **Net cash flow** | **-$32,000** | *Poor cash situation* |

In the illustration above, the income statement indicates a healthy profit of $18,000 while the cash flow statement shows a negative cash flow of $32,000, a very different situation.

2) **Type of transactions that are used when computing each one**. The second important difference between cash flow and profit is the type of transactions included in each. Cash flow considerations include items such as funds borrowed, equipment sold, and loan repayments. These items don't figure into profits and don't show up on your income statement. But such items *do* have a significant impact on your cash flows. Likewise, there are other items such as depreciation which are not considered when computing cash flow but do play an important role when computing profit.

### Tracking Your Cash Flow – The cash flow statement

A crucial detail a business owner must manage is called "cash flow." Through a business tool called "the cash flow statement" one can trace the actual flow of funds into and out of your business. For a small business, a cash flow statement should be prepared, at the very minimum, on a monthly basis. Broadly put, a cash flow statement identifies the cash you had on hand and adds to it the cash you received during the period (your cash inflow). It reduces that amount by the money you paid out (your cash outflow). The resulting amount is your ending cash position.

# Cash Flow Statement Worksheet

For the period _____

**BEGINNING CASH POSITION**      $_____
CASH RECEIPTS

_____    $_____
_____    $_____
_____    $_____
_____    $_____
_____    $_____
_____    $_____
_____    $_____
_____    $_____
_____    $_____

**TOTAL CASH RECEIPTS**      $_____
CASH DISBURSEMENTS

_____    $_____
_____    $_____
_____    $_____
_____    $_____
_____    $_____
_____    $_____
_____    $_____
_____    $_____
_____    $_____
_____    $_____
_____    $_____

**TOTAL CASH DISBURSEMENT**    $_____
**NET CASH FLOW**    $_____
**ENDING CASH FLOW**    $_____

**Success Tip**

The illustration above showed the "direct" method of computing cash flow. Personally, I prefer this method because it provides the business owner with a better feel for business activity. The other method used calculates the cash flow from your income statement and balance sheet, without having to look at your actual receipts and disbursements. This is called the "indirect" method. The "indirect" method calculates cash flow by backing out non-cash line items from the income (like depreciation), and by inferring cash flows from differences between beginning and ending balances of balance sheet items, such as accounts receivable, accounts payable, deferred payments and receipts.

## *Cash Planning (also referred to as Cash Projections, or Cash Budget)*

Cash plans project *cash* activity for the upcoming 12 months. They are an essential part of your financial reporting process. Done correctly, these projections can be instrumental to the success of your business in several ways:

1) Provide the necessary checks, balances, and financial controls to prevent cash shortages.

2) Help spot strengths and weaknesses in your cash management systems (credit policies, payable procedures).

3) Help predict future cash needs to reach your business goals.

Here are 8 simple steps to create a cash flow plan that you can rely on:

1. Compile historical cash plans to understand past trends.

2. Identify your beginning cash position. Know where you are starting from.

3. Forecast cash inflows for the projected period. What do you think you will bring in?

4. Forecast cash outflows for the projected period. What do you think you will pay out?

5. Calculate net cash flow. Determine the difference.

6. Calculate your ending cash position. Know where you end up.

7. Perform a "reality check" to eliminate distortions.

8. Clearly state the assumptions you made while preparing the cash flow plan. Make sure you cover all possibilities.

## CASH PLAN

| | | Month 1 | Month 2 | Month 3 |
|---|---|---|---|---|
| **Net Sales** | | $100,000 | $105,000 | $110,000 |
| **Cash receipts forecast** | | | | |
| Sales for cash (80%) | | $82,000 | $84,000 | $88,000 |
| Cash receipts from A/R | | | | |
| 0-30 days (60%) | | $13,000 | $13,600 | $14,000 |
| 31-60 days (30%) | | $7,000 | $7,100 | $7,200 |
| 61-90 days (10%) | | $3,000 | $3,000 | $3,000 |
| Other cash receipts | | $6,000 | $6,000 | $6,000 |
| **Total cash Receipts** | | **$111,000** | **$113,700** | **$118,200** |
| **Cash disbursements forecast** | | | | |
| Payroll and employee benefits | | $25,500 | $25,000 | $25,500 |
| Debt service (principal and interest) | | $5,500 | $5,500 | $5,500 |
| Business occupancy (rent, utilities) | | $7,500 | $7,600 | $7,700 |
| Material and components inventory | | $33,500 | $34,500 | $36,500 |
| Supplies | | $1,200 | $1,300 | $1,400 |
| Telephone, fax, postage, delivery | | $2,800 | $3,500 | $3,300 |
| Marketing | | $10,800 | $12,000 | $12,200 |
| Sales commissions | | $4,800 | $5,600 | $6,400 |
| Legal and professional services | | $4,000 | $4,000 | $4,000 |
| Dividends to owner and investors | | $8,000 | $8,000 | $8,000 |
| Other disbursements | | | $7,000 | |
| **Total cash disbursements** | | **$103,600** | **$114,000** | **$110,500** |

## THE CASH PLAN VARIANCE REPORT

The cash plan variance report compares the most recent actual cash flow (from your cash flow statement) with your cash plan for the same period, and includes a column showing both dollar and percentage variances for each line item.

The variance report points you toward things that are going right and wrong in your business, and gives you important information regarding what to do about them.

## Cash Plan Variance Report

| Month of March, 20xx | | | | |
|---|---|---|---|---|
| | | | Variance | |
| | Actual | Plan | Dollars | Percent |
| **Net Sales** | $105,000 | $100,000 | $5,000 | 5.0% |
| | | | | |
| **Cash receipts** | | | | |
| Sales for cash (80%) | $82,000 | $85,000 | $(3,000) | -3.5% |
| Cash receipts from A/R | | | | |
| 0-30 days (60%) | $12,500 | $12,000 | $500 | 4.2% |
| 31-60 days (30%) | $7,000 | $6,000 | $1,000 | 16.7% |
| 61-90 days (10%) | $1,000 | $2,000 | $(1,000) | -50.0% |
| Other cash receipts | $3,000 | $5,000 | $(2,000) | -40.0% |
| **Total cash Receipts** | $105,700 | $105,000 | 700.00 | 0.7% |
| **Cash disbursements forecast** | | | | |
| Payroll and employee benefits | $26,000 | $25,500 | $500 | 2.0% |
| Debt service (principal and interest) | $6,000 | $5,500 | $500 | 9.1% |
| Business occupancy (rent, utilities) | $9,000 | $8,000 | $1,000 | 12.5% |
| Material and components inventory | $34,000 | $32,000 | $2,000 | 6.3% |
| Supplies | $1,000 | $1,000 | $0 | 0.0% |
| Telephone, fax, postage, delivery | $3,000 | $2,450 | $550 | 22.4% |
| Marketing | $12,500 | $10,500 | $2,000 | 19.0% |
| Sales commissions | $7,500 | $5,000 | $2,500 | 50.0% |
| Legal and professional services | $3,250 | $4,000 | ($750) | -18.8% |
| Dividends to owner and investors | $6,000 | $7,000 | ($1,000) | -14.3% |
| Other disbursements | $200 | 0 | $200 | 0.0% |
| **Total cash disbursements** | $108,450 | $100,950 | $7,500 | 7.4% |
| | | | | |
| **Net cash flow** | ($2,750) | $4,050 | ($6,800) | -167.9% |
| | | | | |
| **Beginning cash position** | 4,000 | 4,000 | 0 | 0.0% |
| | | | | |
| **Ending cash position** | $1,250 | $8,050 | ($6,800) | -84.5% |

**Practicing Proper Cash Management**

Proper cash management can contribute much to the success of your small business. Cash makes business owners' dreams come true! Managing your cash well means making the best, most productive use of what you have. It involves knowing the following: 1) what your cash needs are; 2) when, during the year, you generally need cash; 3) the best sources for meeting additional cash needs. Proper cash management also means you must be prepared to meet needs when they occur. The quality of relationship you maintain with bankers and creditors will go a long way towards determining your supply of cash. Equipped with the necessary financial statement tools in hand (the cash flow statement, the cash projection and the variance report), you are ready to maximize the cash in your business.

What happens when your cash needs outpace your cash available? The answer is clear – it is difficult, if not impossible, to plan for the future! Even some of the best-managed companies may find themselves vulnerable to cash shortages. Adding employees or inventory too rapidly is one way in which this can occur.

These seven ideas can provide relief and positively influence your cash flow:[4]

**1) Bill promptly:** I find many small-business owners getting caught in the cycle where they may diligently produce the work, but end up not getting paid on a timely basis simply because they did not complete the transaction with an invoice. So the rule to follow is this: Prepare invoices *immediately* after you have delivered your goods or services to each customer.

There are many accounting software packages available that can help you with invoicing. See Chapter 7 for more information.

Your invoice should include the following information:

- The date the invoice was prepared
- The customer's name and address
- A description of the goods or services sold
- The total amount due
- When the amount is due

Once the invoice has been prepared, be sure it is sent immediately to the customer.

**2) Payment in advance:** A number of businesses require payment in advance for some part of the sales price, and often encourage up-front payment with a substantial discount. This leads directly to cash in the bank.

**3) Direct deposits and "auto drafts:"** Direct deposits and "auto drafts" are preauthorized "paperless" checks that permit you to receive payments from your customers electronically. Direct deposits and "auto drafts" offers many cash flow advantages. You don't have to wait for a check, take the time to deposit it, and then wait for the check to clear. The funds are received instantly on the day they are due. The assurance that your customers pay "on time" makes for more productive, predictable, and easier-to-manage cash flow. In addition, utilizing electronic payments reduces the risk of any possible postal service delays in delivering your customers' payments.

**4) Lockbox Banking:** Lockbox banking is a cash flow improvement technique that speeds collection of payments due to you. Your customers' payments are delivered to a special post office box instead of your business address, thus speeding the movement of their payment into your bank account.

**5) Collect on your accounts receivable:** If you do nothing else, make certain that your credit-and-collection system is operating at peak efficiency.

Accounts receivable represent sales you've made, but that have not yet been paid (sales on credit, as it were). If you are on the cash basis with your customers, receivables aren't a worry for you…. you don't have any. But if you extend payment terms or credit to your customers, you have accounts receivable. You can look at your balance sheet to see how much money is tied up in accounts receivable. Reviewing your Aging Accounts Receivable Report allows you to evaluate how old your receivables are. The longer it takes for customers to pay on their accounts, the less available cash you will have to run your business. Accept credit cards!

### Case Study

I recently had a small-business owner come to see me for help on a loan application to finance his cash-strapped landscaping business. It quickly became apparent to me that applying for more debt was not the solution to his acute problem. It was an accounts receivable issue. We devised a collection system consisting of phone calls and letters to expedite his accounts receivable. Within 3 weeks, the much-needed cash started to roll in.

**Credit terms:** The time limit you set for your customers' promise to pay for the merchandise or services purchased represents your credit terms. They affect the timing of your cash inflows. One of the simplest ways to improve cash flow is to make sure that customers pay their bills more quickly.

Small businesses can sometimes significantly cut the time spent waiting for payment by offering a discount for quick payment. I have received bills from businesses offering discounts of 1% to 2% for payment within 10 days. If I were going to pay the bill within 30 days anyway, I'm likely to send out a check right away to get the extra discount. Good for my bottom-line, good for my business' cash flow too.

**Credit policy:** A written credit policy is the blueprint you use when deciding to extend credit to a customer. The correct credit policy is necessary to ensure that your cash flow doesn't fall victim to a credit policy that is too strict or to one that is too generous.

**6) Trim your Inventory:** Inventory describes the extra merchandise or supplies your business keeps on hand to meet the demands of customers. Keeping too much product on hand can tie up a great deal of cash. Too many business owners buy inventory based on hopes and dreams instead of what they can realistically sell. Keep your inventory as low as possible.

**7) Accounts payable:** Accounts payable represent amounts you owe to your suppliers that are payable sometime within the near future. In this case, "near" probably means between 30 and 90 days. To maximize the flow of your cash, you should speed up collection of your receivables, but slow the payment of your bills. There are ways to "stretch" your payables, for instance, paying in installments, or making arrangements in which you agree to use one vendor exclusively in exchange for making payments over an extended period of time.

**8) Minimize Expenses:** The absolute best way to improve your cash flow, and in particular to improve your accounts payable, is to minimize your business' operational expenses and ensure you make the most efficient use of every dollar you spend.

I have 8 suggestions that will help you minimize some of the expenses you may incur in your business:

**a) Keep a lid on spending.** Resist the urge to spend freely! You may like the way a lavish office and expensive furniture looks, but what does it really contribute to your business? In some businesses, a fancy front office is critical; in most it is not. I once had a small-business owner who spent $5,000 on his front office desk in a business operation they had no "office-visits." Needless, to say, this business owner did not survive too long in business due to this and other extravagances. Get as much value as possible out of every transaction, whether you're leasing office space or stocking the company kitchen.

**b) Don't be wasteful**. Recycle and reuse what you can. The savings may not be large on any given item, but they can add up over time.

**c) Comparison shop**. The Internet makes it much easier to compare prices for everything from airplane tickets to office supplies to computers. Start using the Web to get the best deals.

**Success Tip**

As an example, small-business owners can expect to save anywhere from 20% to 70% off bank prices when buying checks from local distributors or catalogs. You can expect to pay $70 to $100 for 1,000 checks. You may also want to order a slightly larger quantity, since prices are significantly higher for quantities of less than 1,000 checks.

**d) Service Contracts.** Smart sellers of equipment will present you with an option to purchase a service contract right before you walk out of their store. They're not just trying to be helpful. Profit margin on the service contract is often greater than the profit margin on the piece of equipment you're purchasing.

A typical service contract will cover the cost of repairing and maintaining a piece of equipment over a certain period of time. Some service contracts can be renewed, while others automatically renew when the contract expires.

If you're like most consumers, you've probably purchased a service contract simply because it made you feel safe and secure knowing that your new office equipment will be fixed at no cost if it should ever break down. After all, you've just spent a considerable amount of money on a new piece of equipment – a few extra dollars for a service contract can't hurt. Wrong! In most cases, the extra money you spent for the service contract is wasted.

Before purchasing or renewing a service contract, reconsider whether or not it makes sense to purchase a service contract on highly reliable equipment. The chances of it breaking down are so slim that it may be worthwhile to take the risk and save the service contract fees.

**e) Pay Employees Every Other Week.** Many small businesses can reduce payroll processing and administrative costs by 20% to 40% by reducing the frequency of the payroll processing to a bi-weekly payroll period. Paying employees every other week spares your cash flow as well, an important consideration when planning for the future.

**f) Lease, don't buy**. Although leasing can be more expensive in the long run, it may prevent unnecessary substantial cash outlays. Look for lease deals on items like office furniture, computers and copiers

**g) Delay hiring employees.** Try to improve the productivity of current employees (without burning them out), use independent contractors and consider outsourcing certain nonessential functions. Employees are expensive, so you should put off adding permanent hires as long as you can – or at least until you're earning the revenue to support them.

**h) Review your vendor invoices, including credit card statements for accuracy**. Credit card companies are notorious for adding hidden fees and charges.

# IN CONCLUSION

Cash is king. Simply put, "no cash equals no business." It is the gas that keeps your business going. As the owner, you must know how much cash comes in and how much goes out on a regular basis. Companies go out of business for cash flow problems over profitability. Even otherwise-healthy companies can go under for lack of cash. It can kill a company if it sneaks up by surprise, but can be easily managed when there is a plan for it. Tracking the amount of cash you have is a vital function that you can never lose a handle on.

# Cash Plan Worksheet

|  | Month | Month | Month |
|---|---|---|---|
| **BEGINNING CASH POSITION** | $_____ | $_____ | $_____ |
| CASH RECEIPTS | | | |
| _____ | $_____ | $_____ | $_____ |
| _____ | $_____ | $_____ | $_____ |
| _____ | $_____ | $_____ | $_____ |
| _____ | $_____ | $_____ | $_____ |
| _____ | $_____ | $_____ | $_____ |
| _____ | $_____ | $_____ | $_____ |
| _____ | $_____ | $_____ | $_____ |
| _____ | $_____ | $_____ | $_____ |
| **TOTAL CASH RECEIPTS** | $_____ | $_____ | $_____ |
| CASH DISBURSEMENTS | | | |
| _____ | $_____ | $_____ | $_____ |
| _____ | $_____ | $_____ | $_____ |
| _____ | $_____ | $_____ | $_____ |
| _____ | $_____ | $_____ | $_____ |
| _____ | $_____ | $_____ | $_____ |
| _____ | $_____ | $_____ | $_____ |
| _____ | $_____ | $_____ | $_____ |
| **TOTAL CASH DISBURSEMENT** | $_____ | $_____ | $_____ |
| **NET CASH FLOW** | $_____ | $_____ | $_____ |
| **ENDING CASH FLOW** | $_____ | $_____ | $_____ |

# Cash Plan Variance Worksheet

For the Period _____

|  | **Actual** | **Budget** | **Variance** |
|---|---|---|---|
| **BEGINNING CASH POSITION** | $_____ | $_____ | $_____% |
| CASH RECEIPTS |  |  |  |
| _____ | $_____ | $_____ | $_____% |
| _____ | $_____ | $_____ | $_____% |
| _____ | $_____ | $_____ | $_____% |
| _____ | $_____ | $_____ | $_____% |
| _____ | $_____ | $_____ | $_____% |
| _____ | $_____ | $_____ | $_____% |
| _____ | $_____ | $_____ | $_____% |
| _____ | $_____ | $_____ | $_____% |
| **TOTAL CASH RECEIPTS** | $_____ | $_____ | $_____% |
| CASH DISBURSEMENTS |  |  |  |
| _____ | $_____ | $_____ | $_____% |
| _____ | $_____ | $_____ | $_____% |
| _____ | $_____ | $_____ | $_____% |
| _____ | $_____ | $_____ | $_____% |
| _____ | $_____ | $_____ | $_____% |
| _____ | $_____ | $_____ | $_____% |
| _____ | $_____ | $_____ | $_____% |
| **TOTAL CASH DISBURSEMENT** | $_____ | $_____ | $_____% |
| **NET CASH FLOW** | $_____ | $_____ | $_____% |
| **ENDING CASH FLOW** | $_____ | $_____ | $_____% |

# Frequently Asked Questions on Cash in on Cash Flow

*Q. I am a small-business owner and seem to be always running at a cash flow deficit. What tips can I use to get out of this situation?*

It can't be said enough. Cash is king! Therefore, you should be aware of several tips to cut costs and boost cash flow. Here they are:

Cash flow tip 1. Offer everyone who owes you money, especially those greater than 30 days, a 5-10% discount for paying within a shortened period of time.

Cash flow tip 2. Make sure every invoice has been forwarded to the appropriate customer.
Don't hesitate to follow up with a phone call.

Cash flow tip 3. Renegotiate credit terms with your vendors. Many will be willing to work with you, especially if you are a frequent customer.

Cash flow tip 4. Location, location, location. Can you run your office from home, or get a smaller office? Reducing overhead is an excellent way to increase your cash flow.

Cash flow tip 5. Consider your workforce. Is it efficient? Productive? Are you getting all that you can from the people you employ? If not, consider reducing your workforce. The cash you save may be put to better use elsewhere.

Cash flow tip 6. Find yourself an "angel". An angel (in this case) is a private investor. In some cases, an angel can exchange equity for much needed cash. Still, it is important to keep in mind that investors generally look for thriving businesses, not those that need rescuing. Before you use this option, make sure your cash problems are not due to business decline.

# CHAPTER 10:

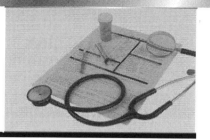

## Fringe Benefits: Why They Benefit You As Much As Your Employees

*"You have to learn to treat people as a resource......you have to ask not what do they cost, but what is the yield, what can they produce?"*
Peter F. Drucker

### *What Are Fringe Benefits?*

Compensation doesn't end with a salary – that's just the first part of the equation. Fringe benefits comprise the second half, and in many ways they are the most important piece of the total compensation package. Fringe benefits provide employers with a "competitive edge" – that is, for the people they hire! But fringe benefits also provide important tax benefits for your business as well. I have discussed below the pros and cons of offering fringe benefits.

**The pros to offering fringe benefits are:**

- Recruiting advantages — you can use and structure benefits packages to attract good employees and reward and thus retain your best employees.

- Tax savings – you can deduct plan contributions.

- Personal gain – you may be able to get benefits for yourself for less money; if you also offer them to your employees, then you would have to acquire them privately for yourself.

- Alternatives to pay — sometimes employees will accept benefits in lieu of higher salaries.

**The cons to offering fringe benefits are:**

- Cost – benefits are costly to large employers and that burden becomes even more significant for the small employer.

- Higher rates – smaller employers will pay higher rates than larger employers for group health coverage because there are fewer employees among whom to spread risk.

- Difficulty in providing life insurance coverage to the employee group.

- Fewer choices – smaller employers have fewer design choices when offering a retirement plan because of high administrative costs.

There are many different types of employee benefits out there. To make matters worse, for each type of benefit, there is a vast array of plans, companies, and administrators that can offer you that benefit in different forms. This chapter deals with the many available fringe benefits. Which benefits are you required to offer? What benefits are optional?

Not all "benefits" are optional. Some are required, even of small businesses. The following is a list of what you are *required* to do as an employer:

1) **Time-off:** You may be required to offer certain time-off benefits, such as to vote, jury duty, and military leave. (There are also other types of time-off that you may choose to offer that are not required by law, such as vacation, sick leave and personal time-off.)

2) **Comply with worker compensation laws:** Worker compensation protects employees against unexpected loss of income due to work-related injury, accident, illness or disease. Check your local state law for specific information.

3) **Withhold for FICA, FUTA and SUTA:** FICA, otherwise known as Social Security taxes, are required of all employers. A portion of an employee's gross salary is withheld from each paycheck (that is, the employee's direct responsibility); employers are required to match the social security withholding. This is an additional expense for employers. FUTA is Federal Unemployment Insurance tax. FUTA is exclusively an employer expense. SUTA is State Unemployment Insurance tax and also is exclusively an employer expense. This rate is specific to your business and set by the State.

4) **Contribute to state unemployment and disability program:** You are required to contribute to state disability programs in states where such programs exist.

The following is a list of *optional* benefits:

5) **Retirement plans**: Retirement benefits are attractive to employees, but they also have specific value to you and your business.

6) **Health plans**. Health insurance is a very common benefit offered by many businesses. Health insurance is a highly competitive area of employee compensation. Most employees have come to expect health insurance as a regular part of their compensation package. It pays to find the right vendor, and to learn details about handling day-to-day administrative issues.

7) **Dental plans:** Dental care plans can be purchased in addition to basic medical care, or as a separate policy from a separate provider.

8) **Life insurance plans:** Life insurance is a wonderful benefit to provide because it offers employees the opportunity to provide additional security for their families at a fairly low cost.

9) **Paid vacations:** Although you are not legally required to offer paid vacation benefits to your employees, most full-time employees will expect to get them.

10) **Paid holidays:** You aren't legally required to give your employees days off for federal or state holidays. However, many employers do have specified holidays when employees do not have to work.

11) **Paid sick leave:** Not required by law. Sick leave, like other time-off benefits, is valuable to employees and, when combined with certain disability insurance benefits, can create an attractive package of benefits that make employees feel secure and valued.

12) **Miscellaneous Fringe Benefits:** Many business owners find that adding special, unique benefits tend to increase employees' level of job satisfaction, and increase their feelings of value to the company.

Let's review more detailed explanations of each benefit listed above, starting with the benefits you are *required* to offer:

**Success Tip**

The key to greater employee loyalty, productivity and reduced turnover is giving your employees what's important to them. And the best way to find out what's important to them is to simply *ask them*. You may be amazed with the outcome. I have often experienced that health benefits may not be that important to part-timers because they are covered from another source (from another full-time job or through a spouse's or parent's health insurance plan). In that case, you might consider offering other, less expensive benefits that would still be considered valuable by employees. Or, you may find that employees have a preference over more cash compensation rather than any particular benefit. The key is to ask them.

# 1) TIME-OFF BENEFITS

As life becomes more stressful and more people feel the pressures of balancing work and family concerns, time-off benefits become more and more valuable to employees.

**Required time-off:** Some types of time-off may not be viewed by employees as "benefits." This is because you, as an employer, are required by law (either federal or state) to provide them. They include:

### a) Time-off to vote:

While there are no federal laws that require you to give employees time-off to vote, 32 jurisdictions have laws that require private employers to give employees time-off to vote, and in many of these states, the employee must be paid for this time.

### b) Jury duty leave:

Employers of all sizes have to provide employees with jury duty leave. Both federal and state laws apply in this area.

**Federal law:** Federal law says that businesses must permit employees the right to serve as jurors in federal courts. As an employer, you must comply with this law or risk legal action.

**State law:** State law says that businesses must permit employees the right to serve as jurors in state and local courts. These laws vary from state to state, and business owners should familiarize themselves with statutes in their local jurisdictions. All states except Minnesota have laws on this subject.

## c) Family and medical leave:

The Family and Medical Leave Act provides that covered employers must allow employees to take the equivalent of 12 weeks of unpaid leave each year due either to a birth or adoption of a child, or to attend to the serious health condition of an immediate family member or to the employee's own serious health condition. A covered employer will have 50 or more employees.

**What is a serious health condition?** A serious health condition under the FMLA is defined as an illness, injury, impairment, or physical or mental condition that involves inpatient care (an overnight stay) in a hospital, hospice, or residential medical care facility. It includes any period of incapacity or any subsequent treatment in connection with the inpatient care, or continuing care, by a healthcare provider that includes one or more of the following:

1) A period of incapacity of more than three consecutive days.

2) Any period of incapacity due to pregnancy or for prenatal care.

3) Any period of incapacity or treatment due to a chronic serious health condition.

4) A period of incapacity that is permanent or long-term due to a condition for which treatment may not be effective.

5) Any period of absence to receive multiple treatments by a healthcare provider, including conditions that are not currently incapacitating but would be if left untreated.

Under the FMLA, an employee must be reinstated to his/her position (or equivalent). Leave may or may not be taken consecutively to qualify.

**State law:** Several states require businesses with less than 50 employees to provide medical leave. Become familiar with the laws in your state, particularly those that affect businesses of a similar size to yours.

Some states require specific benefits for maternity, adoption, or parental leave situations. Where it applies, parental or maternity leave is defined as a period of absence from work for the purpose of caring for a child, either natural-born or adopted. The term parental leave is differentiated from maternity leave because it permits both male and female employees equal access to this benefit. This may be advantageous in that a parental leave benefit would not be subject to scrutiny from anti-discrimination laws.

While your business may not be large enough to be required to provide medical or family leave under a state or federal law, you may choose to give employees some type of leave for these situations; either vacation time or personal time may be substituted.

# 2) COMPLY WITH WORKERS' COMPENSATION

This topic has been covered in detail in Chapter 11. I have discussed here the pros and cons of a state-mandated or voluntary workers' compensation system.

**Advantages and disadvantages.** There are advantages and disadvantages to state-mandated or voluntary workers' compensation system. The advantages are:

- Your liability for on-the-job injuries is limited to the remedies available under the workers' compensation system; you can't be sued for everything you own.

- The types of benefits you have to pay to employees are limited to those available under the laws.

- Your disability planning is made easier because the costs are predictable.

The disadvantages are:

- Your premiums may be high, depending upon your accident record.

- Filing requirements increase your administrative burdens.

- Bogus claims may needlessly take up your time.

# 3) WITHHOLD FOR FICA, FUTA AND SUTA

## a) Social Security and Medicare (FICA) Taxes

It is a federal law that requires you to withhold two separate taxes from the wages you pay your employees: a Social Security tax and a Medicare tax. The law also requires you to pay the employer's portion of these taxes. Unless you have employees who receive tips, the employer's portion will be the same as the amount that you're required to withhold from your employees' wages. The Federal Insurance Contributions Act (FICA) requires businesses to withhold Social Security and Medicare taxes from its employees. It also requires businesses to pay an employer's share for each tax.

> **Example:**
> An employee who earns $1,000 in gross wages will have social security withholding of 6.2%, or $62, and Medicare tax withholding of 1.45%, or $14.50. The business will also owe equal amounts as its employer's portion. The combined FICA liability in this case would be $153 ($76.50 employer's portion plus $76.50 employee's portion).
>
> Employer's obligation to withhold and pay FICA taxes for an employee ends once the employee has earned $118,500 in gross wages (2015). Medicare, however, continues to be paid regardless of the employee's total gross wages.

Starting in 2013, you may be liable for an Additional Medicare Tax if your income exceeds certain limits. Here are a few things that you should know about this tax:

- The Additional Medicare Tax is 0.9 percent. It applies to the amount of your wages, self-employment income and railroad retirement (RRTA) compensation that is more than a threshold amount. The threshold amount that applies to you is based on your filing status. If you're married and file a joint return, you must combine your spouse's wages, compensation, or self-employment income with yours to determine if you exceed the "married filing jointly" threshold.

- The threshold amounts are:

| **Filing Status** | **Threshold Amount** |
|---|---|
| Married filing jointly | $250,000 |
| Married filing separately | $125,000 |
| Single | $200,000 |
| Head of household | $200,000 |
| Qualifying widow(er) with dependent child | $200,000 |

- You must combine wages and self-employment income to determine if your income exceeds the threshold. You do not consider a loss from self-employment when you figure this tax. You must compare RRTA compensation separately to the threshold. See the instructions for Form 8959, Additional Medicare Tax, for examples.

- Employers must withhold this tax from your wages or compensation when they pay you more than $200,000 in a calendar year, without regard to your filing status, wages paid to you by another employer, or income that you may have from other sources. Your employer does not combine the wages for married couples to determine whether to withhold Additional Medicare Tax.

### b) Federal Unemployment Tax

The Federal Unemployment Tax Act (FUTA) imposes a payroll tax on employers, based on the wages they pay to their employees. You don't withhold the FUTA tax from an employee's wages; the business itself must pay this tax.

**Liability for tax:** You must pay the FUTA tax if during the current or the preceding calendar year you meet either of the following tests:

- You pay wages totaling at least $1,500 to your employees in any calendar quarter, OR,

- You maintain at least one employee on any day in each of the 20 calendar weeks (defined as beginning on a Sunday and ending on following Saturday).

Your business must pay FUTA tax for the entire year if you meet either of these conditions.

**Computing the tax:** FUTA tax is imposed on only the first $7,000 paid to each employee. The FUTA rate is 6.0%. When computing the tax, you are generally permitted to claim credits against gross FUTA to reflect state unemployment taxes paid. This credit amounts to 5.4% of federally taxable wages, reducing FUTA tax liability to 0.6%.

## 4) CONTRIBUTE TO STATE DISABILITY AND UNEMPLOYMENT PROGRAMS

Disability insurance taxes are required in some, but not all, states. The jurisdictions where you may have to collect or pay disability insurance taxes include: California,

Hawaii, New Jersey, New York, Puerto Rico and Rhode Island. Colorado has an unemployment tax that the Employer must pay on all eligible employees.

The following provides a more detailed review of the **optional benefits** you may consider providing:

# 5) RETIREMENT PLANS

Having a retirement plan for your employees is simply smart business. Recruiting and retaining good employees, as well as tax advantages, are great reasons to establish a retirement plan. 401(K), Roth IRAs, SEPs, Simple IRAs and Keoghs are all available options. Each has its own unique characteristics, and should be thoroughly researched when considering the right plan.

Business owners may have concerns that retirement plans are too costly and time consuming to administer. The uncertainty inherent in our economic cycles may further increase anxieties. But there are distinct advantages, all of which should be considered, and the implications of NOT having a retirement plan could be far more detrimental. More than one million businesses offer retirement plans – that's almost one in every five!

What follows are the primary advantages to offering a retirement plan:

1) **Attract and retain good employees**: Employees are any business' most important asset. Finding the best often requires giving the best. Offering retirement benefits may indeed increase the pool of qualified candidates for positions you have available.

2) **Gain substantial tax advantages**: Your business may realize tax savings by offering retirement plans to employees. The following are some of them:

   - The amount you contribute is tax-deductible

   - Amounts contributed by employer and employee are tax-deferred

   - Potential to earn higher returns for employer and employees

   - Potential future tax savings if in a lower tax bracket at the time of withdrawal

3) **Improve productivity**: Direct impact on improved productivity – in the case of profits tied to the plan.

4) **Save for retirement**: Retirement plans provide financial security for the future. This is something that everyone certainly thinks about.

# Choosing the right plan

It is important to thoroughly research available plans, and make the right selection for your employees and your business. The IRS governs rules of retirement plans, including the areas of eligibility, vesting, participation, and contribution limits. It is imperative that you provide proper administration of these plans, particularly because of the serious consequences associated with improper handling.

I have identified the following 3 simple steps to consider when selecting the right retirement plan:

> **Step 1**: Identify your needs and goals. Ask yourself these questions: Are there specific key employees (including yourself) that you wish to reward more than others? Are these employees older or younger? Does your business typically employ full-time or part-time workers?

> **Step 2**: Identify the amount you are willing to set aside in employer benefits each year for yourself and your employees. Do you want to fund the plan every year, regardless of profits? Would you like to have the ability to suspend contributions in lean years?

> **Step 3:** Determine the costs involved in establishing and maintaining a retirement plan. Depending on the plan, the costs can be minimal and the plan easy to maintain, or time-consuming, complicated, and costly. It is important to address the complexities and fees related to different types of plans.

## Basic Types of Plans

There are two major categories of pension plans: qualified plans and nonqualified plans.

A **qualified plan** is a program established by an employer under the Employee Retirement Income Security Act of 1974 (ERISA) and the Internal Revenue Code to provide retirement income for employees. If certain requirements are met, a qualified plan is exempt from taxation. Employers are able to deduct contributions made to the plan, while employees are not taxed until funds are distributed to them.

A **nonqualified plan** is one that does not meet ERISA guidelines and the requirements of the Internal Revenue Code. Employees do not receive preferential tax treatment. The main reason nonqualified plans are established is to provide deferred compensation exclusively for one or more executives.

**DEFINED CONTRIBUTION**: Offers a lot of flexibility, but has a minimum annual contribution level. You get the opportunity to sock away higher tax-advantaged savings amounts.

**DEFINED BENEFIT**: This is the most complex and expensive plan to administer. You set or define the output (the guaranteed level of monthly retirement benefit), and the company must contribute whatever it takes to get there.

The following are retirement plan options based on 2014 requirements. The best plan will vary depending on your needs.

| Retirement Plan Options* | | | |
|---|---|---|---|
| **Plan** | **Contribution Limits** | **Phaseout Limits** | **Comments** |
| SEP | 20%*/$52,000 | None | Simple to establish and administer |
| SIMPLE | 3% + $12,000 | None | Simple to establish and administer |
| Keogh | 20%*/$52,000 (or more) | None | Can be designated a profit-sharing plan, or a defined benefit plan. Generally requires a professional to set up, especially if you want a defined benefit plan. You can contribute an extra $5,500 if you are 50 or older. |
| 401(k) | $52,000 | None | High contribution limits mean you can lower your tax bills and generate more tax-deferred earnings for your retirement stash. You can contribute an extra $5,500 if you are 50 or older. |
| Roth IRAs | $5,500 ($6,500 if you are age 50 or older) | $114,000-129,000 for singles, $181,000-191,000 for joint filers | Contributions are nondeductible, but earnings grow tax-free. You can contribute an extra $1,000 if you are 50 or older. |

| | | |
|---|---|---|
| Traditional IRA | $5,500 ($6,500 if you are age 50 or older) | None | Now, if you are covered by a retirement plan, but your spouse isn't, you can make a $5,500 deductible contribution to an IRA for your non-covered spouse, as long as your joint AGI is under $181,000. You can contribute an extra $1,000 if you are 50 or older. |

Based on 2014 limits.

*20% of self-employment income or 25% of compensation for employees.

Let's look at each plan individually.

## Simplified Employee Pension Benefits (SEP)

One of the easiest ways to dip your company's toe into the retirement waters is by starting a Simplified Employee Pension IRA, or SEP-IRA plan. A SEP plan is the simplest, most efficient, and least expensive way for a small business to establish a pension plan for its owners and employees.

**What is a SEP?** SEPs are essentially individual retirement accounts (or IRAs). While they act in many respects like pension plans, they are much easier and less expensive to administer. If you have just a handful of employees and are looking for a plan that is truly low-cost and low-maintenance, then consider a SEP IRA. The plan is funded with tax-deductible employer contributions, and you must cover all eligible employees. Employee contributions are not allowed.

SEPs allow you to contribute and deduct up to 20% of self-employment income (25% of salary if you're an employee of your own corporation). The maximum dollar contribution is $52,000. However, the percentage can be varied each year, so lower amounts (or nothing at all) can be contributed when you turn out to be in need of cash. In contrast, personal IRAs have a $5,500 yearly maximum contribution.

One of the key features of this plan is the ability for you, as the employer, to determine how much will be contributed yearly. This gives you the flexibility to determine contributions according to how well the company is doing. Contributions can vary from year to year. If you hit a lean spell, you aren't locked in. Keep in mind that payouts do need to be evenly distributed, though, with all employees receiving the same percentage contribution in the years that you make contributions.

The SEP-IRA is also the easiest small business retirement plan to administer. The company simply opens an IRA for each participating employee. There are no annual reports that need to be filed with the IRS, as is required by more complex plans like a 401(K) plan. An annual statement to each employee notifying of the total contribution made is the primary reporting requirement. SEPs are also great for latecomers because they can be opened until the extended due date of your income tax return.

As for drawbacks, employees are not allowed to contribute to this plan. In addition, all qualifying employees must be covered by this plan. Qualifying employees include those who are at least 21 years old, have been employed for three or more of the last five years, and have earned at least $550 each year. Under these conditions, this can indicate the required coverage of even part-time employees. With a SEP-IRA, vesting is immediate. This means employees are immediately entitled to whatever money is in their accounts. More complex plans have vesting periods where benefits accrue and are earned by the employee only after a certain period of time. Vesting requirements can encourage employee retention.

Thinking about the future can be difficult when there is so much to handle in the present. Perhaps not surprisingly, 52% of small businesses surveyed in another study are not familiar with SEP-IRAs. Now that you are, you can help make the golden years truly golden.

**Who should set up a SEP?** If you fall into one of these categories, you should consider setting up a SEP:

- Non-employees, that is, independent contractors

- Sole proprietors running businesses without employees

- Businesses whose financial condition will only be known at tax time – SEPs can be established after the close of the tax year.

**Who should NOT set up a SEP?** You should steer clear of SEPs if you:

- Want flexibility. SEPs do not have great degree of it, trading lower costs for few administrative burdens.

## How much will you contribute?

SEPs require you to determine a percentage you will use for SEP contributions. In general, SEP contribution percentages must be the same across the board. Practically, business owners should wait until available funds for contributions are known before establishing the percentage.

**Notices for employees:** Business owners must provide notice to their employees of the percentage contribution by the later of: a) the first January 31st following the contribution year; or, b) 30 days after the contribution is made.

For an example, let's say you operate on a calendar-year (January to December) basis. After the end of the year, you figure out how much you want to contribute to your employees' SEPs and you make those contributions on January 15. You have until February 14 to give your employees the notice.

Now let's say your fiscal year ends September 30. You make contributions to your employees' SEPs on October 20. You have until January 31 to give your employees the notice.

| SEP IRA | | |
|---|---|---|
| | Employers | Employee |
| Eligibility | Any business owner or self-employed individual. | All employees who have worked for you for three of the past five years and who earned at least $550 from you last year. |
| Contribution Limits | 25% of compensation (if you're an employee of your own corporation) up to $52,000; 20% of self-employment income (if self-employed) up to $52,000. | Employees cannot contribute. But the employer must contribute to eligible employee accounts the same salary percentage she contributes to her own. |
| Vesting | Immediate. | Immediate. |
| Pros | Contributions do not have to be made every year. Very easy and cheap to set up and administer. | Vesting is immediate. |
| Cons | Must cover all qualifying employees. Employees cannot contribute. Vesting is immediate. | Employees cannot contribute. |

**SEP IRA**

**Savings Incentive Match Plan for Employees (SIMPLE IRA)**

A Simple IRA allows employee contributions, while mandating that employers match them. For 2014, annual contributions are generally limited to $12,000 ($14,500 if you are 50) each year. Employee contributions can be matched dollar for dollar up to 3% of an employee's compensation or as a fixed contribution of 2% of pay for all eligible employees. Employees are 100% vested in all contributions, decide how and where the money will be invested, and may keep their IRA accounts when they change jobs.

For a business with less than 10 employees, a SIMPLE IRA is a great way to get started.

**Success Tip**
Be aware of the difference between a SIMPLE IRA and the SIMPLE 401(K) – they are different. The SIMPLE 401(K) retirement option is like a traditional 401(K) except it typically has higher fees and less flexibility.

# SIMPLE Plans as Benefits

Employers with no more than 100 employees may set up a savings incentive match plan for employee (SIMPLE). In effect, SIMPLE plans trade off lower annual contribution limits for less burdensome administration. Thus, they're generally cheaper and easier to operate than other retirement options, but you can't save as much for retirement each year as you can with the other options.

Here are the basic rules for SIMPLE plan:

- It must be the only retirement plan you offer.

- The funding mechanism can be either an IRA or a 401(K) plan.

- $12,000 annual contribution in 2014; this amount is adjusted annually. For employees over 50 years of age, an additional $2,500 can be contributed.

- Employer must match up to 3% of employee compensation, or contribute 2% for all eligible employees earning a minimum of $5,000. These are the only permitted contributions.

• Participating employees become vested immediately.

• The difference between IRA and 401(K) forms regarding participation eligibility comes down to previous and expected compensation: two years earning at least $5,000 annually for the IRA, and one year at this level with the 401(K). In each case the employee should be expected to continue earning at least this amount.

• Employers may take a deduction for contributions to the employees' accounts.

• Employee distributions within the first two years are subject to a 25% excise tax.

• Upon separation from employment, distributions may be rolled over tax-free to an IRA or to another SIMPLE plan. SIMPLE plans can still be set up even if none of your employees wants to participate; but you must offer the plan to all eligible employees. Of course, there are strict rules and heavy fines for business owners who don't properly give employees the option of joining.

| SIMPLE IRA | | |
| --- | --- | --- |
| | Employers | Employee |
| Eligibility | Employers with 100 employees or less who do not maintain any other retirement plan. | All employees who have ever earned more than $5,000 in any two years prior and who will earn at least $5,000 this year. |
| Contribution Limits | 3% employer match (in certain situations, the match can be 1% to 2%) or 2% non-elective contribution for all employees up to $5,200 per employee. | $12,000 plus employer match up to 3%. (Employer can contribute $12,000 plus match to her own account.) Additional $2,500 if you are age 50 or older. |
| Vesting | Immediate. | Immediate. |
| Pros | Employees can make contributions. If you have lower salary (or self-employment income), you can make larger contributions than under other types of plans. | Employees can make contributions. |

| Cons | Employer most likely cannot contribute as much as she can to a SEP IRA. Match is mandatory. Vesting is immediate. | None really, unless you have a high salary that would permit larger contributions under other types of plans. |

# Keogh Plans

A Keogh Plan may be established as a defined-benefit or a defined-contribution plan, and can be set up by someone who is self-employed or in a partnership. It must meet the same eligibility and coverage requirements as any retirement plan that covered corporate employees.

A business without employees may still establish a Keogh, but any employees who may join you must be offered the opportunity to participate. Any individual working in a supplemental capacity may open a Keogh; the contribution amount is based on net earnings derived from part-time self-employment.

**Who qualifies?** To be eligible for a Keogh plan you must be "self-employed." Sole proprietorships, partnerships, or limited liability companies (LLC) qualify. Corporations do not qualify. Furthermore, you must actually perform personal services for the business; mere passive investment is not enough.

In addition, the following people are also eligible to set up Keoghs:

- Ministers

- Christian Science practitioners

- Traveling salesmen who work for wholesalers, retailers, contractors, or operators of hotels, restaurants, or other similar businesses

- Drivers who distribute meat products, vegetable products, fruit products, bakery products, beverages (except milk), or laundry or dry cleaning services

- Home workers

**Doctors.** A salaried doctor is not considered to be self-employed, even if a corporation that is owned by the doctor pays the "salary." The doctor, however, becomes eligible to contribute to a Keogh if he or she derives income from other sources.

**Consultants.** Consultants are generally considered to be self-employed. There remains some ambiguity about former employees who are retained as consultants after they retire. Check with an attorney if this applies to you.

## Contribution and Deduction Rules

The amount of the contribution you can make to your Keogh plan is determined by the amount of your "earned income" for the year. Earned income is defined as your gross income from a trade or business, less any allowable deductions. Income received by a passive partner is considered to be investment income rather than earned income.

**Contribution limits.** The limitations on contributions depend on the type of Keogh plan. A *Keogh defined benefit plan* is limited to the amount needed to eventually produce an annual pension payment of the lesser of (1) $210,000, or (2) 100% of your average compensation for your three highest years. The $210,000 limit is for 2014 and may be adjusted for inflation.

A *Keogh defined contribution plan* contribution is limited to the lesser of $52,000 for 2014 or 100% of the participant's earned income for the year.

**Deductions:** The rules for deductions by self-employed individuals are as follows:

- Sole proprietor is eligible for 100% deduction

- A Partner may deduct contribution made on his/her behalf

Partners may not deduct contributions made on behalf of his/her employees.

**When do you have to make contributions?** Keogh contributions can be made after the close of the tax year, provided they are made by the tax filing date. A Keogh must be established, however, prior to the close of the tax year for which you contribute. Remember – a SEP can be established after the tax year ends, unlike a Keogh. But doing so does not mean you can't establish a Keogh at a later date.

# 401(K)

A 401(K) can be established at reasonable cost, with greater benefits to employees and employers. Following recent tax cut legislation, larger contributions can be made, generating lower tax bills and greater tax-deferred earnings for retirement.

In general, up to 100% of the first $17,500 in income can be contributed. Above and beyond that, you can contribute and deduct up to 25% of compensation income, or 20% of self-employment income.

| Tax Year | Under Age 50 | 50 And Older |
|----------|--------------|--------------|
| 2014 | $17,500 | $23,000 |
| 2015 | $18,000 | $23,500 |

You must establish your plan by Dec. 31 if you want to claim a tax deduction in that tax year. You must also generally decide how big the first part of your contribution will be.

## 401(K) Plan Requirements

401(K) plans have certain requirements of which you should be aware:

- Employees must receive written notification about the plan.

- The plan must be for the exclusive benefit of employees or their beneficiaries.

- The plan may not favor highly compensated employees. Highly compensated is considered:

  o Ownership of five percent or more

  o Earnings of more than $90,000 and in the top 20% of employees in terms of compensation

- The maximum amount that an employee may voluntarily defer into the plan is $17,500, for those that are age 50 or over in 2014, can contribute an additional $5,500 for the year.

- Minimum vesting rules must be met. Vested employees have participated for a determined number of service years. As such, he/she is entitled to his/her own contributions, but also those made by the employer.

- The plan must provide for a qualified joint and survivor annuity.

- The plan must contain a spendthrift provision.

- Reports must be filed with the IRS, the Department of Labor, and the Pension Benefit Guaranty Corporation, while other reports must be furnished to plan participants and their beneficiaries, under ERISA, the federal pension law.

- The plan will not qualify as a 401(K) plan if it requires that an employee has more than one year of service with the employer or employers maintaining the plan.

- The plan must provide a separate account for each participant and must separately account for contributions that are subject to the special vesting and distribution rules.

Naturally, any income, expenses, gains and/or losses must be properly allocated, per accounting rules.

| 401(k) | | |
| --- | --- | --- |
| | Employers | Employee |
| Eligibility | Any business. | Employees who worked at least 1,000 hours in the past year; two years, if no vesting period. Age 21 or older. |
| Contribution Limits | Combined employer and employee's contribution cannot exceed $52,000. | $17,500 ($23,000 if you are age 50 or older.) |
| Vesting | Determined by employer. | Determined by employer. |
| Pros | Employee/employer contributions. Match not required. | Employee can contribute. |
| Cons | Administration can be expensive. | Employer contributions usually take years to vest. |

**401(k)**

# Defined Benefit Plan

Although they've been around awhile, a defined benefit plan might still make the most sense. In general, a defined benefit plan works well for older individuals, as it is a great opportunity to save big before retirement. You may contribute as much as is needed to provide annual retirement payouts of the lesser of $210,000 or one hundred percent of the participants compensation averaged over the three highest consecutive pay years. Younger employees have less benefit, because they cannot contribute as much.

There are additional disadvantages. A defined plan is not very flexible, and it can be expensive. Contributions are mandatory. Not being able to fund your plan means you must change the plan document itself. The IRS does not forbid this practice, but it does not look kindly on it either.

| Defined Benefit Plan | | |
| --- | --- | --- |
| | Employers | Employee |
| Eligibility | Any business owner or self-employed individual. | Employees who worked at least 1,000 hours in the past year; two years, if no vesting period. Age 21 or older. |
| Contribution Limits | No set limit. Contributions are based on actuarial assumption. Maximum annual retirement benefit is $210,000 or 100% of the participant's average compensation for his highest three consecutive earning years. | Employees cannot contribute. |
| Vesting | Determined by employer. | Determined by employer. |
| Pros | Older employers looking to put away a lot of money over short time period can do so. | You are guaranteed a set payout after retiring. |

| 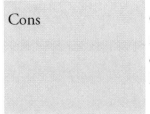 Cons | Can be expensive. Actuary required to determine contribution/deduction limit. Inflexible. | No employee control over investment options. No employee contributions. Vesting takes years in most plans. |

**Defined Benefit Plan**

## Individual Retirement Accounts (IRAs)

Individual Retirement Accounts (IRAs) function as *personal* tax-qualified retirement savings plans. Anyone who works, whether as an employee or self-employed, can set aside up to $5,500 in an IRA for 2014 tax year, and the earnings on these investments grow, tax-deferred, until the eventual date of distribution. Moreover, certain individuals are permitted to deduct all or part of their contributions to the IRA. Certain individuals can also set up Roth IRAs, to which contributions are not deductible, but from which withdrawals at retirement won't be taxed.

IRAs are set up as trusts or custodial accounts for the exclusive benefit for an individual and his or her beneficiaries. You can set up an IRA simply by choosing a bank, mutual fund, brokerage house, or other financial institution to act as trustee or custodian. The institution will give you the necessary forms to complete. A lesser-known alternative is to purchase an individual retirement annuity contract from a life insurance company. An individual cannot be his own trustee.

You must begin taking distributions from an IRA no later than April 1st of the year following the year in which you reach age 70.5. There's an exception to this rule for Roth IRAs, which carry no mandatory distribution requirements.

**Amount:** The most that you can contribute to an IRA in 2014 is the smaller of $5,500 or an amount equal to the compensation includible in income for the year. Those 50 years old and older will also be allowed to make additional $1,000 catch-up contribution to an IRA to help them save more for retirement.

The same limit applies even if the individual has more than one IRA, or more than one type of IRA. When both, a husband and wife, have compensation, the limit applies separately to each, so that as much as $11,000 can be contributed ($13,000 if both are 50 or over).

**Earned income requirement:** The contribution must be from compensation, which means wages, salaries, commissions and other sources of earned income. It does not include deferred compensation, retirement payments or portfolio income such as interest or dividends.

**Nonworking spouses:** Up to $5,500 may be contributed to an IRA on behalf of a nonworking spouse in 2014 ($6,500 if the nonworking spouse is age 50 or older). Separate accounts must be used for each spouse. The couple must file a joint tax return to claim the deduction, and the combined compensation of both spouses must be at least equal to the amount contributed to both spouses' IRAs.

**Timing:** An IRA can be established and a contribution made after year-end. It must be made no later than the due date for filing the income tax return for that year, not including extensions. This generally means that you have until April 15th of the following year to make the contribution and deduct it on your tax return. You don't have to contribute the full amount allowed every year. You may skip a year or even several years. You may resume making contributions in a later year, but you cannot "catch up" for years no contribution was made.

**Excess contributions:** If you contribute more than the allowable amount, a 6% excise tax penalty will be assessed. This penalty is due for the year of the excess contribution and for each year thereafter until corrected.

**Disallowed contributions:** No contributions may be made to an inherited IRA; in a form other than cash; or during or after the year in which the individual reaches age 70.5. For Roth IRAs, however, there is no upper-age limit on when contributions can be made.

**Deductible IRAs:** Everyone is eligible to establish and maintain an IRA, but whether the contributions into the IRA will be deductible depends on the individual's (or, if married, the couple's) income level and whether or not the individual is covered by another retirement plan at work.

If neither the individual nor spouse is covered under another retirement plan, they may take full advantage of the tax deduction for the amount contributed, regardless of their income level.

If the individual making the contribution is covered under another retirement plan, the amount of the contribution eligible for deduction is determined by the filing status and adjusted gross income of the couple.

Ultimately, the phase-out range in 2014 for joint returns will be $96,000 to $116,000, and the range for singles will be $60,000 to $70,000.

If the individual making the contribution is *not* covered by another retirement plan at work, but his or her spouse *is* covered by such a plan, the non-covered individual may make deductible contributions to an IRA. The phase-out range for such contributions is $181,000 to $191,000.

**Roth IRAs:** Some taxpayers can set up an IRA that is back-loaded: that is, the contributions are not deductible, but the withdrawals from the account, including all the buildup in value over the years, are tax-free as long as certain conditions are met. The withdrawals must be made five years or more after the account was opened, and after you attain age 59.5 or have become disabled. Joint filers with income under $181,000 can make full contributions to Roth IRAs; for those with income between $181,000 and $191,000, the contribution amount is phased down, until it is phased out completely at $188,000. For singles, the phase-out range is between $114,000 and $129,000.

You may be able to convert a "regular" IRA to a Roth IRA. The catch is that you must pay current income tax on the entire amount that you convert. The converted amount must remain in the account for five years; if it is withdrawn prematurely, a 10% penalty will apply and any tax due on the conversion that has not already been paid (for instance, if it was to have been spread forward for four years) will become due in the year of the withdrawal.

**Nondeductible contributions:** To the extent that you can't meet the requirements for deductible IRAs or Roth IRAs, you may still make a nondeductible contribution to an IRA. However, your total annual contributions to any type of retirement IRA may not exceed $5,500. The earnings on nondeductible contributions will still accumulate on a tax-deferred basis. To report nondeductible contributions, you must file Form 8606 with your tax return.

**Transfers and rollovers:** The shifting of funds from one IRA trustee/custodian directly to another trustee/custodian is called a transfer. It is not considered a rollover because nothing was paid over to you. A transfer is tax-free and there are no waiting periods between transfers.

A rollover, in contrast, is a tax-free distribution to you of assets from one retirement plan that you then contribute to a different retirement plan. Under certain circumstances, you may either rollover assets withdrawn from one IRA into another, or rollover a distribution from a qualified retirement plan into an IRA. If the distribution from a qualified plan is made directly to you, the payer must withhold 20% of it for taxes. You can avoid the withholding by having the payer transfer the funds directly to the trustee/custodian of your IRA.

A rollover must be made within 60 days of receipt of the distribution. You cannot deduct the rollover contribution, but you must report it on your tax return. Rollovers not completed within 60 days are treated as taxable distributions. On top of the regular income tax, you may also have to pay a 10% excise tax penalty on the premature distribution.

A rollover from one IRA to another enables you to change your investment strategy and enhance your rate of return. This type of rollover may be made only once a year. This rule applies separately to each IRA owned. If property other than cash is received, that same property must be rolled over. Except for an IRA received by a surviving spouse, an inherited IRA cannot be rolled over into, or receive a rollover from, another IRA.

**Withdrawals/distributions from an IRA:** There are rules limiting the withdrawal and use of your IRA assets. Violation of the rules generally results in taxation of the withdrawn amount, plus a penalty equal to 10% of the withdrawal. Generally, you violate the rules if you withdraw assets from your IRA before you reach the age of 59.5. However, there are special exceptions that allow you to take distributions from a regular (non-Roth) IRA if the amounts are used to pay medical expenses in excess of 10% of adjusted gross income or if the distributions are used by certain unemployed, formerly unemployed, or self-employed individuals to pay health insurance premiums. You can take a penalty-free withdrawal of $10,000 from any type of IRA to purchase your first home.

For IRAs, you can also take penalty-free withdrawals before age 59.5 to pay certain education expenses for yourself or your dependents, or if you set up a schedule to take "substantially equal" periodic payments for the rest of your life. You must begin withdrawing the balance from any IRA that is not a Roth IRA by April 1st of the year following the year in which you reach age 70.5 or the year in which you retire.

A withdrawal from your IRA, net of the portion representing return of any nondeductible contributions, is includible in your ordinary income.

**Success Tip**

The more employees you have, the better off you are when it comes to benefits. When you are planning on what benefits to offer, consider your size. It's going to be costly to offer a loaded benefits package to your employees if you have only two or three people working for you. If that is the case, I would advise you to focus on the one or two benefits that you and your employees will value most and that are most cost-effective.

# 6) HEALTH INSURANCE

Health insurance is the most common benefit offered to employees by a small business. To help subsidize the cost, many business owners deduct a portion of the premiums from employee paychecks. In some cases, state laws limit how much of the cost can be passed on to employees. Your insurance agent should have all the forms necessary to set up a group plan, authorize payroll withholding, provide proper employee notification, etc.

To help minimize costs, you can adopt a Section 105 plan, one of the few that require no government filings. The only item you can run through a Section 105 plan is health insurance premiums. You must have a written plan on file to prove that your company has adopted the plan.

If you wish, you may elect a medical reimbursement plan to reimburse employees for costs not covered by health insurance. This provides tax relief, for both the employee and employer. In the event that you provide group health insurance, you are required to offer continuing coverage for as long as 18 months after a person terminates employment with your company. You may, however, bill that employee up to 2% above the premium costs. The law that governs this is called COBRA.

Health insurance can also be provided as part of a more comprehensive package of benefits under a Section 125 plan, usually referred to as a "cafeteria plan." Like the name sounds, the cafeteria plan allows employees to select from a menu of tax-free benefits. Each employee can select something different, or mix and match benefits to meet their own unique needs. The employee pays for the benefits with salary reduction elections via an irrevocable election that is made at the beginning of the year. However, the tax code requires a "use it or lose it" approach - i.e., any unused monies will revert to the employer (not the employee). The types of benefits currently allowed are:

- Group term life insurance premiums

- Disability income and accident insurance costs

- Health insurance premiums

- Dental insurance premiums

- Qualified dependent care costs (up to $5,000)

- Contributions to 401(K) plans

You need not offer all of these benefits. The company can choose which benefits to offer.

The plan will need to file its own annual tax return (a Form 5500), but this type of plan can cut your payroll tax bill, and will save employees both payroll and income taxes. The easiest way to provide a cafeteria plan is to hire a third-party administrator to manage all the paperwork hassle.

**Do you have to offer a health plan?** The law, Prepaid Health Care Act ( PPACA) states that small groups (2-50) do not have to offer health insurance.

Starting in 2015, employers with 100+ need to offer insurance, or may face a per employee penalty of $2,000.

Starting in 2016, employers with 50-99 also face the same penalty.

**Should you offer a health plan?** The first decision to make is whether to offer health insurance at all. To investigate further, consider the following:

## The Pros:

- Attract and retain the most qualified employees

- Gain tax advantages

- Offer employees group purchasing power

- Ensure the wellness of your workers

## The Cons:

- The costs

- Asking employees to share the cost

- The increased administrative workload and cost
- The potential liability

**Success Tip**

The trend in recent years has been pointing toward health insurance as the most important and highly valued benefit for employees. Some employers have found a direct increase in productivity when they initiated health benefits. Health insurance is tax-deductible to the employer and tax-exempt for the employee. You can often purchase it at a lower cost than the employee would ordinarily pay for an individual policy.

## The Affordable Care Act (also known as ObamaCare)

The Affordable Care Act was signed into law to reform the health care industry by President Barack Obama on March 23, 2010 and upheld by the supreme court on June 28, 2012.

ObamaCare's goal is to give more Americans access to affordable, quality health insurance, and to reduce the growth in health care spending in the U.S.

It's a big topic with a lot of information (and misinformation) that's available to people.

For more information, ObamaCare's official health insurance marketplace is www.**healthcare.gov.** However, many states set up their own marketplace. You can find it here: www.obamacarefacts.com/state-health-insurance-exchange.php

## 7) DENTAL CARE

Dental care plan can be purchased in addition to basic medical care, or it can be purchased as a separate policy from a separate provider. Generally, there are two dental plans available: an HMO plan and an indemnity plan. These plans usually cover only basic dentistry services, not orthodontics (braces, for example) or surgical procedures.

**HMO-type plan:** HMO dental plans operate in the same way as an HMO health plan. Employees choose from a list of doctors under contract with the insurance company and are responsible for a co-payment when they visit. Sometimes these plans include free exams and teeth cleaning once or twice a year for insured individuals, as well.

**Indemnity plan:** Like a fee-for-service health plan, these plans allow you to go to the dentist of your choice. The employee must fulfill the deductible before the insurance company will begin payments. Any covered costs that exceed the usual, reasonable and customary fee (UCR) limit must be paid by the employee.

Generally, these plans are big money-makers for the insurance companies that provide them. The premiums are usually small enough to entice people to buy the coverage, although these individuals will seldom use it. For people who require basic preventive services, it may be more economical to put the money they would spend on dental insurance premiums in a medical spending account (if you offer one) and pay dental maintenance bills from that.

## 8) FLEXIBLE SAVINGS ACCOUNTS

An employer health benefit, the Flexible Spending Account, has grown in popularity over the years. FSAs permit employers and employees to use pretax dollars.

---

**Example:**

One of your employees, George Clooney, who earns $40,000 in salary, elects to place $2,500 in a flexible spending account. Income tax, FICA taxes, and FUTA taxes will be paid only on $37,500. The $2,500 in the FSA is not subject to the taxes.

---

**Basic Rules of FSAs**

Here are some of the basic rules for flexible spending accounts:

- Employee must decide how much will be deposited into the FSA for the year.

- The account may not establish a premium payment schedule based on the rate or amount of claims incurred.

- Employee's contributions must be available at all times to reimburse health care expenses.

- Failing to pay premiums will result in termination of FSA coverage, with successive claims subject to non-payment.

- $2,500 maximum contribution in any calendar year. ($5,000 for a dependent care FSA)

- FSA may require minimum to claims before payment will occur.

- Up to $500 can be carried over to the following year.

- The plan administrator should allow 90 to 120 days after the end of the year for participants to submit claims.

- An FSA can be used to pay claims incurred during the plan year. Your administrative system should easily distinguish between plan and other years.

- An employee taking advantage of COBRA benefits must have his/her FSA honored during that time.

## 9) MEDICAL SAVINGS ACCOUNTS

Archer Medical Savings Accounts (MSAs) are a variation of Flexible Spending Account (FSAs). An employee can make tax-free contributions to an account. From that account, the employee pays certain types of medical expenses. The benefit is primarily tax-related; expenses are paid with pre-tax vs. post-tax dollars.

The primary drawback of an FSA is the requirement that only $500 can be carried over despite their being contributed directly by that individual. With an MSA, money can accumulate from year to year, and may be used in later years when medical expenses are higher, or can be saved until retirement.

**Here's how MSAs work.** A business may offer its employees, or a self-employed person may purchase, a high-deductible health insurance plan HDHP. The business has to be an employer who had an average of 50 or fewer employees during either of the last 2 calendar years. The employer and employee may then make tax-free contributions to an MSA.

Total annual contributions are limited to 65% of the deductible for individuals and 75% of the deductible for families.

**Contributions:** In addition to the high-deductible health policy, each employee opens
up a MSA savings/investment account. Contributions to the account by an individual are deductible from adjusted gross income, and contributions made by an individual's employer are excluded from income (unless they're made through a cafeteria plan). Contributions may be made for a tax year at any time until the due date of the return for that year (not including extensions). Employer contributions must be reported on the employee's W-2. Earnings of the fund are not included in taxable income for the current year.

**Withdrawals:** Funds may then be withdrawn from the MSA, tax-free, to pay for minor medical expenses — routine checkups, dental exams, eyeglasses, drugs, even minor surgery. Any funds that are left in the MSA at the end of the year remain in the account, and can be used in succeeding years, or saved until retirement. Thus, unlike flexible spending accounts, there is no "use it or lose it" requirement.

If you have few medical expenses over a period of years, the account may grow to a tidy sum. If funds are withdrawn for non-medical purposes, a 15% penalty will be assessed (plus the funds will be taxed as ordinary income). However, after age 65, you may use your MSA monies for any purpose, just like an IRA, and pay only the tax on withdrawn funds.

**Success Tip**
If you have only a few employees, you may want to look at joining a consortium of other small businesses in purchasing benefits. Contact your local chamber of commerce for information about such groups.

# 10) LIFE INSURANCE BENEFITS

Many businesses offer group term life policies to employees. Although a benefit, the coverage is usually insufficient to meet financial needs. And for many, permanent life insurance is cost-prohibitive. Fortunately, "split-dollar" life insurance fills the gap.

Split-dollar insurance means that premiums for the policy are split between the employee and employer. The employer pays the "cash value" portion, while the employee pays the portion relating to insurance protection.

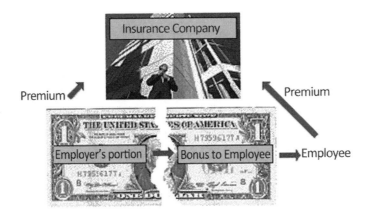

Ultimately, split-dollar insurance costs the employer nothing. Either costs paid by the employer are recovered upon the death of the employee, or through repurchase of premium costs when the employee retires.

The advantages to an owner/shareholder include:

- Low-cost insurance protection

- Benefit of tax-exempt proceeds

- Prevents uninsurability in later years due to illness

- Coverage after retirement, the employee takes a loan for the total of contributions made, then repays the employer; meanwhile, coverage continues

- Lower premiums since policy is based on age at date of issue rather than date of purchase from employer

If the employer pays the employee's part of the premiums and calls it a bonus to the employee, the cost can be deducted by the business, but it will be taxable compensation for the employee.

# 11) VACATIONS

Vacation benefits are not mandated by law, but they are often expected by employees. Small businesses must be especially careful when offering vacation, since a small work force will feel the pinch much more when even one employee is out!

**How much vacation?** How much vacation you decide to give employees is also up to you. In most cases, vacation time earned is directly related to years of service. The greater the service, the more the vacation time earned.

**"Day by day" or "all at once?"** This is entirely dependent upon your type of business – can you afford to have employees on vacation for days at a time? Is your business seasonal, thus requiring "all hands on deck" at certain times of the year? These are important questions to ask when determining vacation policies.

The owner of a small landscaping company gives his employees two weeks per year but makes them take the last week of the year as one of their weeks. They are free to use the other week at any time, subject to approval. Because his business is largely seasonal, he can afford to shut down the entire business for a whole week between Christmas and New Year's Day.

However, allowing employees to take a vacation day here and there without minimum increment requirements allows your employees to take vacation more spontaneously. Advantages to this arrangement are that employees may not take such long vacations, which may mean less interruption in your business.

- There are payroll concerns that you should be aware of if you permit employees to take day-at-a-time vacations. Check with your payroll provider or attorney to ensure that you understand how best to manage this for your business.

- It's best to have a written policy that explains your vacation usage, accrual, and notice policies so that employees can plan most effectively.

# 12) HOLIDAYS

Believe it or not, businesses are not required to give employees holidays off. In fact, depending upon your business, you may even mandate that they work on those days. However, most businesses will offer some holidays to their employees. Here are some things to think about with regard to holidays:

**Whether or not you want to pay employees for them:** Employees who don't get paid for holidays are less likely to take the time off. However, making employees work on a holiday when most others are off, simply because you don't want to pay them for the time, may breed resentment. Time off is a valuable commodity for today's workers.

**What type of business you have:** Naturally, the type of business you have will determine which days you work and which you don't. It is customary to pay employees who do work holidays either time and a half or double time.

**If you want the holiday off:** What the boss does often dictates what the business does. If you are planning to be off on a holiday, consider the impact on morale if you decide to make your employees work. Chances are, when you consider this, you'll close the business and give everyone the day off.

The average number of paid holidays for full-time employees is 9.3. Virtually all companies provide the following as paid holidays:

- New Year's Day

- Memorial Day

- Easter

- Independence Day

- Labor Day

- Thanksgiving Day

- Christmas Day

And they frequently add others from the following list:

- Washington's Birthday or President's Day

- Good Friday

- Dr. Martin Luther King, Jr. Day

- Veterans' Day

- Columbus Day

- The Friday after Thanksgiving

- Christmas Eve

- New Year's Eve

Some businesses add other days, such as a "floating" day, Election Day, or the employee's birthday. Some also have state holidays that they observe.

**Religious holidays:** While the law does not mandate that you give employees paid time off for religious holidays, it is imperative that you accommodate needs of such employees when necessary. Again, although you aren't required to pay them, you should be accommodating.

Here are some options you may want to consider:

- Allow individuals to use vacation (or a floating day off to be taken at the employee's discretion) or other eligible leave pay when observing their religious holidays.

- Grant religious holidays (other than those previously designated as holidays) without pay as an excused absence.

Allow employees to take religious holidays and then make up the time.

## 13) SICK LEAVE

The law does not mandate sick leave benefits, except as dictated by the FMLA. But the truth is, most businesses offer some paid sick leave time for employees.

As with vacation leave, the amount of paid sick leave you offer is entirely up to you. Again, the amount of sick time is often proportional to the employee's years of service. The amount of time:

- Depends on the circumstances, and is at your discretion

- Should be a fixed, predetermined amount, such as ten days each calendar year

- Will mostly likely be based upon the length of service of the employee

If you decide to offer paid sick leave, you might want to have a written policy to explain the procedures and limits of the policy. Some points to include in your policy are:

- How the sick-leave program coordinates with your short-term disability policy, if you have one

- What constitutes a sickness

- Whether the policy extends to a child's or spouse's illness

- Whom an employee should contact in the case of sickness

- Whether employees can accrue and carry over unused sick days from one year to the next

**Personal Leave:**

Personal time off is also a common benefit offered to employees. Personal time off is reserved for situations not included in sick, vacation or other policies. In general, it differs in the following ways:

- Personal time off is usually a few days each year

- Personal time off is given on a "use-it-or-lose-it" basis – employees cannot accrue and carry over personal time

Personal time off is often discretionary. That is, it can sometimes be given "ad hoc" by employers. This is particularly true of long-term, valuable employees. It is important for employers to apply criteria for this as equally and fairly as possible.

**Funeral Leave:**

Funeral or bereavement leave is not legally mandated either. But in many cases, employers will extend this benefit to employees, allowing up to four days for such situations. It is not uncommon for employers to permit taking time off for bereavement, but may require that another form of paid leave be used for compensatory purposes.

If you decide to specifically offer funeral leave, as with all leaves, you may want to have a written policy that will explain the parameters of the program to employees.

**Maternity/Paternity Leave:**

Federal law requires businesses with more than 15 employees to offer women affected by pregnancy, childbirth, or related medical conditions the same benefits as other employees who are unable to work. Pregnant women are to be treated in the same manner as other persons with temporary disabilities for purposes of leave as well as participation in benefit plans and health and disability insurance. Further, if other employees who take disability leave are entitled to get their jobs back when they are able to work again, so are women who are unable to work because of pregnancy.

# 14) MISCELLANEOUS FRINGE BENEFITS

Business owners can offer fringe benefits to their employees pretty much as they wish. In addition to those listed above, many business owners find that adding special, unique benefits tend to increase employees' level of job satisfaction, and increase their feelings of value to the company.

Almost any property or service provided by an employer to an employee as compensation for the employee's performance of services is considered a "fringe benefit." For example, fringe benefits include the following items:

- An employer-provided vehicle

- Free or discounted commercial airline flight through your frequent flyer miles

- Discounts on services or property

- Tickets to a sporting event or other entertainment

- Membership in a country club or social club

Unless fringe benefits are legally excluded from income tax, employees must pay payroll taxes on their value.

---

**Example:**

If you let your sales representatives use a company car for personal purposes, the value of this non-cash fringe benefit must be included in the sales representative's wages as part of his or her compensation.

---

Check with your accountant to determine how to value non-exempt fringe benefits.

What if you don't have any employees? Is it "moot" to consider fringe benefits? Probably not. There may very well be some advantages to your business in the way of available deductions.

**Success Tip**

If you operate your business as a corporation or as a partnership, there may be personal tax implications involved if your business takes a deduction for fringe benefits provided. For example, if your corporation takes a deduction for the cost of certain fringe benefits it gives to you as an employee, you will probably have to include the value of the fringe benefits in your personal income. Depending on what tax bracket you're in, a deduction that your corporation takes could end up costing you money in the long run!

**Certain fringe benefits are exempted from the "taxable wage" rules. They are:**

- No-additional-cost services

- Qualified employee discounts

- Working condition fringe benefits

- Very minimal fringe benefits

- Qualified transportation fringe benefits

Let's discuss each of these in more detail:

### 1) No-Additional-Cost Services

Providing your businesses services/products to employees (and/or their immediate family) for free is an excellent fringe benefit, which many employees appreciate. It is a low or no-cost way to reward your employees.

---

**Example:**

An airline may allow its employees to fly for free when there are empty seats on a plane. Likewise, a hotel chain may allow its employees to use rooms that would otherwise be empty.

---

For these purposes, the definition for the term "employee" applies as follows:

- An individual currently employed by you

- An individual who stopped working for you because of retirement or disability

- A surviving spouse of an individual who died while working for you or who stopped working for you because of retirement or disability

- A partner who performs services for your partnership

An additional "no-cost" benefit is nontaxable, provided it does not add substantial additional cost to provide it. When additional costs are incurred, the employee must be taxed on the entire service.

## 2) Qualified Employee Discounts

Offering employees a price reduction on products or services your company sells is another effective fringe benefit. Most items and services apply, except for personal property usually held for investment, and discounts on real property (buildings or land). These are not considered qualified employee discounts.

Also, there is a limitation on the nontaxable amount of a qualified employee discount you can provide. For property, the nontaxable discount doesn't include any amount that is more than your gross profit percent times the price you charge customers for the property. The gross profit percent is based on all property offered to customers, including your employees that are customers, in the ordinary course of your type of business and your experience during the tax year immediately before the tax year in which the discount is available. To calculate the gross profit percent, subtract the total cost of the property from the total sales price of the property and divide your result by the total sales price of the property. For services, the nontaxable discount doesn't include any amount that is more than 20% of the price you charge customers for the service.

For these purposes, the same definition of the term "employee" applies.

Highly compensated employees may exclude the value of no-additional-cost services and qualified employee discounts ONLY when the benefit is universally available to all employees, and doesn't favor only highly compensated employees. In the event that this standard is not met, the entire benefit is considered taxable.

*A highly compensated employee* is an employee who satisfies either of the following:

- Was a 5% owner of the employer at any time during the current year or the preceding year, or

- Received more than $115,000 in compensation from the employer during the preceding year (employers may use an additional qualification requiring employees to be in the top 20% of employees when ranked by compensation). The $115,000 threshold is for 2014. The threshold amount may be indexed for inflation.

---

**Example:**

As the president of Somerset Apparel Mart, you are the only company employee entitled to a 30% discount on all merchandise. The rest of your employees are entitled to a 10% discount on merchandise purchases. Because of the 20% difference in discount rates (30% less 10%), the IRS will not let you exclude any portion of the discount from your salary because it is discriminatory toward your employees who are not owners. Your employees, on the other hand, will still continue to enjoy the 10% discount and it will not be treated as compensation to them.

---

### 3) Working Condition Fringe Benefits

Certain property or services provided to employees are not considered taxable compensation, provided the employees themselves can deduct the cost as a trade or business expense. Job training, educational assistance programs, meals provided for convenience of employer, and employer provided vehicles used for business fit this category.

The kinds of items that don't qualify as nontaxable working condition fringe benefits include the following:

- Expenses that an employee can deduct under sections of the tax laws other than as trade or business expenses or depreciation

- Physical exams, even if they're mandatory for all or just some of your employees

- Cash payments you make to your employees *unless* you require your employee to use the money for expenses that are deductible in a specific or prearranged activity as trade, business, or depreciation expenses, you verify that the money is used for such expenses, and the employee returns any unused money to you

- Services or property offered through a flexible spending account

For purposes of the working condition fringe benefit, an employee includes:

- An individual currently employed by you

- A partner who performs services for your partnership

- A director of your company

- An independent contractor who performs services for you

**Educational assistance programs.** Educational assistance programs qualify when the cost of the education is job-related. The skills acquired must be for the purposes of maintaining or increasing job-related skills, but that do not qualify the employee for a new occupation.

### 4) Very Minimal Fringe Benefits

A minimal fringe benefit (often referred to as a "*de minimis*" fringe benefit) is any property or service that you provide to your employees that has such a small value that accounting for it would be unreasonable. These benefits are not taxable to your employees.

Minimal benefits must be provided sparingly in order to escape scrutiny by the IRS. Frequency of these benefits is a criterion used by the IRS in determining what does and does not qualify.

The following are some examples of minimal fringe benefits:

- Occasional tickets for entertainment or sporting events

- Holiday gifts (other than cash), with a low fair-market value

- Occasional parties or picnics for employees and their guests

- Coffee, snacks or soft drinks

- Occasional meal money or local transportation fare for employees working overtime (*not* based on hours worked), and for meals provided to enable employees to work overtime

- Typing of a personal letter by the business's secretary or occasional use of a company copying machine

- Group-term life insurance of $2,000 or less payable on the death of an employee's spouse or dependent

**Success Tip**

Cash is never excludable as a minimal fringe benefit, no matter how small the amount. (The only exception is the occasional meal money or local transportation fare listed above.)

## 5) Qualified Transportation Fringe Benefits

Qualified transportation fringe benefits, which are not taxable to the employees but are deductible by you, are the following employee benefits:

- Transportation in a "commuter highway vehicle" (a van pool) if the transportation is between an employee's home and work place. A commuter highway vehicle is any highway vehicle that seats at least six adults, including the driver. Also, you must reasonably expect that at least 80% of the vehicle mileage will be for transporting employees between their homes and the work place. At least half of the vehicle's seats (not including the driver's) must be taken by your employees.

- A transit pass; that is, any pass, token, fare card, voucher, or similar item entitling a person, free of charge or at a reduced rate, to ride mass transit or in a vehicle that seats at least six adults (not including the driver), if the vehicle is operated by a person in the business of transporting persons for compensation or hire. Mass transit can be a publicly or privately operated bus, rail, or ferry service.

- Qualified parking; that is, parking provided to your employees on or near your business premises. Also included is parking provided on or near the location from which your employees commute to work using mass transit, commuter highway vehicles (van pools), or carpools. It doesn't include parking on or near your employee's residence.

Any common-law employee or other statutory employee, including a corporation officer, is eligible for qualified transportation fringe benefits. Self-employed individuals, however, are not considered employees for this benefit.

There are many special rules that apply to qualified transportation fringe benefits. When providing them, it is recommended that you consult with your accountant; he/she will know all special rules that might apply to your business.

# IN CONCLUSION

While the salary you pay a member of your staff is central to his compensation, the fringe benefits you offer will often make the difference between a potential employee choosing to work for you or your fiercest competitor. When it comes to benefits, it is important to take into account many factors about your business. What are the recruiting advantages? Are there potential tax savings? Can you afford it?

In most cases, you will offer your employees at least *some* fringe benefits. Chances are the federal and/or your state governments require that you do. It is critical that you, as a business owner, understand both, the nature of your business – including the competition against which you compete for the best-qualified employees – and the legal requirements regarding fringe benefits. The highly specialized nature of benefits and benefit packages may cause you to consider a "specialist" to help you.  Although there are individuals who specialize only in administration of fringe benefits programs, they are more likely to be found in large corporations.  Consider the services of a human resources administrator, particularly one who is certified in your state.  In most cases, he/she understands the finer points of benefit programs.

# Frequently Asked Questions on Fringe Benefits: Why They Benefit You As Much As Your Employees

### Q. *What does it mean to be "vested" in my retirement plan?*

Vesting refers to one's eligibility to take retirement funds with them when they leave a company.

### Q. *I work for a company and also have a small business of my own. Can I set up a retirement plan for my business even if I'm covered by a plan at work?*

Usually, yes. The restrictions on contributions you can make to a retirement plan are applied to each employer separately. If you work for a company, the company is an employer. If you are self-employed, you are a separate employer, and can have a separate retirement plan for your business. But be careful. If both you and your employer establish some type of salary reduction plan, you might run up against an overall limit on contributions.

The most common types of salary reduction plans are 401(K) plans, tax-deferred annuity or 403(b) plans (these generally cover university professors and public school teachers), and 457 plans (sponsored by state and local governments and other tax-exempt organizations). A SIMPLE IRA is also a salary reduction plan.

Although the amount of your salary or compensation you can defer into each of these plans is limited, the law also puts a limit on the total amount you can defer into all such plans, if you happen to be covered by more than one. The overall limit depends on the type of plan you participate in.

### Q. *Is my retirement plan protected from creditors?*

Thanks to the Employee Retirement Income Security Act of 1974, commonly known as ERISA, Most business plans are safe from creditors. ERISA requires all plans under its purview (generally, qualified plans) to include provisions that prohibit the assignment of plan assets to a creditor. The U.S. Supreme Court has also ruled that ERISA plans are even protected from creditors when you are in bankruptcy.

Unfortunately, Keogh plans that cover only you – or you and your partners, but not employees – are not governed or protected by ERISA. Neither are IRAs, whether traditional, Roth, SEP or SIMPLE.

But even though IRAs are not automatically protected from creditors under federal law, many states have put safeguards in place that specifically protect IRA assets from creditors' claims, whether or not you are in bankruptcy. Also, some state laws contain protective language that is broad enough to protect single-participant Keoghs, as well.

## Q. Is an IRA a retirement plan?

Yes. But it is important to distinguish between a qualified and a non-qualified plan. Qualified plans are established by a business, while certain IRAs are established by individuals. SEPs and SIMPLE IRAs are established by employers. You may have an individual IRA even if you are covered by a business' retirement plan.

## Q. What is the deadline to set up a SEP IRA for my business?

You can set up and fund a SEP IRA through your business's tax filing due date, plus extensions.

## Q. What is the deadline to set up a profit sharing or money purchase plan for my business?

Your company must set up a profit sharing or money purchase plan by the last day of your fiscal year. Contributions may be made through your business's tax filing due date, plus extensions.

## Q. What's the deadline to set up a 401(k) plan?

To allow your employees to get the maximum benefit from salary deferral, it's best to set up your 401(K) as early in the year as possible. 401(K) plans must be established by the last day of your fiscal year, but if the plan is set up late in the year, participants cannot defer compensation already earned. Employee salary deferrals must be sent to the financial institution as soon as possible, and never later than 15 business days after the end of the month. Employer contributions may be made up to the business's tax filing date, plus extensions.

## Q. *What is the difference between a Defined Benefit Plan and a Defined Contribution Plan?*

A defined benefit plan is a company retirement plan in which you expect to receive a fixed amount on a regular basis from your employer, i.e. a pension. The employer is responsible for investing. On the other hand, a defined contribution plan is a company retirement plan in some cases, such as a 401(K) or 403(b), in which the employee elects to defer salary into the plan and directs the investments of that deferral.

## Q. *What is Qualified Retirement Plan (QRP)?*

A tax-deferred plan established by an employer for employees under IRS rules. A qualified retirement plan usually includes provisions for employer contributions (money purchase pension plans) and may also allow employee contributions. Certain deductions and other tax benefits may apply to employer contributions to these plans. The plans build up savings, which are paid out at retirement or on termination of employment. Employees pay taxes only when they withdraw the money.

Examples of qualified retirement plans include 401(K), 403(b), Money Purchase, Profit Sharing, Defined Benefit, and Keoghs.

# CHAPTER 11:

## Insurance: What is Needed and Why

# INTRODUCTION

### Choosing Insurance Coverage

Good insurance coverage is an important part of planning your business' success. When you buy insurance, you secure protection against things that can go wrong. An unexpected event could close your business and ruin you financially. By the same token, don't over-insure. The following pages will help you make the right choice of insurance coverage and carrier. If you have a casualty, that choice can make the difference between losing your business, just scraping by, or being able to carry on with business as usual.

Business insurance is very different from personal insurance. It is important that you consult with a trusted advisor on the subject, and educate yourself about the various options available to you. What do you need? There are many answers to this question, and they will depend solely on the nature and specifics of your business. One thing to keep in mind, however – although separate, your personal insurance is linked to your business' survival. Remember this as you navigate the world of business insurance.

# HEALTH INSURANCE

### Health Insurance Basics

Employees consider health insurance among the most important benefits. Rising healthcare costs and the reigning confusion about health insurance coverage make it essential that business owners understand the various types of plans, and which may be the best fit for your business. Before the advent of managed care plans, fee-for-service plans (FFSs) were the standard form of health care coverage.

## Fee-for-service plans (FFSs)

Fee-for-service plans are the oldest form of health insurance coverage. Also called "indemnity plans", they are the most expensive. If you can afford one, however, FFSs offer the most freedom and flexibility.

Participants choose their own doctors and hospitals, and can refer themselves to specialists with little interference from insurance companies. These plans require large out-of-pocket expenses. Patients pay medical fees up front and then submit bills for reimbursement. Deductibles apply, and preventive services are generally not covered.

## Managed Care Plans

Within the managed care umbrella, you'll find three types of plans — health maintenance organizations (HMOs), preferred provider organizations (PPOs), and point-of-service (POS) plans.

### 1) Health Maintenance Organizations (HMO)

An HMO is the least expensive way to acquire medical insurance. HMOs typically offer a range of health benefits, including preventive care, for a set monthly fee. In exchange for low rates, HMO members give up the freedom to choose their own doctors, being required to use those only within a specific network of physicians. For special needs, primary MDs generally must refer patients – they do not have the luxury of seeking out such practitioners on their own.

### 2) Preferred Provider Organizations (PPO)

A PPO may be more flexible than an HMO, although this plan maintains arrangements/relationships with MDs, hospitals and other healthcare providers. Cost sharing is the basis of a PPO, and practitioners agree in advance to this. Plan members are not required to obtain a reference, but are required to pay the difference between fees for their personal and the network providers.

### 3) Point-of-Service Plan (POS)

Some HMOs offer an indemnity plan known as a POS plan. Members may refer outside of the plan, and in return have a predetermined amount of coverage. If an MD does the referring, the plan pays all or most of the charge.

## Comparing Insurance Options

Be sure to ask the following question when reviewing your insurance options with an agent or broker:

- Is the insurance carrier licensed, accredited, reputable, and financially secure?

- Is the plan easy to administer?

- Are claims processed and paid quickly?

- Are policies renewed every six months or each year?

- Are sufficient financial incentives provided to encourage employees to select network providers?

- Does the insurer provide educational materials to employees?

- Does the insurer underwrite the policy as a group, as individuals, or both?

**Success Tip**
Make sure the insurers submit complete proposals. Competition in the healthcare coverage industry is fierce. Use it to your advantage. Compare. Shop around. Know the companies you are considering.

When comparing healthcare plans, there are three areas you should get complete information on. Here they are and the information you should gather for each:

### Affordability of Coverage

- How much will it cost the company on a monthly basis?

- Should you insure just for major medical expenses or for all medical expenses?

- Are there deductibles to pay before the insurance kicks in?

- After the deductible, what part of the costs is covered by the plan?

- How much more does it cost to see a provider outside the plan?

**Scope of Coverage**

- What doctors, hospitals and other providers are part of the plan?

- Are there enough of the types of doctors you expect to have?

- Are the providers located conveniently for your employees?

- Does the plan require permission for specialist referrals?

- Are there limits to how much will be covered by the plan?

- Does the plan cover the expenses of delivering a baby?

- Does the plan include prescription drugs?

- Does the plan include drug and alcohol treatment, mental-health care, home healthcare, hospice care and physical therapy?

**Quality of Coverage**

- How do independent government organizations rate the plan?

- What do friends and doctors say about their experience with the plan?

# Individual vs. Group Insurance

There are some important, key differences between individual and group insurance plans. While an individual health insurance plan may be highly selective, and seek to limit their liability by denying coverage to those with pre-existing, previously diagnosed or treated health problems, group insurance plans cannot single out high-risk individuals and deny them health coverage. All individuals are covered regardless of their existing health problems, and high-risk individuals are factored into the total cost of the group plan.

The following plan descriptions outline the types of individual and group insurance plans that are widely available:

## Individual Insurance

Individuals can purchase health insurance on their own, but it's usually very costly. This area of coverage is becoming more competitive, and there are some organizations that provide individual coverage at slightly better rates than in the past. Still, it's an expensive option in most cases.

## Group Insurance

Commonly, individuals obtain health coverage through some kind of group plan. Typically, these plans may cover health, dental, vision, life, and disability needs. Other types may include short and long term disability, prescription drug coverage, and even long term and dependent care.

## Indemnity plans.

Individuals pay a set deductible and a percentage of covered expenses with an indemnity plan. After a predetermined out-of-pocket amount is reached, the health plan pays further expenses. Participants with indemnity and other fee-for-service plans are free to use any doctor or hospital and file claims for reimbursement.

## Medical savings accounts.

A medical savings account (MSAs) is a tax-free trust from which medical bills and deductibles are paid. Individuals use funds in their MSA to cover small medical bills, and instead use health insurance for major, catastrophic needs. In some cases, health insurance premiums can actually be reduced.

## Managed care

Financial incentives in the form of reduced co-payments are offered in managed care plans. Typically, these plans establish a network of doctors and other providers who agree to limit their fees in return for a guaranteed number of patients. As discussed earlier, HMOs and PPOs are common types.

**Success Tip**

The success of a small business, whether it's a tiny enterprise run out of your home or a large corporation, is dependent on many factors discussed throughout this book. However, no matter how industrious you are at implementing these strategies, one disaster can wipe out all your profits and even destroy your business. The key to making sure that all the effort and money you have invested in a business don't disappear when a disaster strikes is to protect it with the appropriate insurance.

# BUSINESS OWNER'S INSURANCE

### Business Owner's Policy (BOP) Basics

Basically, there are three types of insurance that are available to protect your business: property, general liability and workers' compensation. In addition, laws in all 50 states require workers' compensation insurance.

Packages of insurance for business owners provide property and liability coverage, usually at a reasonable price. This may be the first insurance consideration for any business owner, since it is quite basic. In some cases, large companies and businesses considered "high risk" may not meet the criteria for a BOP. Your insurance advisor can help you determine what your business may or may not be qualified for.

### What Does a BOP Cover?

A BOP typically protects business property and property brought onto your premises by others. Fire, theft, floods, and earthquakes are typically included in the BOP coverage. A business selects the amount of liability coverage it needs based on its assets. Liability coverage pays for the cost of defending the business in a lawsuit and pays damages if the business is sued for injury or property damage. The liability policy also pays the medical expenses of those injured, other than employees, as a result of business operations.

Business interruption insurance is part of a BOP. This type of insurance covers income lost from disasters and also provides coverage for operating expenses – payroll and other business activities, for example.

In addition to the basic BOP policy, businesses may purchase add-on coverage based on the particular risks associated with the company. You might consider coverage for employee dishonesty, for example, which covers loss of business property due to embezzlement, fraud, or another criminal act.

Business insurance is intended to provide full and complete coverage for the business. As such, it is critical that you understand how to make insurance purchasing decisions. Make sure your advisor understands your needs, and that you understand what you're buying. It is important to be sufficiently insured, but not over (or under) insured.

# PROPERTY INSURANCE

### Property Insurance Basics

When damage, theft, or loss occurs, property insurance will cover your work premises and contents of your workspace. Inventory, furniture, machinery, supplies, etc. – all are covered.

Many insurance companies offer special insurance supplements, and depending on your needs, geographical location, risk, etc., you may want to consider them. Multiple peril policies can often provide additional essential coverage, specific to your needs.

As a business owner, you have control over your own level of risk. Take steps to prevent loss – hire security personnel to prevent shoplifting, install a sprinkler system to contain fires or use an alarm system to protect against theft – each of these, and other measures, can help control the cost of property insurance.

## Optional Coverage

Two types of optional coverage in a property insurance policy that protect a business after a loss occurs are:

> **Business-interruption insurance** provides payments for expenses such as salaries, taxes and debts, as well as any loss of profit due to the interruption of business.

**Extra-expense insurance** pays the costs of temporarily relocating a business when a covered peril occurs.

---

**Example:**

A fire at Edison Office Supplies last year destroyed a major part of their inventory, fixtures, and office equipment. Thanks to their insurance advisor, the owner, Bob had purchased the optional extra-expense insurance coverage. The insurance company paid Bob $28,000 to resume operations and cover such expenses as buying or leasing equipment, re-stocking the inventory, and notifying their customers about changes that have occurred.

---

**Success Tip**

Although a BOP (discussed earlier) bundles property and liability insurance into one policy and some BOPs also include business-interruption and extra-expense insurance, it is advisable for companies that require a lot of coverage to stick with a separate policy.

# GENERAL LIABILITY

### General Liability Insurance Basics

General liability insurance is a key part of any business' insurance defense plan. In today's litigious society, even small mishaps can result in large lawsuits. For this reason, general liability insurance, along with property and worker's compensation insurance, are crucial for most companies. Liability insurance protects the business when it is sued for something it did or didn't do to cause an injury or property damage.

As with property insurance, general liability insurance can also be purchased separately or as part of a business-owner's policy (BOP). A BOP bundles property and liability insurance into one policy; however, the liability coverage limits are generally pretty low. Businesses that need more coverage usually purchase liability insurance as a separate policy. The amount of coverage a business needs depends on two factors:

- **Perceived risk.** Business owners should first consider the amount of risk associated with their business. For example, a business that manufactures heavy machinery is at a greater risk of being sued than a company that manufactures linens and would therefore need more liability insurance.

- **The state in which you operate.** Businesses that operate in states with a history of awarding high damage amounts to plaintiffs typically need to carry liability insurance with higher coverage limits.

## How General Liability Works

Under a general liability insurance policy, the insurer is obligated to pay the legal costs of a business in a covered liability claim or lawsuit. Covered liability claims include bodily injury, personal injury, property damage, advertising injury, compensatory damage, and general damages. Punitive damages aren't covered under general liability insurance policies because they are considered punishment for intentional acts.

General liability policies specify a maximum to be paid in the event of a claim. For example, a $2 million occurrence cap would mean that an insurer would pay no more than $2 million, despite what a claim award might be.

Many companies purchase "umbrella liability insurance", which picks up where their general liability coverage ends. Umbrella liability provides additional coverage for liabilities not covered in a standard liability insurance policy.

Taking precautions before an accident can help keep your liability and your insurance rates down. All businesses can take certain steps to lower the chance of a liability insurance claim:

- Set a high standard for product quality control.

- Make sure all employees are properly trained.

- Make sure all company records are complete and up-to-date.

- Get safety tips for your type of business from your insurance company.

**Success Tip**
General liability insurance tends to have a lot of exclusions. Be sure you understand exactly what your policy does and doesn't cover. You may want to purchase additional liability policies to cover specific concerns, such as product liability insurance, auto liability insurance, errors and omissions liability, and directors and officers insurance.

# WORKERS' COMPENSATION

Every state has enacted workers' compensation laws to protect employees against loss of income and for medical payments due to a work-related injury, accident, illness, or disease. In the vast majority of states, workers' compensation coverage is mandatory. This section will give you guidance in determining what is required. Still, you should spend quality time with your insurance agent or broker to ensure that you understand the coverage details and expectations.

### Do the laws apply to you?

In most states, all employers who have at least one employee are covered. While some states exempt very small employers, they don't all have the same definition of what constitutes a small employer.

Some states require that all employers provide for the payment of obligations to injured employees or to the dependents of deceased employees through a workers' compensation insurance policy or through self-insurance approved by the Commissioner of the Department of Banking and Insurance. Sole proprietorships, partnerships and limited liability companies (LLCs) are exempt from this rule if the only employees are the business owner or partners or members of the LLC.

### How Can You Control Workers' Compensation Costs?

The best way to control the cost of workers' compensation insurance premiums is to avoid injury claims. A safe environment, effective safety training and ongoing programs are keys to preventing employee injury.

In most states, workers' compensation is "no fault." This means that on-the-job injuries are covered by workers' compensation insurance regardless of the cause of the accident. In other words, if employees are injured on the job due to their careless or foolish behavior, those accidents are covered by your workers' compensation insurance. This is why it is very important to continually promote safety awareness and safe work habits.

An important factor in controlling workers' compensation rates is by using the proper industry classification codes for your employees. There are over 600 different codes that identify professions with the maximum risk of on-the-job injury. I frequently see employers make the mistake to classify their entire staff under a single code.

Another common error is to assign the code of office clerk to all administrative personnel. Your administrative personnel may not perform the same job duties, and there are different classifications that carry different levels of risk. For instance, a filing assistant typically doesn't use a keyboard. A data entry clerk, on the other hand, generally runs a much higher risk of carpal tunnel injury due to a heavy use of the computer keyboard.

**Success Tip**

Use the most up-to-date classification codebook for your state to be certain you're classifying employees correctly, and familiarize yourself with the appropriate codes for your employees.

## What Happens When You Don't Have Enough Workers' Compensation Insurance?

Due to being heavily regulated on the state level, the workers' compensation system ensures that businesses carry enough insurance to cover the costs of work-related injury. Thus, unlike most types of business and personal insurance, it's very difficult to find yourself underinsured.

Workers' compensation insurance is directly related to the size of your work force and is calculated by your payroll. Each state performs mandatory audits to ensure that companies are carrying the appropriate level of workers' compensation coverage.

# AUTO LIABILITY

Auto insurance for business works similarly to personal coverage. It covers damages when your vehicle is involved in an accident resulting in injury and/or property damage. Commercial auto coverage may cost much more than personal insurance. But without it, your insurance company may leave you high and dry. Consider adding affordable coverage for hired and non-owned autos; this covers rental cars and employees using their own cars, for example.

# DISABILITY INSURANCE

### Do you need Disability Insurance?

The statistics in this paragraph should help you answer the question whether you need disability insurance. Do you know that at the age of 25, your chances of having at least one long-term disability that will put you out of action for three months or more before you reach the age of 65 is 44%. Those are pretty high odds. 35? A 41% chance of long-term disability! It doesn't go away as you get older, either. One in seven people will be disabled for at least 5 years before reaching age 65. Although we often insure against death, disability is twice as likely to happen to people between the ages of 25 and 50. Unless you are prepared for it to happen, financial stress can be added to the pain of your disability.

Unfortunately, Social Security can be difficult to qualify for because you must be unable to work at any job, period. Even if you do qualify for Social Security disability, it will be at least six months before you can begin to collect it. Workers' compensation will only cover injuries and illnesses that occur on the job and, only if you have coverage.

As a practical matter, though, not everyone can afford disability insurance. Some insurance agents won't even recommend it unless the insured is making at least $40,000 per year. Instead, they suggest that you have 6 months' worth of replacement income set aside in a bank or money market account in case of trouble, then rely on Social Security to cover longer term problems.

Disability insurance guarantees you will be paid if you are unable to run your business. Still, it does not replace all of your income. In general, disability insurance will cover up to 65% of your current salary.

Finding the right policy involves making sure you understand what it means to be "disabled." If you own a small construction company and are no longer able to work in the field but could do a desk job, the broadest coverage would probably pay you. Some policies will pay benefits if the individual cannot work at a job "consistent with one's education, training, and experience." There is also replacement income, which pays if you can continue work in the same field but only with reduced earnings.

The least protective policies would only cover you if you cannot work at all. How much should you buy? Look at your day-to-day living needs and how much you have "in reserve." What do you need to pay the bills? What kinds of features should you consider when shopping for disability coverage? Let's start with inflation. If costs go up and you have a long-term disability, you could lose ground every year. Look at a policy that offers cost of living adjustments that go up with the Consumer Price Index. Another option is to find a policy that goes up by a certain amount per year, say 5% a year for 5 years.

Guaranteed insurability is an important feature to consider when purchasing an insurance policy. With this feature, you can buy more insurance as your need goes up without having to prove that you're still in good health.

You can save money on premiums by extending the waiting period for your policy to pay you. It's less expensive if you can wait 90 days before getting your first payment. For short-term insurance, payment doesn't usually start until at least 30 days after the disability. Long-term insurance can take up to six months to begin payments.

In each case, it is critical that you cover yourself. You are the principal business owner, and thus, your presence is essential to the successful operation of your business. What happens in the event you are unable to work? What happens if you lose the business as a result? Answering these questions should make it clear why you should take care of yourself FIRST.

Disability insurance as an employee benefit can be critical to retaining employees. In addition to a disability plan that covers all qualified individuals, you may want to offer a disability wage continuation plan to key employees. In this case, the employee is covered by an additional individual policy. Usually, the employee applies for and owns the individual plan and your company pays part or the entire premium to them. Your contributions to a wage continuation plan can be excluded from the employee's income and part or all of your payments may be tax deductible to your company as reasonable compensation.

As a small-business owner, you may want to consider two additional disability coverages. One is for business overhead expense, which, during your disability, pays for ongoing expenses. Examples are paying employees, rent, leases, taxes, worker's compensation, utilities, professional dues, insurance, and other costs of keeping your business operational while you are disabled. In the case of multiple ownership of a business, you may have a buy-sell agreement that you might want to implement if one of the owners becomes disabled and can no longer work. A disability buyout policy can be purchased that would pay for the buyout.

**Success Tip**

Pay close attention to your policy when you buy it. Make sure that you understand the definition of disability in the contract and what it means to your coverage. Research and find out the answers to these questions:

How long will it be between a disability and the first payout? How long will payments continue? Under what circumstances does an insured individual lose disability payments? What happens if the insured person returns to work and the disability is re-triggered? Can an employee, or yourself, convert it to an individual policy if the business changes its insurance coverage plans? Are there any disabilities that the policy doesn't cover, like carpal tunnel syndrome?

## CASE STUDY

Integrated Matrix, Inc. (IMI), a small corporation, provided highly specialized computer programming services to banks. The firm was founded and run by 2 shareholders, Joseph Levitt and Michael Ross. Ross was responsible for the marketing and management side of the business while Levitt was the senior programmer involved with customer interface and design. Eleven years after the start of the business, Levitt was disabled in an accident. As a result of losing Levitt, the company also lost its technical programming capability. Levitt, who had been involved in several high dollar value computer projects, was not available to complete them or be there to train his replacement. As a result, the company lost considerable sums of money and had to file for bankruptcy. This could have been easily avoided with a "key-man" policy.

# LIFE INSURANCE

### What Would Happen To Your Company If You Died Or Became Disabled?

Unfortunately, most small-business owners do nothing to plan for the event of an untimely death or disability. One recent survey of family businesses revealed that only 57% of business owners have buy-sell agreements among shareholders, and of those, 92% do not set aside funds to purchase the shares. Most assume their families will deal with those issues and see the threat as remote. In the event of your untimely death or disability, chances are your family, partners, key employees, rank and file, suppliers, and customers will depend on your success and the smooth continuation of your business.

How does one appropriately plan for this? You implement a buy-sell agreement. Buy-sell agreements can provide an effective way to transfer ownership of a closely held company back to the business or to the partners or key employees. This type of contract between owners of a business can help the surviving owners buy out the interest of a deceased or disabled co-owner. This strategy can be beneficial to provide for the family of the deceased owner and to ensure the continuation of the business for the remaining owners.

A well-drafted and properly funded buy-sell agreement will set a value for the business, or at least designate a specific formula to use in determining the value. And it will also specify the funding vehicle to be used for the buyout. These measures take much of the guesswork out of the transfer of ownership and reduce the amount of strain put on the business and the family of the deceased business owner

There are three main types of buy-sell agreements:

### a) Cross-Purchase Plan

Also referred to as a "survivor purchase plan." Under this plan, the surviving owner purchases the deceased owner's share of the business. A well-liked funding approach is for each business owner to have a life insurance policy on the other owner. By having the cross-purchase plan in place, the family of the deceased owner is paid a fair price in a timely manner for its interest in the business. And the remaining owners preserve their control over the business without the threat of outside intervention.

### b) Entity Plan

Under an entity plan, the difference compared to the cross-purchase plan is that the business itself agrees to purchase the interest of a deceased or disabled owner. Like is the case with the cross-purchase plan, the value of the business and all other details of the sale are agreed to in advance. This approach achieves the same objectives of providing for the family of the deceased business owner as well as the continuation of the business itself.

### c) Hybrid Plan

Also referred as a "Wait and See Plan," a hybrid agreement is set up similar to a cross-purchase plan. This type of agreement ensures the owner's family of a ready market for its share of the business when one of the business owners dies. The eventual buyer is typically not specified at the time the agreement is made but done so at the owner's death. This gives the surviving owner the freedom to choose the best funding option at that time. A hybrid agreement offers flexible purchasing options.

# FUNDING A BUY-SELL AGREEMENT

## A small business or its owners can fund a buy-sell agreement in several ways:

**1. Existing Funds.** If sufficient capital is readily accessible, the corporation could buy the deceased or disabled owner's shares of the company with existing funds. The reality is that many business owners often have their assets invested in assets that are not liquid or easily exchanged for cash. Because there is no assurance that sufficient funds will be available, using existing funds may be the riskiest approach.

**2. Borrowed Funds.** If funds are to be borrowed, it is important to recognize that the buyer will automatically pay more than the original cost of the purchase. The company will have to determine the impact this added burden will have on the business.

**3. Sinking Fund.** This approach requires the business to make deposits to a fund that can be used to redeem a shareholder's stock. The problem with this approach is that if the owner is disabled or passes away in the early years following the agreement, a sinking fund may prove inadequate. This may force the business to scramble for cash to fund the buyout and scale back on some of its business plans to meet this need.

**4. Not Funded.** An alternative approach is not to fund the buy-sell agreement at all. Instead, installment payments from the after-tax earnings of the corporation could be used to purchase a deceased owner's share of the business. The benefit of this approach for the buyer is that it stretches out the cost of purchasing the business over a period of time. This can make a buyout more affordable on an annual basis. But in some cases, the estate of the former owner may need all the proceeds up front to pay estate taxes and other expenses. In these instances, installment payments would be an unfavorable choice. And once again, the ability of the buyer to make future payments depends on the future success of the business.

**5. Life and Disability Insurance.** One of the most widely accepted ways to fund the purchase of an owner's shares in a business is through the use of insurance. Life insurance and disability insurance can provide complete financing in the event of death or a long-term disability. Cash will be available at the time of need, regardless of the timetable. This can help give the owners and the business a confident feeling about the transfer of ownership. The policy proceeds are generally free of income tax to the beneficiary. This preserves the buying power of the benefits. However, you should be aware that life insurance benefits could potentially be subject to the alternative minimum tax. This is generally my preferred approach to fund a buy-sell agreement.

**Success Tip**
There are several ways to fund a buy-sell agreement. Begin by evaluating your business finances. Do you have excess cash reserves? What is your credit rating? What is the outlook for the business's future success? Most important, always consider the choices and preferences of your family. Seek the advice of a financial professional to help narrow down the list of appropriate choices.

# PROFESSIONAL LIABILITY INSURANCE

This insurance protects you in the event your advice/counsel results in a negative event for one of your clients. Professional liability insurance covers professional negligence or errors and omissions; in most cases it is inexpensive.

**Success Tip**
If you buy this policy, make sure that legal costs are covered. In my mind, that's probably the most important coverage – payment for your legal counsel. Even if a lawsuit has no merit, you lose both time and money defending yourself.

# DIRECTORS AND OFFICERS COVERAGE

This coverage protects your board members and company officers in lawsuits where misrepresentation or mismanagement is alleged. It also covers errors or omissions (but not negligence) in disclosing financial information.

# EMPLOYMENT PRACTICES LIABILITY

With this insurance, your defense and damages are covered up to the policy limit when you are challenged for ending employment, sexual harassment, discrimination for age, sex, ethnicity, religion, pregnancy, or disabilities. These claims are usually not covered under general liability and may or may not be covered under workers compensation.

# KEY EMPLOYEE LIFE INSURANCE POLICY

The loss of a key person can be a major blow to a small business if that person is the key contact for customers and suppliers and the management of the business.

Losses caused by the death of a key employee are insurable. Such policies will compensate the business against significant losses that result from that person's death or disability. The amount and cost of insurance needed for a particular business depends on the situation and the age, health and role of the key employee.

Key employee life insurance pays a death benefit to the company when the key employee dies. The policy is normally owned by the company, which pays the premiums and is the beneficiary.

**Success Tip**
Deductibles are a part of most insurance policies. A "deductible" refers to the amount of any claim that must be paid for out of pocket by the business. In general, policies with higher deductibles have lower premiums. Your first instinct might be to select an insurance policy with a low deductible, but this might not save you money in the long run. Think carefully before you choose a policy with a lower monthly premium and a higher deductible; if you opt for this type of plan, you'll have to pay a higher deductible when an accident or incident occurs.

## Insurance Rating Services[5]

When choosing an insurance company, it is important to pick one that's financially secure. Several rating agencies evaluate the financial strength of a given insurer. The ratings are similar to grading for students, generally running from a low of "F" to a high of "A." However, take note: there are many different levels of "A" – therefore, weaker insurers can still tout the "A" ranking.

Below you will find some tried and true ways of deciphering insurance ratings systems. Be familiar with these when shopping for insurance, and as always, check with your broker or agent.

- ## A.M. Best

This rating agency publishes the annual Best's Insurance Reports, which rates the insurers. Unlike the other services, A.M. Best rates only insurance companies, and it rates the entire market. Top financial-strength ratings fall in the categories of superior (A++, A+) and excellent (A, A-). http://www.ambest.com/.

- ## Standard & Poor's

Standard & Poor's offers a less comprehensive rating service of insurers. However, private financial data is analyzed by the company when determining the rating. Companies that earn their highest ratings are virtually sure to be solid. Highest financial-strength ratings are AAA (extremely strong) and AA (very strong). Standard & Poor's also designates certain companies as Security Circle insurers. These companies must rank in the top four categories for financial strength and submit to a comprehensive initial review and undergo ongoing monitoring.

- ## Duff & Phelps

This agency specializes in rating small to medium size insurers. Companies with high claims paying ability get marks of AAA, AA+, AA and AA-. In addition to its ratings, Duff & Phelps' Solvency Seal identifies companies that have been in operation five years or longer and show strong long- and short-term capacity to pay claims.

- ## Moody's

Moody's ratings cover global life, property and casualty, mortgage and title insurers, and reinsurers plus financial guarantors. Look for companies with financial strength ratings of Aaa (exceptional) or Aa (excellent).

- ## Weiss Research

This company sticks to a straight report-card style rating system. Excellent financial strength ratings are A+, A and A-. Ratings aren't available online, but you can call 800-291-8545 to find a library near you that carries Weiss ratings books.

**Success Tip**

In addition to researching the ratings of an insurance company, you should also examine how a company ranks across its entire range of services and from agency to agency. This will give you a better idea of its overall financial stability. Ratings tell you only how able a company is to pay claims – not how willing. A personal referral or your agent's advice can help you get a feel for how quickly claims are settled. Another important source is your state insurance department because it collects complaints from consumers against their health carriers.

# When choosing an insurance provider, should I focus more on the reputation of the company or on the insurance agent / broker?

Your focus should essentially be on both. Here are various questions you should ask in each case.

### Insurance agents/brokers

Using an insurance broker can help sort out the confusing world of business insurance. A local broker knows the insurance carriers in your area and can help you find the best plan for your business. Check with friends, colleagues, and others whom you trust in order to select a good insurance broker.

Interestingly, most brokers' services are free. Insurance carriers pay brokers for connecting them with customers, so brokers don't pass any costs along to you. Yet another reason to seek out the advice of one who is qualified, and enlist that person to serve your insurance purchasing needs. Here are some questions to ask when interviewing an agent/broker:

- How long have you been in business?

- Which insurance companies do you work with?

- How are you compensated?

- What insurance carrier do you do the most business with?

- How much clout do you have to resolve a tough claim or coverage dispute?

- Which insurers specialize in covering my type of business?

- Do you have errors and omissions coverage?

- What are the industry segments you serve?

If the agent is unwilling to answer these questions, find somebody else.

**Insurance companies**

Ask an agent the following questions about individual insurance companies:

- What is their reputation for paying claims?

- What is their financial rating?

- Have they been in and out of the market or are they a long-term player?

- Can they offer multiple year policies?

# IN CONCLUSION

Businesses, like people, need protection from the unexpected. If longevity and perpetuity are goals for your business (and why wouldn't they be?), the time and care you take to purchase business insurance will prove an extremely important endeavor. True, researching and buying insurance coverage may not be the most exciting thing on your "to do" list. Woody Allen said, "There are many things worse than death. If you've ever spent an evening with an insurance salesman, you know exactly what I'm talking about."

But when it comes to worthwhile pursuits, it's hard to argue that anything else is more important or necessary. Tragedies can happen. They will occur. And when they do, not having proper insurance coverage can end in the complete destruction of your business. Business insurance is available to prevent this very tragedy, and is so readily accessible and affordable; there is no need to take such risks.

There is a lot to learn. Take your time. Do your research. Talk to people who know about the subject. And in doing so, you will assure yourself (and your loved ones) of complete protection from unforeseen events. When you do decide to purchase business insurance, you will have the benefit of this knowledge behind you, and most importantly, peace of mind to know that longevity and perpetuity are very attainable goals.

# Frequently Asked Questions on Insurance

### Q. What type of insurance coverage should I obtain for my business?

Business owners should have adequate liability, property/casualty, loss of use, unemployment, workers' compensation, and product insurance. A qualified agent should review your commercial coverage needs annually.

### Q. What is property insurance?

Property insurance protects your buildings and equipment, stock, furniture, and fixtures. In some policies, equipment breakdown and loss of income are also covered.

### Q. How much property insurance does my small business need?

Insurance needs are based on property's actual value (replacement minus depreciation), its full replacement value, or a mutually agreeable amount.

### Q. How does liability insurance coverage protect my small business?

Business liability insurance may protect you from claims arising from someone's bodily or personal injuries. Other items that could be covered are damage to the property of others, products-completed operations, advertising, premises operations, fire, legal liability, and related legal defense costs.

### Q. What exactly does the term "bodily injury" in a liability insurance policy mean?

This refers to the injury, sickness, disease, or even death, of any person that occurs during the policy period.

### Q. What does "personal and advertising injury" mean in general liability insurance coverage?

Personal and advertising injury refers to libel, slander or any defamatory or disparaging material, or a publication or utterance in violation of an individual's right of privacy; wrongful entry or eviction, or other invasion of the right of private occupancy; false arrest, wrongful detention, false imprisonment, or malicious prosecution; which occurs during the policy period.

## Q. *What's the difference between claims-made coverage and prior acts coverage?*

Claims-made refers to claims during the policy period; prior acts refers to events that may have occurred before the inception of a policy, but are not yet known.

## Q. *How does an umbrella insurance policy work?*

An "umbrella" policy provides protection over and above other general coverage policies – liability, auto, etc. Umbrella coverage kicks in when other coverage limits have been met.

## Q. *What does workers' compensation insurance do?*

Workers' compensation pays for the rehabilitation, recovery and medical bills of employees' work-related injuries, as well as lost time when they are unable to work because of a work-related injury. Workers' compensation is not a substitute for health or medical insurance, since employees are only covered for on-the-job injuries.

## Q. *When do I need to buy workers' compensation insurance?*

In most states, workers' compensation is required when you have one or more employees. There are a few states that do not require employers to carry workers' compensation coverage.

## Q. *Where do I buy workers' compensation?*

In most states, coverage is underwritten by private insurers; other states are considered to be "closed" or "monopolistic" - the coverage is underwritten by a state-sponsored fund (ND, OH, WA, WV, WY). In an open market, the rates for workers' compensation are competitive.

## Q. *How much does workers' compensation insurance cost?*

Workers' compensation pricing is based upon your employee payroll, the number and job classification of the employees, classification of your business and past loss experience. The employer pays for the cost of the workers' compensation.

## Q. *Why should I purchase commercial auto insurance?*

A commercial auto policy provides coverage for autos owned by a business if these vehicles are in an accident. Personal auto insurance does not.

## Q. *Will my employees' personal cars be covered under a commercial auto policy if they are using their cars for business?*

Most commercial auto insurance policies cover the liability for a business if employees use their own cars for business, provided that the business owner has purchased coverage for non-owned liability. In most cases, however, the employees' personal auto policy would be the primary coverage for damage to their automobiles.

## Q. *What is errors & omissions insurance?*

"E&O" is also referred to as professional liability or malpractice insurance. This type of liability insurance would cover you and your employees in the event someone claims you incorrectly performed or failed to perform your professional duties. In general, E&O insurance covers those who dispense advice, make recommendations, design solutions, or represent others.

## Q. *What is a business owners' policy or a "BOP"?*

BOP combines property and liability insurance in one policy, and usually includes additional coverage at little or no additional cost. It provides only broad coverage, and is available as a customized package of coverage, depending on your business. It is very important that business owners be properly insured. Keep in mind – BOP coverage may not be enough. Check with your independent agent, who is most qualified to advise you on what coverage your small business needs.

## Q. *What is business income insurance?*

This insurance may reimburse you for the net income that would have been earned if, for example, a fire or other covered causes of loss had not occurred. Losses due to down time or extra expenses needed to restore operations (such as additional property rental) also may be covered.

## Q. *What is employment practices liability insurance?*

Employment practices liability insurance (EPLI) is designed to protect employers against claims of employee sexual harassment, discrimination, wrongful termination and other employment-related litigation. Many insurance companies offer employment practices liability insurance as part of their business owners' policy or as a stand-alone policy.

# CHAPTER 12

## Planning the Exit:
## Leaving Your Business

## INTRODUCTION
### What is an "exit from a business"?

There will be some point in the future when you may want to "get out" of your business, that is, exit it. It may be that you want to retire or have received a "good offer" for the business and it may be time to get into something else. It could be that your business has done so well that it's time to jump on the "early retirement" bandwagon and transfer the responsibilities to your children.

On the contrary, perhaps your business is more than what you had bargained for: it's requiring too much time and energy for the profits it is generating. Exiting it will be "a weight off your shoulders." Other common reasons for exiting a business might include divorce, the death of a partner or co-owner, pressure from family members who think you ought to retire, or your own health.

Don't wait until one of these events described above confronts you. Start thinking about your exit strategy now, even though it might be a long time before you actually need to make it. That way, you'll have lots of time to consult with professionals and put your plan in place. Importantly, you will also optimize your chances of getting the most financial and personal satisfaction from the results. The degree of care and effort you put into the sales process could have a huge impact on the price you receive and how long it will take to complete that sale and leave you free to pursue your pleasures!

It's probably going to take you a lot of time and effort to sell your business. Anyone who makes an offer is going to demand a great deal of information regarding the business. You are going to have to determine how much you want to divulge prior to the sale. And you are going to have to spend an extensive amount of time with prospective buyers explaining the "ins and outs" of your particular business.

Remember that during this process it will continue to be necessary for you to devote enough energy, time, and other resources to maintaining the business in good shape. And don't forget to carefully weigh the impact of announcing that the business is for sale to your employees, customers, vendors, bankers, and other people you do business with.

Selling a business also involves handling a lot of legal issues. You should prepare to consult an attorney before you draw up a prospectus, which, typically describes the business right up to the time the sale closes.

## Exit Routes

There are 3 typical exit strategies. They are:

1) Pass the business on to children or other family members.

2) Sell the business as a going concern or liquidate the business and sell the assets.

3) File for bankruptcy, if all else fails and the business has substantial debts.

If your heirs aren't interested or qualified to take over your business, it may be time to sell the business as a going concern or to sell the assets of the business. For some, the third choice, bankruptcy, however unfortunate, may be an option.

## i) Passing the business on to children or other family members

Transfer of a business to family members can be challenging. There are numerous issues to deal with: family, tax and estate issues, to name a few. Proper planning for succession in a family business is a priority. The record shows that less than 30% of family businesses survive into the second generation and fewer than 15% of them endure into the third. This is a sad fact for the families who, for the most part, took decades to build their business. Since much of our economy is made up of small, family-owned businesses, this is also bad news for the nation's economic health. If the business of succession is not done by *process* (through planning), it will be done by *crisis* (a failure to plan), with perhaps devastating consequences.

**Success Tip**
Attention is required in 2 areas when transferring a family owned business. The first is the *transfer of power*, a process during which control over the business's operation is transferred to those best suited to exercising it. The second is the *transfer of assets* whereby the ownership of the assets in the business is transferred to designated family members.

## ii) Selling the Business

An entrepreneur may not experience his greatest challenge until he attempts to sell the business. This action, perhaps more than any other, typically has far-reaching financial and emotional consequences.

When you started your own business, you probably weren't thinking ahead to the day you would sell it. But after years of hard work spent building your enterprise into a success, that time has now come. You'd like to move on to the next phase of your life.

Selling your business is a one-time event. You get one chance to put a price tag on years and years of effort – and once you sign the sales documents, it's over. You'll come out way ahead, both financially and personally, if you make an effort to understand the steps in selling, formulate your plan carefully with the help of your professional advisors and, when the time comes, take the time to negotiate a price and terms that satisfy your reasons for getting out of the business.

Even if you think you're many years away from selling out, you should consider what your heirs or successors would have to do if you died unexpectedly. If you don't have a workable exit strategy in place, you (or your heirs) may have no choice but to liquidate the business and sell off the assets one at a time, getting little or *nothing* for the goodwill you've built up over the course of the years.

**Success Tip**

Too often, I see genuine hardworking people who have struggled and persevered to build up a good successful business become disappointed and confused when they realize, following the sale, that they failed to reap the richly deserved benefits of all their hard work.

When selling, they don't know what to do or where to go and without knowledge, failed to present their business effectively to potential buyers.

Even if you are not yet intending to sell, reading this section of the chapter will not only give you a better appreciation of your own business, but also exposure to some pertinent principles.

Here are some things to think about now, long before you ever consider selling:

# 1) Preliminary planning

## a) Develop an understanding of your potential buyer

Begin to develop a list of potential buyers – your customers, suppliers, employees, community, or industry competition. Do any seem to be possible candidates to be interested in purchasing your company? Are there any you would rule out as someone you would *not* want to sell to?

## b) When would you like to sell your business?

What is the best time to sell your business? How long it will take? After looking at other businesses sold in your industry, how long do you anticipate it will take?

## c) What terms will your offer the potential buyer?

How much of the purchase price do you want to receive at closing? Will you consider an installment sale? Will you hold a promissory note? To what extent will you remain involved in the business after the sale?

## 2) Put your business in order

a) **Records should be formalized** with all transactions clearly documented, so that a new manager can take over with minimal training. Eliminate idiosyncrasies: If you have similar vendors or customers who are receiving different payment terms, or if you've been generous and forgiving to friends and relatives, try to establish more unilateral rules. The new owner will not want to face the customer who expects special treatment or, worse yet, be the ogre who cancels a long-standing verbal agreement with the company's oldest customer. If handshake pacts cannot be canceled, document the arrangement so the buyer is not surprised.

b) **Examine all supplier and customer contracts**. Make sure terms and conditions will not expire or require renegotiation just as a new owner unpacks. Terminate contracts that might trouble a potential buyer or that drain the company financially or serve little purpose.

As you examine records, **codify current company policies and procedures.** Eliminate all "unwritten rules." If necessary, create a procedure manual that documents exactly how to best run the business, and be sure to include your unspoken, undocumented techniques.

c) **Review your real estate leases**, especially if your business is tied to its location. Make sure the lease does not expire or require renegotiation at the same time you plan to sell the company. If the company's location will discourage buyers, consider moving the location before you place the business for sale.

Equipment leases require the same scrutiny. **Analyze the lease** from the buyer's perspective. Don't saddle a new owner with leases that include high interest rates or leases that have already earned tax advantages for you. Such leases will diminish the company's value.

d) You must also **fully evaluate and catalog company assets**, from property to warehouse inventory to employees. Potential buyers will want to see records and assess your tracking system. If you delayed investing in computer upgrades designed to manage and control the flow of inventory, now is the time to modernize. For one to three years before the sale, keep inventory at a minimum to demonstrate company efficiency and maximize profit. If advisors suggest a complete sell-off of inventory, do it.

e) **Assess your computer systems**. If you aren't already on the Net, it may be wise to evaluate and document what it will take to Web-enable your IT systems. Although many small companies have yet to make the switch to e-commerce, companies that are ready to move online will bring a higher price.

f) If company assets include real estate, **separate or sell the property** before your company hits the market. Real estate can devalue a business simply because it complicates the financial records, which in turn can make potential buyers hesitant to assume a new business with added expense.

g) Finally, **don't forget about your employees**. The loss of key employees during a sale can kill a deal. Key employees may be crucial to the new owner's success, so it's important to determine which employees are prepared to stay with the company during and after the transition. It is important that your employees hear about the pending sale of the company from you and not a third party in order for the new owner to retain as many employees as possible and ensure a smooth transition.

## 3) Add Value Before the Sale

There is any number of things that you can do to perk up your business's appeal to buyers before the sale. Many of these things take time. If you need to sell right away, you're not going to be able to add much value.

**a) Improve your income.** One of the first questions that a buyer will typically have is "what are the revenues and the net income of your small business?" The most vital step you'll want to take is to clean up your income statement. You can have your accountant recast your financials to reflect the way the company should look with new owners. This may mean simply increasing your advertising expenditures, hiring another salesperson on a commission basis, or keeping your store open an extra 8 hours per week to generate more revenues. Also take a hard look at your expenses to see whether you can reduce them. You may also want to have your accountant capitalize certain items that might otherwise have been expensed, and review your depreciation and inventory reporting methods.

**Success Tip**
I mentioned earlier that there are a number of things that one could perform to improve the value of his or her company. Because these take time, the ideal situation is to start working on them three years before the sale, since most buyers will want to see three years of financials.

**b) Improve your assets.** Assess the assets of the business. You'll want to sell off or dispose of any unproductive assets or inventory that isn't selling. The buyer won't want to pay for them, and they will only drag you down — better to get what you can from them now, and write off any losses that may result. The business may own certain assets that are primarily there for your personal use (the most common example is a company car) but that you want to retain after the sale; now's the time for you to "buy" the asset from the business, perhaps at the current book value.

If the business owns real estate, you might consider removing it and placing it in a limited liability company so that it will not be transferred in the sale. You can continue to lease it to the new owners, or to someone else, and retain an income stream. This is a judgment call — for some businesses, the real estate provides the main appeal to buyers and you won't get much for the business without it. Your business broker, if you have one, should be able to tell you whether this is true for you.

Another move you may want to make is to replace any machinery that's nearing the end of its useful life, and do any necessary repairs and upgrades. The average buyer wants to purchase a turnkey operation, meaning that all they have to do is walk in, turn on the lights, and the business will operate with no immediate need for investment on their part.

**c) Clean up potential liabilities.** You should make an effort to clear up any pending or potential legal problems, such as product liability claims, employee lawsuits, IRS audits, insurance disputes, etc. A buyer who purchases only the assets of your business (instead of corporate stock) generally won't get stuck with inherited legal problems; however, the very existence of lawsuits or other problems may raise red flags in potential buyers' minds. One concern that buyers increasingly have is whether there might be any lurking environmental problems on your property. When problems turn up, it's possible that any and all former owners can be held accountable by the government for very expensive cleanup costs.

If real estate will be part of the sale of your business, you should make every effort to ensure there are no leaking underground storage tanks, asbestos, lead paint, hidden hazardous waste, or other nasty surprises around the property. If it's reasonable to conclude that problems are unlikely, an environmental transaction screen conducted at your attorney's direction may be all that's necessary. This is one area where your lawyer's advice will be very important.

## 4) Recast the Company's Financials

If you are like most small businesses, you have probably shown lesser profits to minimize your tax burden. That's good for tax purposes, but bad when it comes time to determine the value of your business. To obtain the highest price for your small business, you will want to make your company look as profitable as possible to prospective buyers.

The best way to do this is to have your accountant recast the profit-and-loss statements to reflect adjustments for what the business owner takes out of the business in terms of compensation and fringe benefits. This can be especially useful when dealing with a buyer who would operate the business himself.

Here is a list of adjustments your accountant can make to your current financial statements so they can be reflected upon in an even more positive light:

Adjustments to your profit and loss statement

- Remove your salary and fringe benefits. Fringe benefits include any car allowance, health insurance, and perks that you receive.

- Remove interest payments on any money you loaned your business. Since you will be removing such loans from the books, any corresponding interest expense should also be removed, thus increasing the net profits in your recast profit and loss statements.

- Remove any expenses not expected to recur after the sale. An example of this would be a loss in the sale of assets or losses from discontinued items.

Adjustments to your balance sheet

- Remove debts that will not be assumed by the new owner.

- Value your balance sheet assets at fair market value.

- Reclassify any items that were expensed off and re-categorize them to capital assets.

- Remove any assets that will not be part of the company after it's sold.

The next thing is to take these recast financial statements and prepare projected financial statements for the next five years. Remember that the prospective buyer is looking at the future potential growth and profitability of your business, and your projections could serve as an important basis for the prospective buyer to pay top dollars for your business.

## 5) Determine a value – the selling price of your business

After going through the 4 steps explained above, you are now ready to figure the asking price of your small business. The important question is: How much is your business worth? There are many formulas for valuing a business. Buyers may base an offer to buy your business in part on the value of the assets in your business, net profits, gross revenues, future earning capability, and other factors.

Though many formulas and tools can help you determine the selling price for your small business, there isn't one right way to come up with the correct price for every instance. The final price ultimately depends on how much the buyer wants to buy and how much the seller wants to sell.

Yet there are a number of ways to value your company and determine your asking price. For example, find out the selling prices of similar businesses in your area and use them as a starting point. Or contact the national trade association for your industry (if one is available). These organizations usually keep detailed statistics and are more than willing to provide information to members or potential members.

You can also consider employing the services of a professional business appraiser. This may lend more credibility to your initial asking price and allow you to keep the reins on sale-price negotiations.

Here's a rundown of the major approaches commonly used to put a price tag on small businesses. My objective is simply to give you a feel for the process that your appraiser will be going through. Appraisals must be done with full knowledge of the facts, circumstances, and all relevant factors pertaining to the subject company. A particular valuation technique that is appropriate for one company at one point in time may not be appropriate for another.

Common valuation methods include:

a. **Market-based valuation**. There are essentially 2 approaches that come under this valuation. The first one is called the **"comparable sales" approach**. This approach values your business based on recent sales of similar businesses in your area and industry. It attempts to locate similar businesses that have recently sold in your area, and uses those sales figures to set a comparable price for your business, adjusting appropriately for differences. While widely used for real estate sales, this method is difficult to apply to business valuations because of the problems in gathering information about small-business sales and because of the unique character of each business. Although this is not a comprehensive valuation tool, it is quick, economical, and makes sense to buyers, so it's common practice for the sale of small businesses.

The second approach is the **"multiple of earnings"** approach. This approach places a value of the business based on a certain multiple of revenue or net profit. However, a rule of thumb does not take into account any of the factors that make your business unique, and using one can result in setting a price for your business that's way too high or too low. Nevertheless, small businesses are often sold at a price based on a rule of thumb, simply because it's a relatively fast, cheap method to use, and because it will result in a price that seems reasonable to buyers who have been looking around at a lot of similar businesses. The multiple selected is not an arbitrary number. One rule of thumb is: -- if you buy a new machine for a factory, you should be able to pay for it five years from the resulting labor savings. Likewise, a business should be able to pay for itself in three to five years, assuming that the earnings remain exactly the same for that period of time. To go one step further, a prudent person might expect a 20% return on an investment in a company with steady earnings. On that basis, the company could be paid for in five years at the same earnings level. Therefore, higher or lower multiples are affected by the corresponding difference in the rate of return. Historically, however, a five-year payback has been a de-facto standard.

The multiplier you select is driven by market conditions, comparables, and value in the eye of the beholder. The value the buyer sees in the company affects the market multiplier: Paying 10 times earnings for a company provides the buyer with a 10% return on the invested capital based upon historical financial performance. Paying 5 times earnings results in a 20% return on invested capital; 4 times earnings results in a 25% return. The EBIT is most commonly used as the constant of the multiplier. One needs, however, to separate the acquisition and financing features of the deal. Buyers will use their own capital structure as a model to finance the acquisition of the seller, and will look at the company from that perspective.

**b) Asset-based valuation.** This method takes into consideration figures such as the book value and liquidation value of the business. At a minimum, your company should be valued at the sum of the value of its easily salable parts. Two commonly used business valuation methods look primarily at the value of your hard assets.

- **Book value** is the figure you arrive at when you deduct all your liabilities from your assets. This figure is also known as "owner's equity." There are two limitations of using this approach. The first one is that since the balance sheet reflects historical costs and depreciation of assets rather than their current market value, this figure is not very useful. However, if you adjust the book value in the process of recasting your financials, the current adjusted book value can be used as a "bare minimum" price for your business. The second limitation is that it ignores the future return the assets can produce, and is calculated using accounting practice that does not reflect how much the business is worth to someone who may buy it as a going concern.

- **Liquidation value** refers to the amount left over if you had to sell your business quickly, without taking the time to get the full market value, and then used the proceeds to pay off all debts. There's little point in going through all the trouble of negotiating a sale of your business if you end up selling for liquidation value — it would be easier to simply go out of business.

**c) Future Earnings-based valuation.** The most extensively used method is the earnings approach, which measures the worth of earnings. Three separate valuation methodologies have been developed from this approach. They are:

**Capitalization of earnings.** Considering the company's "earning potential" via the capitalization rate, this method assumes earnings consistency in a near-future term. Tax profits by year are multiplied by a "capitalization rate" to determine value. Your accountant should research an appropriate "cap" rate.

**Discounted cash flow.** As with the capitalization method, discounted cash flow considers earnings when determining value. This method projects future earnings, usually over a 3-to-10 year period of time, and then discounts them at a specific rate. The complexity in this method comes from subjective considerations of how a potential buyer would change the business, and your accountant should definitely work this through.

**The IRS-recommended method.** The IRS suggests you:

1. Determine average annual returns on tangible assets (for a period of not less than five years). If history is not available, assume a rate of 8% to 10%.

2. Determine average earnings for the preceding five years.

3. Subtract returns from earnings. This is the amount attributed to intangibles, such as goodwill, which is the value of the business that is above and beyond the value of the assets.

4. Capitalize at a rate of 10% to 20% for high-risk business, 8% to 15% for low-risk businesses.

5. Add the goodwill results to the book value of assets.

However, this method, established in the 60s is considered to be archaic by some and tends to overvalue businesses. Still, the IRS suggests buyers always consider the following:

- Economic environment for overall economy and specific industry

- Nature and history of the business

- Book value, financial condition, and earning capacity

- Capacity to pay dividends

- Intangible value

- Prior sales of company stock

- Market price for similar businesses

## iii) Bankruptcy: The Last Resort

Individuals, who may be burdened by debt, have the option of "starting fresh." This is a completely legal process, and is available to almost anyone who needs it. Bankruptcy helps people avoid the kind of permanent discouragement that can prevent them from ever reestablishing themselves as hard-working members of society. Through the bankruptcy process, creditors are ranked so that the debtor's nonexempt property can be fairly distributed according to established rules guaranteeing identical treatment to all creditors of the same rank.

The discussion that follows is intended only as a brief overview of the types of bankruptcy filings, what a bankruptcy filing can and cannot do, and the effect bankruptcy can have on your credit rating. I strongly suggest that you seek the advice and assistance of an attorney specializing in bankruptcy law if you are considering this course of action.

We will explore the following three areas:

1. Types of bankruptcy

2. What bankruptcy can and cannot do

3. Bankruptcy's effect on your credit rating

## Types of Bankruptcy

The Bankruptcy Code is divided into "chapters." The chapters that usually apply to consumer debtors are Chapter 7, known as Liquidation, and Chapter 13, known as an Adjustment of the Debts of an Individual with Regular Income.

An important feature applicable to all types of bankruptcy filings is the <u>automatic stay</u>. The automatic stay means that the mere request for bankruptcy protection automatically "stays" or forces an abrupt halt to repossessions, foreclosures, evictions, garnishments, attachments, utility shut-offs, and debt collection harassment. It offers debtors and the trustee assigned to the case time to review the situation and develop an appropriate plan. Creditors cannot take any further action against the debtor or the property without permission from the bankruptcy court.

- **Chapter 7.** The chapter of the Bankruptcy Code providing for "liquidation," i.e., the sale of a debtor's nonexempt property, and the distribution of the proceeds to creditors. In a Chapter 7 liquidation case, the bankruptcy court appoints a trustee to examine the debtor's assets, and divide them into *exempt* and *nonexempt* property. Exempt property is limited to a certain amount of equity in the debtor's residence, motor vehicle, household goods, health aids, life insurance, specified future earnings such as social security benefits and alimony, and certain other personal property. The trustee may then sell the nonexempt property and distribute the proceeds among the unsecured creditors. Although a liquidation case can rarely help with secured debt (the secured creditor still has the right to repossess the collateral), the debtor will be discharged from the legal obligation to pay unsecured debts such as credit card debts, medical bills and utility arrearages. However, certain types of unsecured debt are allowed special treatment and cannot be discharged. These include some student loans, alimony, child support, criminal fines, and some taxes.

- **Chapter 13.** With a Chapter 13 bankruptcy, the debtor puts forward a plan, following the rules set forth in the bankruptcy laws, to repay all creditors over a period of time, usually from future income. A Chapter 13 case may be advantageous in that the debtor is allowed to get caught up on mortgages or car loans without the threat of foreclosure or repossession and is allowed to keep both exempt and nonexempt property. The debtor's plan is a simple document outlining to the bankruptcy court how the debtor proposes to pay current expenses while paying off all the old debt balances. The debtor's property is protected from seizure from creditors, including mortgage and other lien holders, as long as the proposed payments are made. The plan generally requires monthly payments to the bankruptcy trustee over a period of three to five years. Arrangements can be made to have these payments made automatically through payroll deductions.

## What Bankruptcy Can and Cannot Do

Bankruptcy may make it possible for financially distressed individuals to:

- Discharge liability for most or all of their debts. Once the debt is discharged, the debtor has no further legal obligation to pay the debt.

- Stop the repossession of a car or other property, or force the creditor to return property even after it has been repossessed.

- Stop foreclosure actions on their home and allow them to catch up on missed payments.

- Reduce the monthly payments on debts.

- Stop wage garnishment and other debt collection harassment.

- Restore or prevent termination of utility service.

- Allow debtors an opportunity to challenge the claims of certain creditors who have committed fraud or who are otherwise seeking to collect more than they are legally entitled to.

Bankruptcy, however, cannot cure every financial problem. It is usually not possible to:

- Get rid of certain rights of secured creditors. Although a debtor can force secured creditors to take payments over time in the bankruptcy process, a debtor generally cannot keep the collateral unless the debtor continues to pay the debt.

- Discharge debts that are incurred after bankruptcy has been filed.

- Discharge types of debts singled out by the federal bankruptcy statutes for special treatment, such as child support, alimony, some student loans, criminal fines, certain court ordered payments, and some taxes.

- Protect all cosigners on their debts. If relative or friend co-signed a loan, which the debtor discharged in bankruptcy, the cosigner may still be obligated to repay the loan.

## Bankruptcy's Effect on Your Credit

According to federal law, a bankruptcy can remain part of a debtor's credit history for 10 years. Whether or not the debtor will be granted credit in the future is unpredictable. In some cases it may actually be easier to obtain future credit, because new creditors may feel that since the old obligations have been discharged, they will be first in line. They also realize that the debtor cannot again file bankruptcy for at least the next six years.

## Is it time to close your business?

Here are five tell-tale signs that may indicate that you need to do things differently if you want to stay in business, or else exit the business.

## 1. Your debt-to-asset ratio is on the rise

Businesses often borrow money to purchase equipment, buildings and other assets. But if debt as a percentage of assets is increasing, you could be on the road to being what is called, "over-leveraged". Some business consultants consider it a sign of trouble if the debt-to-asset ratio is floating above 50%. A rising debt ratio is seldom a good sign.

Similarly, a rising level of debt-to-shareholder equity indicates your business's overall leverage is increasing. But the greater your leverage or debt ratios, the more debt you have to service, the greater the drain on your profitability, and the less equity you have in your venture.

## 2. You're losing money and the losses are increasing

Some aspects of the tax code make it possible for businesses to reduce their profit or show a loss even though the business is healthy.

It's usually not a concern when a solid venture shows a tax loss. But if your business is losing money in real terms, and your tax is only magnifying that loss, you've likely got a problem. Businesses do often lose money in the first few years of operation as they ramp up and try to take advantage of economies of scale.

However, if the losses are increasing, not dwindling, there comes a point where you have to look at your business model and decide whether it's realistic to assume you're going to be able to "grow out" of your losses.

## 3. Your inventory turnover is slowing down

If your business is selling a product or products, having those items on the shelves longer than usual is indicative of a business slowdown. Not a good sign.

## 4. You're unable to raise more money for the business

We've all heard stories about how a venture was doing all right until a loan application or line of credit renewal was turned down. But looking at it from another angle, a recalcitrant banker actually may be helpful in letting you know that the business is not as good as you think it is. Lenders sometimes keep borrowers out of trouble - or at least, from getting in deeper trouble. A loan rejection can be a reality check for someone who thinks his or her current problems are only temporary.

I've seen this most often in the case of prospective real estate ventures -- when a businessperson has found what he thinks is a good piece of investment property but the bank won't approve a loan. Maybe the bank's analysis indicates the property is not profitable at the purchase price. Maybe the bank feels the numbers don't leave enough margin of error to protect it against a decline in a currently inflated real estate or rental market. But if the result is that the entrepreneur doesn't get into a real estate venture that turns out to be riskier than he thought, both borrower and lender have benefited.

### 5. You're not having any fun

Having fun is important. If you get up in the morning and you can't stand the thought of going in to run your business, or if the dream of self-employment has become your own personal little nightmare, then it's time to take a hard look at shutting down. Chances are you'll benefit at least in terms of your mental health - and it's hard to put a monetary value on that.

## Tax Concerns When Selling Your Business

As soon as you begin to think about selling your business, you should also start thinking about the tax consequences of the sale.

After you sell your business, the amount of tax you owe will depend on the internal structure of your company and how you structure the sale. If you plan wisely, you can minimize your tax liability.

Your tax advisor or accountant can help you determine what's best for your company. They can also assist you with the following tax issues that you'll confront when you sell your business.

### Structuring your Company

If you operate as a sole proprietorship or a partnership, think about incorporating. If you incorporate your business, the corporation – not the individual owners – is responsible for tax liabilities and debts. Incorporating the business also allows you to structure the transaction as a sale of stock.

## Structuring the Sale

It's important to structure the sale so that you minimize the tax liability on the gain from the sale. For example, if you provide seller financing by accepting installment payments or shares of the purchaser's stock, you should structure the transaction so you don't pay tax on the gain until you receive the installment payments or shares of the stock.

The seller will pay tax based on two different income tax rates – an ordinary income tax rate, and a capital gains rate lower than the ordinary tax rate.

When you sell stock, gains or losses are generally treated as capital gains or losses. Some items – goodwill, most real property gains and any appreciation over the original cost of equipment – qualify as capital gains.

On the other hand, when you sell individual business assets, such as inventory or equipment, much of the gain is considered ordinary income. Gains from inventory, publicly traded securities, and depreciation recapture are not eligible for installment reporting. And if you offer seller financing, you should know that if the total value of installment payments exceeds $5 million in a year, interest is charged on deferred taxes.

If the seller has held the assets of the business for over one year, the assets are long-term capital assets. That means a lower tax rate for most taxpayers. However, there is an exception made for property that is used in the trade or business. In this case, the gain related to these items is taxed at the generally higher ordinary income tax rates. Regardless of how long the assets are held, the result is the same for these assets – a higher tax rate.

Examples of property that the IRS states must be excluded from the capital gains are inventory, stock in trade, and property held primarily for sale to customers in the ordinary course of the taxpayer's trade or business.

From the seller's perspective, it's most advantageous if you can convince your buyer to buy the stock in your corporation. In this case, the entire amount will be taxed at the lower capital gains tax rate. A stock sale also allows the seller to take advantage of the special provisions of Section 1202, if you qualify. It is important to consult with a professional regarding this.

## Assigning a Price to Business Assets

As you negotiate the purchase of a business or its assets, you will be evaluating each of the major assets. That's good, because the tax code requires that you and the seller jointly agree on allocations of the purchase price to each asset or group of assets. These amounts allocated must be at the "fair market value" and reported to the IRS by each side on Form 8594, Asset Acquisition Statement. You will also use these values to calculate your depreciation deduction for each asset, and to figure the taxable gain or loss when you sell or dispose of it.

It is not always easy to precisely value business assets; you may need to bring in a professional appraiser for real estate or some other assets. There is usually room for flexibility in valuing assets. The overall price paid for a business or its assets usually reflects how eager the parties are to make a deal, not how much each item is worth. Obviously, these allocations have tax significance to both parties — but especially to a buyer.

---

**Example:**

Abdul buys Woodbridge Bakery from Laura for $100,000. With the help of a business appraiser, they agree to allocate the purchase price as follows: $70,000 for equipment, and $30,000 for goodwill. Both parties report this to the IRS when they file their tax returns. In the event either Abdul or Laura is audited, they can each produce a report from the appraiser backing up the allocations.

---

**Success Tip**

If you are selling the assets of your business, negotiate for increased allocated value to capital gains assets so you pay less tax.

Don't forget the IRS requires a form filed with tax returns for both the buyer and the seller for a newly sold business.

# Important facts to know when selling a business

## How Do You Determine Who Is a Qualified Buyer?

Selling your business is a difficult and time-consuming task, particularly if you're not using a broker. It's important not to waste too much time with "buyers" who are going to do just that - wasting your time.

The best method of separating the serious buyer from the time-waster is to determine the strength of their financing ability. A prospective buyer with little or no chance of raising the necessary capital to complete the sale is usually not going to be a qualified buyer. Simply ask prospective buyers about their financing plans. If they can't provide concrete, educated answers, they may not be serious buyers.

Also consider a buyer's initial offer. If it is as low as 50% of your original asking price — or even lower — the prospect may just be looking for desperate owners in the hopes of scooping up a bargain.

**Success Tip**
One option that I have seen many small-business owners use to expand their base of qualified buyers is to offer financing themselves. If you choose to offer seller financing, have the buyer sign a loan agreement drawn up by your lawyer. Remember that when you offer financing yourself, you risk the buyer defaulting on the loan. One precaution is to ask for significant collateral on the amount of the loan. Even though you may have run your business profitably, there are no guarantees that the new owner will be able to do the same.

## Legal Ramifications of Selling a Business

The single most important thing that you can do to protect yourself legally when selling a business is to make a complete disclosure to the buyer about all aspects of the business.

Open up the books for inspection. Show them all leases and other relevant contracts. Let the buyers see everything, warts and all.

Business sales most often go awry when the buyer later feels that the seller failed to disclose an important aspect of the operation — an act that may constitute fraud. By making a full disclosure, you ensure that no one can accuse you of anything down the road.

### Business brokers

A business broker acts as an agent for an owner looking to sell a business. They can be found through telephone listings or advertisements in local newspapers or trade magazines. Charges vary, but a business owner can usually expect to pay up to 10% of the final sales price.

There are several advantages to using a business broker. The broker will allow you to maintain confidentiality if you don't want the public to know your intent to sell. Having one saves you the time of talking to potential buyers, thus allowing you to focus on running your business. Good business brokers deal directly with those interested in your business, and often have excellent contacts with which to lure prospective buyers.

### Partial sale

You may decide to sell part of the business, rather than all of it. If one segment of your operation is growing much more quickly than another, you may want to consider placing the less successful portion on the market. If you are able to sell it, you will have more money and time to invest in the remainder of your company.

In order to make a partial sale, you will have to separate out financial information and prepare a two-year profit and loss statement for the separate business segment you are selling. This may be tricky, and you might want to consider having an independent accountant perform the work or at least check your figures.

### Financial statements

The basic financial information needed to sell most small businesses are: 1) profit and loss statements, and 2) balance sheets from the last five years of operation. If you are three or four months into a new fiscal year, you should also provide an interim financial statement.

Even if you have prepared your own statements in the past, you should consider having an outside firm prepare or review them for the sale. This will increase the value of the business in the eyes of potential buyers. If you decide against using an outside accounting firm, offer to show copies of your corporate or, in the case of a sole proprietorship or partnership, personal or partnership tax returns to serious potential buyers. This will help to substantiate your businesses profitability.

### Management agreements

Often, a prospective buyer will express an interest in having the current owner continue to run the business after the sale takes place. If you are interested in doing this, be sure to get any such agreement in writing.

### Selling to larger corporations

Sometimes it is possible to sell your business to a larger corporation for more than it is worth to an individual buyer.

A larger corporation that is active in the same business area may be able to improve on existing profit margins in a variety of ways. Any corporation with which you are currently engaged in any type of cooperative effort should be targeted as a potential buyer.

### Attorneys

There are two areas where it is strongly suggested that you consult with an attorney when selling a business. First, when you prepare a circular or prospectus summarizing your business for potential buyers, and second, when you prepare a purchase and sales agreement.

While you may have operated your business successfully year after year, a new buyer without your unique skills, expertise, or personality may easily run into problems. If the business turns out to be less successful or easy to run than the buyer anticipated, he or she might assume that the business was fraudulently represented. One way to reduce the risk of litigation in this is to have an attorney review your circular or prospectus. The attorney will undoubtedly advise you to avoid projecting future sales or profits, or at least be extremely careful when doing so. Even if you are selling a very small business, you should have your attorney review, if not actually prepare, the purchase and sales agreement.

## Employees

Make sure that employees hear about a potential sale of the business from you and not a third party. Rumors breed nervousness. If you decide to advertise your business openly, tell your employees before the advertisements run. If you expect to find a buyer who will keep all or most of your employees on the payroll, tell this to your staff. Remain truthful, but emphasize the positive. If you decide to advertise the business confidentially, make a concerted effort to avoid any leaks to employees. Consider using a business broker and have any interested buyers sign a nondisclosure agreement. Potential buyers should also visit your operation during off hours. You may also decide that one or more of your employees are the best potential buyer for your business. Employees know the business better than outsiders and may be able to persuade investors or lending institutions to help them finance a leveraged buyout

## Seller Financing

One of the biggest obstacles in selling a business, especially for the price you want, is finding a buyer who has or can borrow the cash to buy the business. Hence, it is very common for businesses to be sold with seller financing. If you do decide to provide financing, have the buyer sign a loan agreement with you and be sure to get an attorney to write up the documentation. It will cost you more in the long run if you don't use an attorney. Try to get as much solid collateral as you can in order to protect your loan. If your business includes real estate, motor vehicles, machinery, or other hard assets, you may want to consider selling them separately or even leasing them to the new owner. This could increase the pool of qualified prospects, increase your chances of completing a sale, and decrease the need for seller financing.

# IN CONCLUSION

Why should I be thinking about exiting my business when I'm just getting started? A good question deserves a good answer. Because planning your business does not just mean getting started and getting going – it also means thinking about what the ending might look like – how will it finish?

Your business has many stakeholders – family, employees, customers, and partners. And each has an interest in the business. Each will want and need to know how they are affected, particularly if something unexpected happens to you, or if you decide to sell or transfer the business.

An "exit strategy" involves thinking about contingencies in the event of expected or unforeseen circumstances. The exit planning process suggests the consideration of alternative approaches, ones that add value to your business and others that preserve its value. Planning your exit now, in the early stages of your business, provides peace of mind for those whose lives are or will be tied into the heart of it.

# Frequently Asked Questions on Succession Planning

## Q. *What Is Goodwill?*

A business' reputation and relationship with its customers represents its goodwill. When a business is sold, any amount of sale exceeding fair market value is considered to be goodwill by the IRS.

---

**Example:**

Sam pays $100,000 for Honest John's Network Communications Emporium. The cash and tangible assets of the business add up to $69,000: $1,000 in the cash drawer, $15,000 in inventory on hand, $3,000 worth of machinery and a building worth $50,000. Why is Sam willing to pay $31,000 above the value of all of its identifiable assets? Because Honest John's has a good reputation and has made a decent profit for several years, and Sam thinks that a lot of John's customers will stick with the business. He pays this premium for the business's goodwill.

---

## Q. *What is a Letter of intent?*

It is a formal notification that a buyer intends to buy a business or a property. It is not legally enforceable.

## Q. *What is an agreement of sale?*

A document in which a property's buyer and seller approve the price and other terms of the transfer of title.

# CONCLUSION

## My parting words

In this book, I have shared with you some of the insights gained in the process of starting and operating my own business, advising hundreds of small-business owners on theirs, and the wealth of knowledge I have accumulated from studying some of the greatest minds in the fields of entrepreneurship.

I hope the previous pages have answered many questions, but I want to use these closing sentences to make my mission clear. I have a passion for entrepreneurship and am committed to helping you – and anyone who wishes to succeed as a small-business owner – to achieve your goals. And I know from my own experience in running a business and from studying the great entrepreneurial minds that it takes more than number-crunching to achieve the joy and independence (and not just the frustration and hard work!) of business ownership.

That's why my role as author encompasses the entire process of successfully launching, growing and closing a business. I want to share my enthusiasm as well as my expertise, which includes advising hundreds of small-business owners such as yourself about the pleasures and potential pitfalls that await

One secret (warning) about running your own small business that you MUST know is this: Entrepreneurship is addictive. Like me, you may already be hooked. Once you work for yourself, it is hard to ever work for anyone else. This makes it especially important – crucial – that you succeed! Your initial motivation for wanting to start your own business might have varied – perhaps you had a business idea you couldn't follow through while working a regular corporate job, perhaps you were fired, or perhaps you simply tired of watching everyone but you get wealthy from your ideas. But as soon as you join the "small-business owners club", you'll want to be a lifetime member! And this is terrific, because your determination to succeed will drive you to astounding levels of success.

But achieving goals and finding happiness do *not* necessarily go hand in hand. I want your addiction to be a happy, healthy one; I want you to avoid some of the struggles and stresses I endured – the same ones that discourage thousands of entrepreneurs a year. I want to help you reach your goals, and to be prepared for the success that awaits you. Your success will bring both wealth and responsibilities you may not have anticipated before reading this book. Money does not diminish your problems. On the contrary, it creates a whole new set of them.

When I first boarded the train with other entrepreneurs bound for success, I had no idea how rough the journey would be. I kept looking up the tracks, focusing all my energies on the treasure chest of happiness that I believed awaited my arrival at the station. But I discovered that I couldn't just "ride the train" and magically arrive at my business-goal destination. I had to learn some of my lessons the hard way – but there's no reason why you should.

You can take advantage of the earlier entrepreneurs who blazed the trail before you. When you do, you will find that the rewards far outweigh the costs. Nothing worth having is ever easy, as they say, but having gone through this book, chapter by chapter, you now know everything you *need* to know to create your own happiness. I hope this book has helped you to learn various techniques, strategies and concepts so that your journey to success will be as smooth and as joyful as possible.

If you encounter rough patches or potholes, don't give up! And don't ignore the problems either. Seek professional help from other successful business owners (but not your competitors!), from a financial advisor or a business coach. Call me, if you'd like, and I will gladly offer my assistance or provide a referral. Your business may be small, but the world of small-business owners is large, and filled with people who, like me, are rooting for your success!

# GLOSSARY OF BUSINESS TERMS

An important aspect of understanding the financial side of your business consists of nothing more than learning the business language. Once you're familiar with basic terms, you will be well prepared to make sense of basic written reports and better able to communicate with others about important financial information.

**Accelerated Depreciation** – Any method that records greater depreciation than straight-line depreciation in the early years, and less depreciation than straight-line in the later years of an asset's holding period.

**Account Payable** – short-term debts incurred as the result of day-to-day operations.

**Account Receivable** - monies due your enterprise as the result of day-to-day operations.

**Accountants' Report** - Formal document that communicates an independent accountant's: (1) expression of limited assurance on financial statements as a result of performing inquiry and analytic procedures (*Review Report*); (2) results of procedures performed (*Agreed-Upon Procedures Report*); (3) non-expression of opinion or any form of assurance on a presentation in the form of financial statements information that is the representation of management (*Compilation Report*); or (4) an opinion on an assertion made by management in accordance with the Statements on Standards for Attestation Engagements (*Attestation Report*). An accountants' report does not result from the performance of an audit.

**Accounting** - Recording and reporting of financial transactions, including the origination of the transaction, its recognition, processing, and summarization in the financial statements.

**Accounting Change** - Change in (1) an accounting principle; (2) an accounting estimate; or (3) the reporting entity that necessitates disclosure and explanation in published financial reports.

**Accrual Basis** - Method of accounting that recognizes revenue when earned, rather than when collected. Expenses are recognized when incurred rather than when paid.

**Accumulated Depreciation** - Total depreciation pertaining to an asset or group of assets from the time the assets were placed in services until the date of the financial statement or tax return. This total is the contra account to the related asset account.

**Additional Paid in Capital** - Amounts paid for stock in excess of its par value or stated value. Also, other amounts paid by stockholders and charged to equity accounts other than capital stock.

**Alternative Minimum Tax (AMT)** - Tax imposed to back up the regular income tax imposed on corporations and individuals to assure that taxpayers with economically measured income exceeding certain thresholds pay at least some income tax.

**American Depository Receipts (ADRs)** - Receipts for shares of foreign company stock maintained by an intermediary indicating ownership.

**Amortization** - Gradual and periodic reduction of any amount, such as the periodic write-down of a bond premium, the cost of an intangible asset, the periodic payment of mortgages or other debt.

**Annual Report** - Report to the stockholders of a company which includes the company's annual, audited balance sheet and related statements of earnings, stockholders' or owners' equity and cash flows, as well as other financial and business information.

**Auditors' Report** - Written communication issued by an independent certified public accountant (CPA) describing the character of his or her work and the degree of responsibility taken. An auditors' report includes a statement that the audit was conducted in accordance with generally accepted auditing standards (GAAS), which require that the auditor plan and perform the audit to obtain reasonable assurance about whether the financial statements are free of material misstatement, as well as a statement that the auditor believes the audit provides a reasonable basis for his or her opinion.

**Bad Debt** - All or portion of an account, loan, or note receivable considered to be uncollectible.

**Balance Sheet** – A financial statement that lists the assets, liabilities, and equity of a company at a certain point in time.

**Bankruptcy** - Legal process, governed by federal statute, whereby the debts of an insolvent person are liquidated after being satisfied to the greatest extent possible by the debtor's assets. During bankruptcy, the debtor's assets are held and managed by a court appointed trustee.

**Board of Directors** - Individuals responsible for overseeing the affairs of an entity, including the election of its officers. The board of a corporation that issues stock is elected by stockholders.

**Book Value** - Amount, net, or contra account balances that an asset or liability shows on the balance sheet of a company. Also known as carrying value.

**Breakeven Analysis** - An analysis tool that models how revenue, expenses, and profit vary with changes in sales volume. Breakeven analysis estimates the sales volume needed to cover fixed and variable expenses.

**Break-Even Point** - the point at which revenues are equal to expenses.

**Budget** - Financial plan that serves as an estimate of future cost, revenues, or both.

**Bylaws** - Collection of formal, written rules governing the conduct of a corporation's affairs (such as what officers it will have, what their responsibilities are, and how they are to be chosen). Bylaws are approved by a corporation's stockholders if a stock corporation, or other owners if a non-stock corporation.

**Capital Gain** - Portion of the total gain recognized on the sale or exchange of a non-inventory asset, which is not taxed as ordinary income. Capital gains have historically been taxed at a lower rate than ordinary income.

**Capital Stock** - Ownership shares of a corporation authorized by its articles of incorporation. The money value assigned to a corporation's issued shares. The balance sheet account with the aggregate amount of the par value or stated value of all stock issued by a corporation.

**Capitalized Cost** - Expenditure identified with goods or services acquired and measured by the amount of cash paid or the market value of other property, capital stock, or services surrendered. Expenditures that are written off during two or more accounting periods.

**Capitalized Lease** – Lease recorded as an asset acquisition accompanied by a corresponding liability by the lessee.

**Carrying Value** - Amount, net, or contra account balances, that an asset or liability shows on the balance sheet of a company. Also known as book value.

**Carryovers** - Provision of tax law that allows current losses or certain tax credits to be utilized in the tax returns of future periods.

**Cash Basis** - Method of bookkeeping by which revenues and expenditures are recorded when they are received and paid.

**Cash Equivalents** - Short-term (generally less than three months), highly liquid investments that are convertible to known amounts of cash.

**Cash Flows** - Net of cash receipts and cash disbursements relating to a particular activity during a specified accounting period.

**Certificate of Deposit (CD)** - Formal instrument issued by a bank upon the deposit of funds, which may not be withdrawn for a specified time period. Typically, an early withdrawal will incur a penalty.

**Certified Public Accountant (CPA)** - Accountant who has satisfied the education, experience, and examination requirements of his or her jurisdiction necessary to be certified as a public accountant.

**Collateral** – Asset pledged by a borrower that will be given up if the loan is not paid.

**Common Stock** - Capital stock having no preferences generally in terms of dividends, voting rights, or distributions.

**Comparative Financial Statement** – Financial statement presentation in which the current amounts and the corresponding amounts for previous periods or dates are also shown.

**Compilation** - Presentation of financial statement data without the accountant's assurance as to conformity with generally accepted accounting principles (GAAP), or an other comprehensive basis of accounting (OCBOA).

**Compilation Report** - See accountants report.

**Continuing Professional Education (CPE)** - Educational programs for certified public accountants (CPAs) to keep informed on changes that occur within the profession.

**Contra Account** – Account considered to be an offset to another account. Generally established to reduce the other account to amounts that can be realized or collected.

**Corporation** - Form of doing business pursuant to a charter granted by a state or federal government. Corporations typically are characterized by the issuance of freely transferable capital stock, perpetual life, centralized management, and limitation of owners' liability to the amount they invest in the business.

**Cost Accounting** - Procedures used for rationally classifying, recording, and allocating current or predicted costs that relate to a certain product or production process.

**Credit** - Entry on the right side of a double-entry bookkeeping system that represents the reduction of an asset or expense or the addition to a liability or revenue

**Creditor** - Party that loans money or other assets to another party.

**Current Asset** – Cash and any other asset, which can be converted to cash or consumed in operations within 1 year.

**Current Liability** – Debts of a business that must be paid within 1 year.

**Debit** - Entry on the left side of a double-entry bookkeeping system that represents the addition of an asset or expense or the reduction to a liability or revenue.

**Debt** – The amount, which a business owes to another. Also known as liability.

**Debtor** - Party owing money or other assets to a creditor.

**Default** - Failure to meet any financial obligation. Default triggers a creditor's rights and remedies identified in the agreement, and under the law.

**Deferred Income** - Income received but not earned until all events have occurred. Deferred income is reflected as a liability.

**Deficit** - Financial shortage that occurs when liabilities exceed assets.

**Defined Benefit Plan** - See EMPLOYEE BENEFIT PLAN.

**Defined Contribution Plan** - See EMPLOYEE BENEFIT PLAN.

**Demand Loan** - Loan repayable on demand. Also known as a call loan.

**Depreciation** - Expense allowance made for wear and tear on an ASSET over its estimated useful life.

**Disbursement** - Payment by cash or check.

**Discount Rate** - Rate at which interest is deducted in advance of the issuance, purchasing, selling, or lending of a financial instrument. Also, the rate used to determine the current or present value, of an asset or income stream.

**Discounted Cash Flow** - Present value of future cash estimated to be generated.

**Dissolution** - Termination of a corporation.

**Distributions** - Payment by a business entity to its owners of items such as cash assets, stocks, or earnings.

**Dividends** – In a corporation, a proportionate share of the net profits of a business, which the board of directors has determined, should be paid out to shareholders, rather than held as retained earnings.

**Double-Entry Bookkeeping** – An accounting system in which each transaction is entered in two or more accounts, and involves two-way, self-balancing posting. Total debits must equal total credits.

**Earned Income** - Wages, salaries, professional fees, and other amounts received as compensation for services rendered.

**Earnings Per Share (EPS)** - Measure of performance calculated by dividing the net earnings of a company by the average number of shares outstanding during a period.

**Employee Benefit Plan** - Compensation arrangement, generally in writing, used by employers in addition to salary or wages. Some plans such as group term life insurance, medical insurance, and qualified retirement plans are treated favorably under the tax law. Most common qualified retirement plans are: (1) defined benefit plans - a promise to pay participants specified benefits that are determinable and based on such factors as age, years of service, and compensation; or (2) defined contribution plans - provide an individual account for each participant and benefits based on items such as amounts contributed to the account by the employer and employee and investment experience. This type includes profit-sharing plans, employee stock ownership plans and 401(k) plans.

**Employee Stock Ownership Plan (ESOP)** - Stock bonus plan of an employer that acquires securities issued by the plan sponsor.

**Equity** - Residual interest in the assets of an entity that remains after deducting its liabilities. Also, the amount of a business' total assets less total liabilities. Also, the third section of a balance sheet, the other two being assets and liabilities.

**Equity Account** - Account in the equity section of the balance sheet. Includes capital stock, additional paid in capital and retained earnings.

**Escrow** - Money or property put into the custody of a third party for delivery to a grantee, only after fulfillment of specified conditions.

**Estate Tax** - Tax on the value of a descendant's taxable estate, typically defined as the decedent's assets less liabilities and certain expenses, which may include funeral, and administrative expenses.

**Excise Tax** - Tax on the manufacture, sale, or consumption of a commodity.

**Exclusions** - Income item, which is excluded from a taxpayer's gross income by the internal revenue code or an administrative action. Common exclusions include gifts, inheritances, and death proceeds paid under a life insurance contract. Also known as excluded income.

**Exempt Organization** - Organization, which is generally exempt from paying federal income tax. Exempt organizations include religious organizations, charitable organizations, social clubs, and others.

**Exemption** - Amount of a taxpayer's income that is not subject to tax. All individuals, trusts, and estates qualify for an exemption unless they are claimed as a dependent on another individual's tax return. Exemptions are also granted to taxpayers for their dependents.

**Extension** - Time granted by a taxing authority, such as the Internal Revenue Service (IRS), a state or city, which allows the taxpayer to file tax returns later than the original due date.

**External Reporting** - Reporting to stockholders and the public, as opposed to internal reporting for management's benefit.

**Extraordinary Items** - Events and transactions distinguished by their unusual nature and by the infrequency of their occurrence. Extraordinary items are reported separately, less applicable income taxes, in the entity's statement of income or operations.

**401(K) Plan** - employee benefit plan authorized by internal revenue code section 401(k), whereby an employer establishes an account for each participating employee, and each participant elects to deposit a portion of his or her salary into the account. The amount deposited is not subject to income tax. This is the most common type of salary reduction plan.

**Face Value** - Amount due at maturity from a bond or note.

**Factoring** - Selling a receivable at a discounted value to a third party for cash.

**Fair Market Value** - Price at which property would change hands between a buyer and a seller without any compulsion to buy or sell, and both having reasonable knowledge of the relevant facts.

**Favorable Variance** - Excess of actual revenue over projected revenue, or actual costs under projected costs.

**Fiduciary** - A person who is responsible for the administration of property owned by others. Corporate management is a fiduciary with respect to corporate assets, which are beneficially owned by the stockholders and creditors. Similarly, a trustee is the fiduciary of a trust, and partners owe fiduciary responsibility to each other and to their creditors.

**Financial Statements** - Presentation of financial data including balance sheets, income statements and statements of cash flow, or any supporting statement that is intended to communicate an entity's financial position at a point in time, and its results of operations for a period then ended.

**First in, First out (FIFO)** – The inventory value is based on the cost of the latest item purchased.

**Fiscal Year** – A 12 month accounting period used by a business, which may or may not be a calendar year.

**Fixed Asset** - Any tangible asset with a life of more than one year used in an entity's operations.

**Forecast** - Prospective financial statements that are an entity's expected financial position, results of operations, and cash flows.

**Franchise** - Legal arrangement whereby the owner of a trade name, a franchiser, contracts with a party that wants to use the name on a non-exclusive basis to sell goods or services, franchisee. Frequently, the franchise agreement grants strict supervisory powers to the franchisor over the franchisee, which, nevertheless, is an independent business.

**Gain** - Excess of revenues received over costs relating to a specific transaction.

**General Ledger** – In double entry accounting, the central listing of all accounts of a business.

**General Partnership** - A partnership with no limited partners.

**Going Concern** - Assumption that a business can remain in operation long enough for all of its current plans to be carried out.

**Going Public** - Activities that relate to offering a private company's shares to the general investing public, including registering with the SEC.

**Goodwill** – The accounting term for amounts paid for assets over and above their fair market value. Goodwill arises, for example, when a company purchases another business and pays a price higher than the value of the acquired assets alone. Goodwill theoretically represents the value of the business's name, reputation, and customer relations, which increase the true value of the business beyond the value of its assets alone.

**Governing Documents** - Official legal documents that dictate how an entity is operated. The governing documents of a corporation include articles of incorporation and bylaws; a partnership includes the partnership agreement; a trust includes the trust agreement or trust indenture; and an LLC includes the articles of organization and operating agreement.

**Guaranty** - Legal arrangement involving a promise by one person to perform the obligations of a second person to a third person, in the event the second person fails to perform.

**Historical cost** - Original cost of an asset to an entity.

**Improvement** - An expenditure directed to a particular asset to improve its performance or useful life.

**Income** - Inflow of revenue during a period of time.

**Income Statement** – Financial statement that shows the income and expenses for a business.

**Income Tax Basis** - (1) For tax purposes, the concept of basis determines the proper amount of gain to report when an asset is sold. Basis is generally the cost paid for an asset plus the amounts paid to improve the asset less deductions taken against the asset, such as depreciation and amortization. (2) For accounting purposes, a consistent basis of accounting that uses income tax accounting rules while generally accepted accounting principles (GAAP) does not.

**Initial Public Offering (IPO)** - When a private company goes public for the first time.

**Insolvent** - When an entity's liabilities exceed its assets.

**Installment Method** - Tax accounting method of reporting gain on the sale of an asset exchanged for a receivable. In general, the gain is reported as the note is paid off.

**Intangible Asset** – Non-physical assets having no physical existence such as trademarks, patents, and goodwill.

**Interest** - Payment for the use or forbearance of money.

**Interim Financial Statements** - Financial statements that report the operations of an entity for less than one year.

**Internal Audit** - An audit performed within an entity by its staff rather than an independent certified public accountant.

**Internal Control** - Process designed to provide reasonable assurance regarding achievement of various management objectives such as the reliability of financial reports.

**Internal Rate of Return** - Method that determines the discount rate at which the present value of the future cash flows will exactly equal investment outlay.

**Internal Revenue Code** - Collection of tax rules of the federal government. Also referred to as Title 26 of the United States Code.

**Internal Revenue Service (IRS)** - Federal agency that administers the internal revenue code. The IRS is part of the United States Treasury Department.

**Inventory** - Tangible property held for sale, or materials used in a production process to make a product.

**Joint Venture** - When two or more persons or organizations gather capital to provide a product or service. Often carried out as a partnership.

**Journal** - Any book containing original entries of daily financial transactions.

**Key Person Insurance** - Business-owned life insurance contract typically on the lives of principal officers that normally provides for guaranteed death benefits to the company, and the accumulation of a cash surrender value.

**Kiting** - Writing checks against a bank account with insufficient funds to cover them, hoping that the bank will receive deposits before the checks arrive for clearance.

**Last in, First out (LIFO)** – Value of inventory is based on the costs of the earliest items purchased.

**Lease** - Conveyance of land, buildings, equipment, or other assets from one person (lessor) to another (lessee) for a specific period of time for monetary or other consideration, usually in the form of rent.

**Leasehold** - Property interest a lessee owns in the leased property.

**Ledger** - Any book of accounts containing the summaries of debit and credit entries.

**Lessee** - Person or entity that has the right to use property under the terms of a LEASE.

**Lessor** - Owner of property, the temporary use of which is transferred to another (lessee) under the terms of a lease.

**Letter of Credit** - Conditional bank commitment issued on behalf of a customer to pay a third party in accordance with certain terms and conditions. The two primary types are commercial letters of credit and standby letters of credit.

**Liability** - Debts or obligations owed by one entity (debtor) to another entity (creditor), payable in money, goods, or services.

**Limited Liability Company (LLC)** - Form of doing business-combining limited liability for all owners (called members) with taxation as a partnership. An LLC is formed by filing articles of organization with an appropriate state official. Rules governing LLCs vary significantly from state to state.

**Limited Liability Partnership (LLP)** - General partnership, which via registration with an appropriate state authority, is able to enshroud all its partners in limited liability. Rules governing LLPs vary significantly from state to state.

**Limited Partnership** - Partnership in which one or more partners, but not all, have limited liability to creditors of the partnership.

**Liquid Assets** - Cash, cash equivalents, and marketable securities.

**Liquidation** - Winding up an activity by distributing its assets to the appropriate parties and settling its debts.

**Long-Term Debt** - Debt with a maturity of more than one year from the current date.

**Loss** - Excess of expenditures over revenue for a period or activity. Also, for tax purposes, an excess of basis over the amount realized in a transaction.

**Lower of Cost or Market** - Valuing assets for financial reporting purposes. Ordinarily, "cost" is the purchase price of the asset, and "market" refers to its current replacement cost. Generally accepted accounting principles (GAAP) requires that certain assets (e.g., inventories) be carried at the lower of cost or market.

**Management Accounting** - Reporting designed to assist management in decision-making, planning, and control. Also known as Managerial Accounting.

**Margin** - Excess of selling price over the unit cost.

**Matching Principle** - A fundamental concept of basic accounting. In any one given accounting period, you should try to match the revenue you are reporting with the expenses it took to generate that revenue in the same time period, or over the periods in which you will be receiving benefits from that expenditure. A simple example is depreciation expense. If you buy a building that will last for many years, you don't write off the cost of that building all at once. Instead, you take depreciation deductions over the building's estimated useful life. Thus, you've "matched" the expense, or cost, of the building with the benefits it produces, over the course of the years it will be in service.

**Materiality** - Magnitude of an omission or misstatements of accounting information that, in the light of surrounding circumstances, makes it probable that the judgment of a reasonable person relying on the information would change or be influenced.

**Net Assets** - Excess of the value of securities owned, cash, receivables, and other assets over the liabilities of the company.

**Net Income** - Excess or deficit of total revenues and gains compared with total expenses and losses for an accounting period.

**Net Lease** - In addition to the rental payment, the lessee assumes all property charges such as taxes, insurance, and maintenance.

**Net Sales** - Sales at gross invoice amounts less any adjustments for returns, allowances, or discounts taken.

**Net Worth** - Similar to equity, the excess of assets over liabilities.

**Non-for-profit organization/tax-exempt organization** - An incorporated organization which exists for educational or charitable purposes, and from which its shareholders or trustees do not benefit financially. Also called not-for-profit organization.

**No-Par Stock** - Stock authorized to be issued but for which no par value is set in the articles of incorporation. A stated value is set by the board of directors on the issuance of this type of stock.

**No-Par Value** - Stock or bond that does not have a specific value indicated.

**Operating Agreement** - Agreement, usually a written document that sets out the rules by which a limited liability company (LLC) is to be operated. It is the LLC equivalent of corporate bylaws or a partnership agreement.

**Operating Cycle** - Period of time between the acquisition of goods and services involved in the manufacturing process and the final cash realization resulting from sales and subsequent collections.

**Ordinary Income** - One of two classes of income (the other being capital gains) taxed under the internal revenue code. Historically, ordinary income is taxed at a higher rate than capital gains.

**Paid in Capital** - Portion of the stockholders' equity, which was paid in by the stockholders, as opposed to capital arising from profitable operations.

**Partnership** - Relationship between two or more persons based on a written, oral, or implied agreement whereby they agree to carry on a trade or business for profit and share the resulting profits. Unlike a corporation's shareholders, the partnership's general partners are liable for the debts of the partnership.

**Par Value** - Amount per share set in the articles of incorporation of a corporation to be entered in the capital stocks account where it is left permanently, and signifies a cushion of equity capital for the protection of creditors.

**Passive Activity Loss** - Loss generated from activities involved in the conduct of a trade or business in which the taxpayer does not materially participate.

**Pension** - Retirement plan offered by an employer for the benefit of an employee, usually at retirement, through a trustee who controls the plan assets.

**Perpetual Inventory** - System that requires a continuous record of all receipts and withdrawals of each item of inventory.

**Personal Financial Statements** - Financial statements prepared for an individual or family to show financial status.

**Personal Property** - Movable property that is not affixed to the land (real property). Personal property includes tangible items such as cash, cars and computers, as well as intangible items, such as royalties, patents and copyrights.

**Pledged Asset** - Asset placed in a trust and used as collateral for a debt.

**Prepaid Expense** - Cost incurred to acquire economically useful goods or services that are expected to be consumed in the revenue-earning process within the operating cycle.

**Preferred Stock** - Type of capital stock that carries certain preferences over common stock, such as a prior claim on dividends and assets.

**Premium** - (1) Excess amount paid for a bond over its face amount. (2) In insurance, the cost of specified coverage for a designated period of time.

**Present Value** - Current value of a given future cash flow stream, discounted at a given rate.

**Prime Rate** - Rate of interest charged by major U.S. banks on loans made to their preferred customers.

**Principal** - Face amount of a security, exclusive of any premium or interest. The basis for interest computations.

**Profit Sharing Plan** - Defined contribution plan characterized by the setting aside of a portion of an entity's profits in participant's accounts.

**Pro Forma** –Financial forms (Profit and loss statements, balance sheets, etc.) based on future expectations.

**Projection** - Prospective financial statements that include one or more hypothetical assumptions.

**Promissory Note** - Evidence of a debt with specific amount due and interest rate. The note may specify a maturity date or it may be payable on demand. The promissory note may or may not accompany other instruments such as a mortgage providing security for the payment thereof.

**Proprietorship** - Business owned by an individual without the limited liability protection of a corporation or a limited liability company (LLC). Also known as sole proprietorship.

**Pro Rata** - Distribution of an expense, fund, or dividend proportionate with ownership.

**Prospective Financial Information** (forecast and projection) - Forecast: Prospective financial statements that present, to the best of the responsible party's knowledge and belief, an entity's expected financial position, results of operations, and changes in financial position. A financial forecast is based on the responsible party's assumptions reflecting conditions it expects to exist, and the course of action it expects to take.

**Projection**: Prospective financial statements that present, to the best of the responsible party's knowledge and belief, given one or more hypothetical assumptions, an entity's expected financial position, results of operations, and changes in financial position.

**Prospectus** - Major part of the registration statement filed with the Securities and Exchange Commission (SEC) for public offerings. A prospectus generally describes securities or partnership interests to be issued and sold.

**Ratio Analysis** - Comparison of actual or projected data for a particular company to other data for that company or industry in order to analyze trends or relationships.

**ROI** - (Return on Investment) Net Profit divided by Net Worth. A financial ratio indicating the degree of profitability.

**Real Property** - Land and improvements, including buildings and personal property that is permanently attached to the land or customarily transferred with the land.

**Receivables** - Amounts of money due from customers or other debtors.

**Reconciliation** - Comparison of two numbers to demonstrate the basis for the difference between them.

**Related Party Transaction** - Business or other transaction between persons who do not have an arm's-length relationship (e.g., a relationship with independent, competing interests). The most common is between family members or controlled entities. For tax purposes, these types of transactions are generally subject to a greater level of scrutiny.

**Restricted Assets** - Cash or other assets whose use in whole or in part is restricted for specific purposes bound by virtue of contracted agreements.

**Restructuring** - Reorganization within an entity. Restructuring may occur in the form of changing the components of capital, renegotiating the terms of debt agreements, etc.

**Retained Earnings** - Accumulated undistributed earnings of a company retained for future needs or for future distribution to its owners.

**Return on Investment (ROI)** - Ratio measure of the profits achieved by a firm through its basic operations. An indicator of management's general effectiveness and efficiency. The simplest version is the ratio of net income to total assets.

**Revenue Recognition** - Method of determining whether or not income has met the conditions of being earned and realized or is realizable.

**Revenues** - Sales of products, merchandise, and services; and earnings from interest, dividend, rents.

**Review** - Accounting service that provides some assurance as to the reliability of financial information. In a review, a CPA does not conduct an examination under generally accepted auditing standards (GAAS).

**Review Report** - See accountants' report.

**Risk Management** - Process of identifying and monitoring business risks in a manner that offers a risk/return relationship that is acceptable to an entity's operating philosophy.

**S-corporation** - An S-corporation is a corporation, which, under the Internal Revenue Code, is generally not subject to federal income taxes. Instead, taxable income of the corporation is passed through to its stockholders in a manner similar to that of a partnership.

**Salvage Value** - Selling price assigned to retired fixed assets or merchandise un-salable through usual channels.

**Security** - Any kind of transferable certificate of ownership including equity securities and debt securities.

**Security Interest** - Legal interest of one person in the property of another to assure performance of a second person under a contract.

**Short-Term** - Current; ordinarily due within one year.

**Sole Proprietorship** - an enterprise that is owned by a single individual.

**Start-up Costs** - (1) Costs, excluding acquisition costs, incurred to bring a new unit into production, (2) Costs incurred to begin a business.

**Stated Value** - Per share amount set by the board of directors to be placed in the capital stock account upon issuance of no-par value.

**Statement of Cash Flows** - A statement of cash flows is one of the basic financial statements that is required as part of a complete set of financial statements prepared in conformity with generally accepted accounting principles. It categorizes net cash provided or used during a period as operating, investing, and financing activities, and reconciles beginning and ending cash and cash equivalents.

**Statement of Financial Condition** - Basic financial statement, usually accompanied by appropriate disclosures that describe the basis of accounting used in its preparation and presentation as of a specified date, the entity's assets, liabilities and the equity of its owners. Also known as balance sheet.

**Stock Compensation Plan** - Fringe benefit that gives employees the option to purchase the employer's stock at a specified price during a specified period.

**Straight-Line Depreciation** – Accounting method that reflects an equal amount of wear and tear during each period of an assets useful life.

**Tangible Asset** – Assets having a physical existence, such as cash, land, buildings, machinery, or claims on property, investments or goods in process.

**Tax** - Charge levied by a governmental unit on income, consumption, wealth, or other basis.

**Tax Lien** - Encumbrance placed on property as security for unpaid taxes.

**Tax Shelter** - Arrangement in which allowable tax deductions or exclusions result in the deferral of tax on income that would otherwise be payable currently.

**Term Loan** - Loan for a specified time period.

**Total Gain** - Excess of the proceeds realized on the sale of either INVENTORY or non-inventory goods.

**Treasury Stock** - Stock reacquired by the issuing company. It may be held indefinitely, retired, issued upon exercise of stock options or resold.

**Trust** - Ancient legal practice where one person (the GRANTOR) transfers the legal title to an ASSET, called the principle or corpus, to another person (the TRUSTEE), with specific instructions about how the corpus is to be managed and disposed.

**Trustee** - Person who is given legal title to, and management authority over, the property placed in a trust.

**Unaudited Financial Statements** - Financial statements, which have not undergone a detailed, AUDIT examination by an independent certified public accountant (CPA).

**Unearned Income** - Payments received for services, which have not yet been performed.

**Unqualified Opinion** – Audit opinion not qualified for any material scope restrictions nor departures from generally accepted accounting principles (GAAP). Also known as clean opinion.

**Variable Rate Loan** - Loan whose interest rate changes over its life in relation to the level of an index.

**Variable Cost** - Expenditures that change in proportion to increases or decreases in sales or production volumes

**Variance** - Deviation or difference between an estimated value and the actual value.

**Venture Capital** - Investment company whose primary objective is capital growth. New assets invested largely in companies that are developing new ideas, products, or processes.

**Vesting** - Point at which certain benefits available to an employee are no longer contingent on the employee continuing to work for the employer.

**Withholding** - Amount withheld or deducted from employee salaries by the employer and paid by the employer, for the employee, to the proper authority.

**Working Capital** – The money available for immediate business operations. It is the excess of current assets over current liabilities.

# Recommended Reading

For your progress, I am enclosing an appendix of recommended reading. A number of years ago, I came across the following advice. It goes as follows:

*"When I get a little money I buy books, and if any money is left I buy food and clothes."*

These words stayed with me, and from that advice, I have amassed my business success library. The following list is a trimmed-down version so you can get the greatest impact by starting here.

Abraham, Jay. *Getting Everything You Can Out of All You've Got.* New York: St. Martin's Press, 2000.

Blanchard, Ken, and Sheldon Bowles. *Big Bucks.* New York: HarperCollins, 2000.

Blanchard, Ken, and Sheldon Bowles, *Raving Fans.* New York: William Morrow, 1993.

Carnegie, Dale. *How to Win Friends and Influence People.* New York: Simon & Schuster, 1937.

Clason, George S. *The Richest Man in Babylon.* New York, Hawthorn, 1955. Reprint, New York: Signet, 1988.

Covey, Stephen R. *The Seven Habits of Highly Effective People.* New York: Simon & Schuster, 1989.

Gerber, Michael E. *The E-Myth Revisited.* New York: HarperCollins, 1995.

Hill, Napoleon. *Think and Grow Rich.* New York: Hawthorn, 1966. Reprint, New York: Ballantine, 1983.

Hopkins, Claude. *My Life in Advertising.* New York: NTC Publishing Group, 1987.

Kennedy, Dan. *The Ultimate Sales Letter.* Holbrook, Mass.: Adams Media Corporation, 2000.

Kennedy, Dan. *The Ultimate Marketing Plan.* Holbrook, Mass.: Adams Media Corporation, 2000.

# End Notes and References

## Chapter 2
[1]http://www.family-business-experts.com/swot-analysis.html
[2]http://www.startinbusiness.co.uk/buyingbiz.htm

*Other References:*
Pollan, Stephen. *The Field Guide to Starting a Business*. New York: Fireside, 1990.
http://www.entrepreneur.com/Your_Business/YB_Node/0,4507,107,00.html
http://www.startinbusiness.co.uk/buyingbiz.htm

## Chapter 3
Montgomery, Vicki. *The Smart Woman's Guide to Starting a Business*. Bookmart Press, 1998, 2nd edition.
www.businesstown.com
www.entrepreneur.com
www.inc.com

## Chapter 4
Cohen, William A. *The Entrepreneur & Small Business Problem Solver*. John Wiley & Sons Inc, 2nd edition, 1990.
http://www.nolo.com
http://www.mycorporation.com
http://www.irs.gov

## Chapter 5
Abraham, Jay. *Getting Everything You Can Out of All You've Got*. New York: St. Martin's Press, 2000.

## Chapter 6
[3]http://www.businesslendingsolutions.org/forms/Loan%20Comparison%20Chart%20-%20Jan%202011.pdf

*Other References:*
Mancuso, Joseph R. *How To Start, Finance, and Manage Your Own Small Business*. New York: Prentice Hall Press, 1986.

Sherman, Andrew J. *Running and Growing Your Business*. Times Books, 1997. 1st Edition.

## Chapter 7

*Other References:*
Sitarz, Daniel. *Simplified Small Business Accounting*. Nova Publishing Company, February, 1996, 1st Edition; 2nd printing.
Kravitz, Wallace W. *Bookkeeping the Easy Way: Assets, Liabilities, Owner's Equity*. Woodbury, New York/London/Toronto/Sydney: Barron Educational Series, 1983.

## Chapter 9
[4]http://www.allbusiness.com/articles/content/3041.asp
http://www.smartmoney.com/tax/workbusiness/index.cfm?story=smallbiz

*Other References:*
Sullivan, Robert Allen. *The Small Business Start-up Guide*, Information International, Virginia, 1996.

## Chapter 10

*Other References:*
www.smartmoney.com
http://www.helpbizowners.com/hr/hrfrng.htm
http://www.uschamber.com

## Chapter 11
[5]http://www.allbusiness.com/articles/content/3282.asp

*Other References:*
Parson, Mary Jean. *Financially Managing The One-Person Business*. The Putnam Publishing Group, 1991.
http://www.techinsurance.com/
http://www.buyerzone.com/business_insurance/
http://www.allbusiness.com/articles/INS_articles.asp

## Chapter 12

*Other References:*
Sales, Dr. Michael J. Ed. D, "Succession Planning in the Family Business." *Small Business Reports*, Feb. 1990, pp 31-40.
http://www.uschamber.com/sb/business/P11/P11_0100.asp
http://www.score.org/5_tips_bp_7.html

# APPENDIX

## Specifics on Florida

### Why Florida?

Location, location, location!

Florida boasts an unbeatable location for business. There is the sunshine and beaches, lakes, rivers and oceans, not to mention many theme parks, zoos and the Everglades National Park. Florida has been the site of many historic space launches and the closest place in the US to be subject to nuclear war (Cuban Missle Crisis).

Florida also boasts a population of almost 20 million people and is very diverse with ethnicity. With all of the fun vacation spots in Florida, almost 95 million people visit the "Sunshine State" each year.

The climate in Florida allows you to be outdoors all year long. There are plenty of outdoor activities to enjoy. Kayaking, swimming, boating, fishing, hunting, running, biking, and outdoor sports like baseball, football and soccer. Of course there are plenty of indoor activities to do as well and they are usually air-conditioned.

So with all of this fun and sunshine, Florida becomes one of the best places to do business as well. Especially if you cater to the tourist industry like lodging, restaurants, rental cars, etc. In addition, it has been said that for every 13 tourists that visit Florida, 1 job is created. Of course that job could be in a theme park or hotel, but it also is in the doctor's office, the dentist, teachers, police or even the CPA that supports the people in these other jobs.

Florida by far is one of the most business friendly places to be. Most small businesses operate as a sole proprietorship, partnership or as an S corporation. These entities are not taxed in Florida nor do they file a state income or franchise tax return as in many other states. In addition, individuals are not taxed on their personal income. Now Florida does have its other taxes that they have to get down to business about, along with a few squirrelly rules and regulations that we will talk about a little later, but overall it is a great place to open a business.

# Starting Your Business in Florida

To start a business in Florida, you must first decide on a name of your business (unless you are not going to use your own name as a sole proprietor) and register your business with the state. You will also need to decide the entity type you wish to have. Do you want or need to be an LLC, Inc., Corp., LLP, LLLP, LP, PA, PLLC, etc. It is always recommended that you consult your attorney and tax advisor before creating the entity to determine the best legal and tax structure for your business.

## Business Under Your Own Name

### Step 1:

If you intend to do business under your own name (e.g. Dan Henn) , you are not required to register a trade name. If trading under any name other than your own as a sole proprietor, the law requires you to register a fictitious name with the state. To register your business for tax and employer purposes with the Florida Secretary of State, you do so by going to www.sunbiz.org or contact an attorney or licensed paralegal to get your articles of formation created.

### Step 2:

If you will have employees, you will need to obtain an Employer Identification Number (EIN). Fill out Form *SS-4* which can be found at www.irs.gov or you can search for "SS-4 Online" and complete the online wizard which will give you the EIN at the completion of the application.

To obtain federal business tax information, contact the Internal Revenue Service Office in your area, or call toll-free: 1 (800) 829-1040. To request forms only, call (800) 829-3676.

### Step 3:

To register your business for tax and employer purposes with the Florida Department of Revenue, please go to dor.myflorida.com. Here you need to download Form

DR-1 or apply online. Form DR-1 will allow you to register for reemployment tax (formerly unemployment tax), sales and use tax, communication services tax, solid waste fees, documentary stamp tax, or fuel taxes. We will discuss the most common taxes (reemployment tax and sales and use tax) later in this appendix.

When you have completed and filed your application you will be registered with the Departments of Revenue; your business will be registered for taxes and for employer contributions for unemployment tax, sales and use tax or any other appropriate tax for your business. The State will send you the forms and information you will need for compliance with Florida tax laws and if you elected to file online, they will send you the appropriate online access.

## Local Registration

If you are starting a business and it is located in the county or city limits, you need to obtain a Business Tax License in each county you have a business location as well as each city if you are located within an organized city. In addition, if you have a business that uses licensed individuals such as attorneys, mortgage representatives, real estate agents or CPAs, each individual will also need to obtain a Business Tax License in the respective jurisdiction.

## Dan's Words of Wisdom

Before you actually start your business and open your doors to customers or clients, make sure that you have completed a Business Plan. There are plenty of books out there to help you with this. The one I recommend the best is "*Business Plan In A Day*" by Rhonda Abrams. Determine your goals, your target market, your marketing plans and most of all, write up a proposed budget. Don't instantly think that you need to be in the Yellow Pages, pay for Facebook advertising, or be in your local newspaper advertising without first figuring out a plan. Also, I know sometimes this is a difficult to think of but as Stephen Covey says in his book "*Seven Habits of Highly Effective People*", <u>Begin with the End in Mind</u>. Which means that you need to understand what your exit plan is. How are you getting out of this business? Do you plan on selling it to a third party or passing it on to a family member? Do you want to hire someone to grow with you internally and sell to them? Oh, and don't forget that you always need to "Sharpen the Axe", a quote from Abraham Lincoln. This means to keep educating yourself and keep your mind a sharp tool to make things easier in your business. Do not rest on your laurels and think you know it all. Always be looking for new products, new ideas and more efficient ways to get things done.

## Doing Business in Florida

The Florida Deparment of Revenue is the state entity that deals with most taxes in the state of Florida. Their main phone number (800) 352-3671 or you can find forms, publications or the Revenue Law Library at dor.myflorida.com/dor.

In order to commence business in the state of Florida you must register with the Secretary of State Division of Corporations. You register as a For-Profit entity or Not-for-Profit entity. In addition, you will register as a domestic entity (headquartered and registered initially in Florida) or a foreign entity (headquartered and registered initially in another state or country). You are required to file an Annual Report for your entity after January 1st of each year and on or before May 1st of each year. If you do not file this timely, the state will assess a $400 penalty for late filing that cannot be reduced or eliminated.

## Florida Income Taxes

Florida does not have an individual income tax but does have an income tax on corporations formed only as C Corporations that you will file on Form F-1120. The tax is assessed at a rate of 5.5% of income less an exemption of $5,000. If you have activity in multiple states, Florida applies apportionment factors at a rate of 50% toward sales, 25% toward payroll and 25% toward property, inventory and rent. This return is due on the 1st day of the 4th month after the end of your fiscal year. You may file an extension for up-to-six months. Florida does not accept the federal extension so you will need to file a separate Florida extension on Form F-7004. If an extension is not filed and if there is no tax due, there will be a $50 per month penalty for each month or part of a month the return is late not to exceed $300. However, the good news is there is no minimum tax.

S corporations, Partnerships, Single-Member LLCs, and sole proprietors do not pay income tax, franchise tax or a minimum taxes in the state of Florida nor do they file income tax returns.

# Florida Payroll Taxes

The only payroll taxes that are of concern for Florida is the Reemployment Tax (formerly Unemployment Tax). The Reemployment Tax is paid on the first $7,000 of wages for each employee on an annual basis. The tax rate is called an experience rate and is multiplied by the taxable wages to determine the tax due. The initial experience rate for new businesses is 2.7%. Depending on the number of reemployment claims against your business, the rate can range from .102% to 5.4%.

This tax is paid quarterly on Form RT-6 and is due the month following each quarter (the same due date as federal Form 941). You can also register to file Form RT-6 electronically. There is also an option to spread your tax payments out over the year paid on a quarterly basis. If you need to amend this return you will use Form RT-8.

# Florida Sales and Use Taxes

Since Florida does not have an individual income tax, sales and use taxes are the primary source of income to fund government activities. Due to this fact, the Florida Department of Revenue aggressively reviews, audits and collects this tax.

Florida has a base rate of 6% of sales tax on most tangible items purchased within the state. Of course there are some exemptions for certain purchases such as medical or food items. Various counties within Florida can assess an additional 1% discretionary surtax on sales taxable items. This surtax is assessed up to a taxable purchase maximum of $5,000. As an agent for the state in collecting this tax the state gives you a collection allowance of 2.5% of tax due to a cap of $30 for each filing.

If you are responsible for collecting and remitting sales and use tax, you must file Form DR-15 or DR-15EZ on a frequency that is based on your collections from the previous year. New businesses generally start filing on a quarterly basis but it can be as often as monthly. These returns are due by the 20th of the month following the month of collection. If the due date falls on a weekend or holiday, then the due date falls on the business day. Please note that this is the due date for filing. If you are remitting tax electronically, it must be initiated the day before the due date. Also, it is considered timely if remitted before 5pm of the due date.

There are certain items that are taxable in Florida that other states do not assess tax. For example, Florida assesses sales tax on commercial rental income but not residential rental income (except for written residential lease agreements that are less than 6 months). Here is a list of some additional sales taxable items. This list is meant to be an example and may not be all inclusive of the various items that are sales and use taxable in Florida.

- Commercial cleaning (but not residential cleaning)

- Purchase of tangible items not exempted by law

- Online purchases of tangible items that are brought into and used in the state (i.e. use tax)

- Online software sales (if you receive any tangible items as part of the purchase (i.e. books, manuals, CDs or DVDs)). Meaning if you receive the software all electronically, then sales tax does not apply

- Vending machine sales

- Restaurants and bars

- Hotel/Motel lodging

- Real Property contractors (i.e. cabinets, HVAC, sign companies) pay sales tax on their purchases of supplies and materials and do not assess a sales tax to their customers.

## Electronic filing

The state of Florida is always looking for efficiencies to save taxpayer money. Effective July 1, 2012, in order to qualify for the sales and use tax collection allowance, you must file your return electronically. If you file the paper form, you will no longer be allowed to receive the collection allowance.

# BUSINESS NETWORKING

If you plan on expanding your business through networking the local business chamber in your area or local chapters of professional networking groups are the best way to reach your target market.

### 1. Chambers of Commerce

*Florida Chamber of Commerce*
*136 S. Bronough Street*
*Tallahassee, Florida 32301*
*Phone: (850) 521-1200*

# Local Chambers

- Each county usually has at least one chamber of commerce, however, there are many cities or regional areas that have a chamber of commerce. In addition, there are many chambers of a specific industry or ethnicity located throughout the state.

Below are the chambers by county for the East Central Florida Area

# Brevard

Cocoa Beach Regional Chamber of Commerce
400 Fortenberry Rd
Merritt Island, FL 32952
Phone: (321) 459-2200
Fax: (321) 459-2232
Website: http://www.cocoabeachchamber.com

Melbourne Regional Chamber of East Central Florida
1005 E Strawbridge Ave
Melbourne, FL 32901
Phone: (321) 724-5400
Fax: (321) 725-2093
Website: http://www.melbourneregionalchamber.com

Greater Palm Bay Chamber Of Commerce
4100 Dixie Hwy NE
Palm Bay, FL 32905
Phone: (321) 951-9998
Fax: (321) 473-8904
Website: http://www.palmbaychamber.com

Titusville Area Chamber of Commerce
2000 S Washington Ave
Titusville, FL 32780
Phone: (321) 267-3036
Fax: (321) 264-0127
Website: http://www.titusville.org

## Indian River

Sebastian River Area Chamber of Commerce
700 Main St
Sebastian, FL 32958
Phone: (772) 589-5969
Fax: (772) 589-5993
Website: http://www.sebastianchamber.com

Indian River County Chamber Of Commerce
PO Box 2947
Vero Beach, FL 32961
Phone: (772) 567-3491
Fax: (772) 778-3181
Website: http://www.indianriverchamber.com

## Orange

East Orlando Chamber of Commerce
2860 S Alafaya Trl Ste 130
Orlando, FL 32828
Phone: (407) 277-5951
Fax: (407) 381-1720
Website: http://www.eocc.org

Orlando, Inc.
PO Box 1234
Orlando, FL 32802
Phone: (407) 835-2451
Fax: (407) 835-2500
Website: http://www.orlando.org

West Orange Chamber of Commerce
12184 W Colonial Dr
Winter Garden, FL 34787
Phone: (407) 656-1304
Fax: (407) 656-0221
Website: http://www.wochamber.com

Goldenrod Area Chamber Of Commerce
4755 N Palmetto Ave
Winter Park, FL 32792
Phone: (407) 677-5980
Fax: (407) 677-4928
Website: www.goldenrodchamber.com

Winter Park Chamber of Commerce
PO Box 280
Winter Park, FL 32790
Phone: (407) 644-8281
Fax: (407) 644-7826
Website: http://www.winterpark.org

## Osceola

Kissimmee/Osceola County Chamber Of Commerce
1425 E Vine St
Kissimmee, FL 34744
Phone: (407) 847-3174
Fax: (407) 870-8607
Website: http://www.kissimmeechamber.com

St. Cloud Greater Osceola Chamber of Commerce
1200 New York Ave
Saint Cloud, FL 34769
Phone: (407) 892-3671
Fax: (407) 892-5289
Website: http://www.stcloudflchamber.com

## Polk

Lakeland Area Chamber of Commerce
PO Box 3607
Lakeland, FL 33802
Phone: (863) 688-8551
Fax: (863) 683-7454
Website: http://www.lakelandchamber.com

Greater Winter Haven Area Chamber of Commerce
401 Avenue B NW
Winter Haven, FL 33881
Phone: (863) 293-2138
Fax: (863) 297-5818
Website: http://www.winterhavenfl.com

Haines City-Northeast Polk County Regional Chamber of Commerce
35610 Hwy 27
Haines City, FL 33844
Phone: (863) 422-3751
Fax: (863) 422-4704
Website: http://www.hainescity.com

Greater Mulberry Chamber Of Commerce
PO Box 254
Mulberry, FL 33860
Phone: (863) 425-4414
Fax: (863) 425-3837
Website: http://www.mulberrychamber.org

**Seminole**

Sanford Chamber of Commerce
400 E First St
Sanford, FL 32771
Phone: (407) 322-2212
Fax: (407) 322-8160
Website: http://www.sanfordchamber.com

Seminole County Regional Chamber of Commerce
1055 AAA Dr Ste 153
Heathrow, FL 32746
Phone: (407) 708-4610
Fax: (407) 708-4615
Website: http://www.seminolebusiness.org

Casselberry Chamber Of Commerce
894 State Road 436
Casselberry, FL 32707
Phone: (407) 831-1231

Maitland Area Chamber of Commerce
110 N Maitland Ave
Maitland, FL 32751
Phone: (407) 644-0741
**Fax: (407) 539-2529**

**Volusia**

Chamber of Commerce of Holly Hill
PO Box 250615
Daytona Beach, FL 32125
Phone: (386) 255-7311
Fax: (386) 267-0485
Website: http://www.hollyhillchamber.com
Email: office@hollyhillchamber.com

Daytona Beach/Halifax Area Chamber of Commerce
PO Box 2676
Daytona Beach, FL 32115
Phone: (386) 255-0981
Fax: (386) 258-5104
Website: http://www.daytonachamber.com

DeLand Area Chamber of Commerce
336 N Woodland Blvd
DeLand, FL 32720
Phone: (386) 734-4331
Fax: (386) 734-4333
Website: http://www.delandchamber.org

Ormond Beach Chamber of Commerce
165 W Granada Blvd
Ormond Beach, FL 32174
Phone: (386) 677-3454
Fax: (386) 677-4363
Website: http://www.ormondchamber.com

2.  Networking

Networking is a vital portion of pretty much every business. This is where you develop connections with future customers, clients, vendors, suppliers, referrals sources and future employees. It is important to do networking to tell your story. Why did you get started doing what you are doing? What is your passion?

We just listed various Chambers of Commerce in the previous section. You should find the chamber that is closest to you and the one the fits your organization the best.

Below is a list of other networking organizations or networking tips that you should consider for your business.

A.  Business Network International (BNI)

B.  LeTip International (LeTip)

www.letip.com

C.  Meetup.com

This is a site that you can go to find people who share a love or passion that you do. You can find personal and business groups in which you can get involved.

D.  Join business trade or professional organizations in which your target market customers or clients belong. If you were marketing toward doctors or realtors, you would join their state and/or local professional organizations. Usually they have what is called an affiliate membership. Going to these functions to get to know the members is a real good way to get business. But always keep in mind that this is a marathon and not a sprint.

Here are the top 7 do's and don't related to networks.

1)  Ask someone connected to the organization or event coordinator for an introduction to your top prospects or for people in your target market. This will be a great way to get started.

2) Listen more than you talk. There will be time for you to talk about yourself, but if you ask questions of your new "friend", like how did you get started in your business? Where do you find your passion for your business? What are you biggest challenges?, and you genuinely listen to them, you will start the workings of a great relationship.

3) Make personal connections. Try to ask questions about personal stories that people discuss, especially if you have a similar interest, hobby or passion.

4) Be sure to create a short "elevator" speech that rolls off of your tongue and doesn't feel rehearsed or memorized. It should come from the heart.

5) Take notes. But be sure to take notes about people and conversations after they leave you. While they are in your presence, they should have your full undivided attention.

6) Introduce new people in the room to people you know. They will never forget that you did that for them.

7) Follow-up. Send a thank you note. Include something special in that note, a gift card, a newspaper article on a topic that you discussed, but do not send them anything about your business. Call them up and invite them to breakfast, lunch or just a cup of coffee. Be sure to pick up the tab. But be sure that they know that you want to know more about their business. Your time will come for you to talk about your business.

# ABOUT DAN HENN
# BIOGRAPHY AND FACT SHEET

Dan Henn is a CPA who enjoys seeing others succeed financially and in all areas of their lives, being especially gratified when they do so based on his advice, encouragement and support.

He has more than 20 years' experience advising clients on their finances, having worked both in large global accounting firms and more recently with his own practice.

Dan is actively involved in IRS tax resolution, comprehensive tax planning and preparation of tax returns for corporations, partnerships and high wealth individuals. He has worked on many issues related to tax consulting, IRS representation, payroll, sales tax and multi-state income taxation.

He set up his own practice because he was unhappy working for the larger firms, becoming tired of the politics and pettiness.

He says: "Running my own practice makes me master of my own destiny and allows me to be more passionate, caring, and attentive to my clients. I treat them as I would want to be treated. I treat everyone in a supportive and non-judgmental manner. I give them peace of mind to help them sleep better at night."

Outside business, Dan is married with two daughters who have been home-schooled since day one. He is active in church activities and is a sport enthusiast. He enjoys watching both American football and European soccer. He also enjoys woodworking, spending time with his family and traveling with them all over the US and globe.

Dan comments: "As a parent, I discovered a passion for a sport that I did not play as a kid. I have become involved in coaching soccer and coached my daughters from age 6 through 17. I even became a soccer referee and liked that as well."

Dan was awarded Speaker of the Year in 2009 by the Florida Institute of CPAs for his talks to local high school students about becoming a CPA.

He says, "As a business owner myself for five years now, I feel better able to service my clients as I have the same experience of being in the trenches as they do."

Commenting on the book he says, "I hope this will help more business owners succeed, give them encouragement to move forward, and ensure them that they are not afraid to seek advice when it is needed."